# Murder and Moral Decay in Victorian Popular Literature

# Nineteenth-Century Studies

Juliet McMaster, Series Editor

University Professor
University of Alberta

Consulting Editor:

James Kincaid

Professor of English
University of Colorado, Boulder

## Other Titles in This Series

# Murder and Moral Decay in Victorian Popular Literature

by
Beth Kalikoff

 Research
Press

Ann Arbor, Michigan

Produced and distributed by
UMI Research Press
an imprint of
University Microfilms, Inc.
Ann Arbor, Michigan 48106


Library of Congress Cataloging in Publication Data

**Kalikoff, Beth.**
   Murder and moral decay in Victorian popular
literature.

   (Nineteenth-century studies)
   Revision of: Murder and the erosion of authority
in Victorian popular literature. Thesis (Ph.D.)—
Indiana University, 1983.
   Bibliography: p.
   Includes index.
   1. English literature—19th century—History and
criticism.   2. Murder in literature.   3. Crime and
criminals in literature.   4. Moral conditions in
literature.   5. Social ethics in literature.
6. Authority in literature.   7. Popular literature—
Great Britain—History and criticism.   I. Title.
II. Series: Nineteenth-century studies (Ann Arbor,
Mich.)
PR468.M85K3   1986        820'.9'355          86-16153
ISBN 0-8357-1762-3 (alk. paper)

*To my parents,*
*Elaine and Stanley,*
*with love and gratitude*

Broadside for the Newgate Novel, *Eugene Aram*, 1831
*(Courtesy of the Michael Sadleir Collection, Lilly Library)*

# Contents

**Part III: "The Night-Side of Nature"**

# Acknowledgments

I owe thanks to many people and institutions. The Indiana University Graduate School and the Eastern Illinois University Foundation provided financial assistance. During the final rash of revisions, the Ragdale Foundation offered a timely residency. I would also like to thank the staff of the Lilly Library. David Warrington and Joel Silver have been especially patient and helpful; their efforts brought the most grisly woodcuts of the Michael Sadleir Collection to the light of the Lilly reading room.

I have also received much friendly advice from other scholars. Deborah Clarke, Ruth Hoberman, Constance M. Perry, M. Jeanne Peterson, David Raybin, Richard Sylvia, and Albert Wertheim gave me detailed, useful suggestions on drafts. Patrick Brantlinger helped me to see the popular works I read in a broader cultural context. He also directed me to a number of significant sources. As Editor of *Victorian Studies* while I served as Managing Editor, he gave me ideas and encouragement. Both were very welcome.

Donald J. Gray deserves special thanks. Many writers seek and receive his knowledgeable suggestions, but he read every version of this manuscript as though it were the only one on his desk. His comments were imaginative, acute, and careful. I looked forward to deciphering his pencilled remarks; they were always so much more incisive than the paragraphs they illuminated. Don shares his learning with great good humor. His wit and generosity have been inspiriting, and his help has been invaluable.

Lastly, I would like to thank Linda Calendrillo and John Guzlowski for their unwavering encouragement, Ron Wray for his affectionate patience, and my sister, Hedy Kalikoff, for everything.

# Prologue

*Who ever heard the like of it—in the nineteenth century, mind;*
*in an age of progress, and in a country which rejoices in the*
*blessings of British constitution?*

Franklin Blake in *The Moonstone*

Throughout the nineteenth century, murder captured and held the attention of the English public. Lurid homicides and their circumstances were subjects for "gallows literature" of the streets, sociological articles in middle-class magazines, crime melodramas, and popular novels. As Garrett Stewart writes in *Death Sentences,* "characters die more often, more slowly, and more vocally in the Victorian age than ever before or since."[1] Detective fiction did not emerge as a separate genre until Doyle's tales of Holmes, but many nineteenth-century genres featured murder regularly. "The age was fascinated by crime and its nemesis," Ian Ousby has noted, "by mysteries and their solution."[2] Sensational crimes have riveted readers and playgoers for centuries, and surely homicides were not more grotesquely or frequently committed in the Victorian period than at any other time in history. Yet there was a "sustained enthusiasm for murder" all through the nineteenth century and a corresponding emphasis on homicide in a variety of popular genres, both of which invite attention from the scholar of Victorian literature and culture.[3]

Even the most desultory browse through current writing on Victorian crime will reveal that murder and detection have not been ignored by critics. In *Victorian Studies in Scarlet,* Richard Altick traces "the crimson thread that runs through the fabric of Victorian social history" (Altick, 9) by surveying murder and its influences in drama, street writing, mainstream literature, and many kinds of entertainments; he also analyzes numerous accounts of murder trials of the period. The detective has been the focus for several studies, including Ian Ousby's *The Bloodhounds of Heaven,* which examines the history of the detective in nineteenth-century British literary contexts, and *The Lady Investigates* by Patricia Craig and Mary Cadogan. Michael Booth includes a chapter on crime drama in his *English Melodrama*. Mid- and late-century detective fiction is the starting point for several works of literary theory in *The Poetics of Murder*, edited by Glenn W. Most and William W. Stowe. Historians such as Mary S. Hartman and J. J. Tobias make notable contributions to scholarship on murder and crime in Victorian Britain. Individual authors—Dickens, Collins, Doyle—have received detailed attention for their novels featuring murder, and individual works—*Caleb Williams, Lady Audley's Secret,* and *The Bells*—have been tackled more than once in studies of detective fiction, sensation novels, or melodrama.

Murder in Victorian popular literature nevertheless remains a provocative and significant topic for study. Although scholarship on popular genres increases in quality and quantity every year, many areas have yet to receive critical attention. Few works have been written on street literature, and the number of essays on murder in "gallows literature" may be counted hurriedly on one hand. Although melodrama attracts some theatre historians and literary scholars, it is rarely discussed in the context of other kinds of popular writing. Few works compare several popular Victorian genres; fewer still attempt to trace a theme through a number of popular genres.

In choosing to study the discussion and enactment of murder in street literature, newspapers, middle-class journals, melodrama, and fiction, I hoped to discover its significance at different times and for different audiences. How are the murders focal? What does the identity of the victim—and the killer—reveal about the values and purposes of the work? How does the treatment of murder change over the period? What themes are common to several genres? What do those themes suggest about the fears and hopes of the reading and playgoing public? Like detective stories, works featuring murder are often "concerned with moral issues"[4] and function as weathervanes we may use to try and understand the direction of Victorian beliefs and fears.

I selected works on the basis of their popularity rather than the degree to which they were representative. The unusual popularity of some, like *Maria Martin; or, Murder in the Red Barn* and *The String of Pearls,* insisted on their inclusion, and I would be the last to suggest that Sweeney Todd of the latter play represents anything but his own distinctively energetic compulsions. Yet the popular ballads, essays, melodramas, and novels that attracted my attention seem to address common anxieties and to employ similar themes. As Kirby Farrell observes in an essay on *The Sign of the Four,* "the best-seller, like the camera, cannot lie."[5] Throughout popular literature on murder, for example, runs a fear of unrestrained sexuality, especially women's, a fear of being attacked by members of the family or social circle, and a growing belief in the decay of morality. What are the social messages implied by these murders? How do the character of the crimes and their messages change over the period?

I hope that this study begins to answer these questions, while suggesting others for future research.

With the appearance of Sherlock Holmes in 1887, detective fiction emerged to spend years imitating or rejecting Doyle's model. Literary critics and cultural historians have done much work on Holmes, Jack the Ripper, and other late-century figures. As fascinating as the eighties and nineties are for the reader of crime literature, early and mid-Victorian popular works featuring homicide have their own appeal, and not only as forerunners of Holmes and modern detective fiction. In this study I linger over the earlier works and less familiar late-century writings, spending as much time on *The Big Bow Mystery* by Israel Zangwill as I do on Doyle's *A Study in Scarlet,* bypassing Jack the Ripper to focus on rarely read nonfiction concerning murder. Dickens, Collins, and Doyle have long been the maintstays of scholarly writing on nineteenth-century British crime and murder, but the wealth of "minor" or undiscovered works—or works that have yet to be discussed from the perspective of homicide—should not be neglected. I hope that this study contributes to a greater appreciation of these works and to scholarship on crime in nineteenth-century popular literature.

# Part I

# "Barbarious and Horrible Murder"

JUST OUT.    PRICE ONE PENNY.

# SWEENEY TODD OUTDONE.

THE

# UNDERTAKER

SUPERSEDED; OR,

## NOVELTIES IN THE ART OF

# BURIAL.

## HORRIBLE PROPOSALS

OF

### MR. HADEN & THE DUKE OF SUTHERLAND

FOR THE

## DISPOSAL OF THE DEAD.

## TERRIBLE CONSEQUENCES

OF PLACING THE

## CORPSE IN A BASKET.

*The brutalizing results of this New System,*

WITH A DESCRIPTION OF THE

## COFFINS AS EXHIBITED AT STAFFORD HOUSE.

LONDON : PUBLISHED BY E. MORRIS, 66, LEVER STREET, GOSWELL ROAD, AND
W. JENKINSON, 1, SHOE LANE, FLEET STREET.

Political Broadside, ca. 1850
Sweeney Todd, like many early Victorian criminals, became a familiar
part of the cultural landscape.
*(Courtesy of the Michael Sadleir Collection, Lilly Library)*

# Introduction to Part I

One of Henry Mayhew's informants in *London Labour and the London Poor* observes that notorious murders are "great goes" in the sale of street literature.[1] Real and imaginary homicide also helped to sell theatre tickets, magazines, newspapers, and books in the 1830s and 1840s. There are important differences as well as central similarities in the treatment of murder in three characteristic genres of the early Victorian period: street ballads, melodrama, and fiction. In street literature, for example, motive is secondary or irrelevant, while in some melodrama and in most fiction, causes of crime are central to the action and structure of the work. These genres also differ greatly in the presentation of social environment. Criminal melodramas and the gallows literature of the street tend to provide rather terse and perfunctory details of class, occupation, and status, although social messages are implied for both victims and criminals. In fiction, on the other hand, murders are often prescribed by the very environments in which they occur.

The homicides in popular street ballads, melodramas, and novels are strikingly similar in three ways. They are marked by extreme violence; narratives emphasize the murderer's emotional psychology, rather than setting a puzzle about the identity of the killer; and criminals are punished with divine justice or artistic symmetry, illustrating a belief or hope that transgressors against traditional authority are punished with the violence that characterizes their crimes.

Murders in the popular literature of the 1830s and 1840s, particularly in street literature and melodramas, tend to be excessively violent and irrational. In some ways they seem immune to both explanation and prevention. The African blowpipe and the detective capable of identifying its obscure poison belong to the last decade of the Victorian era; earlier murderers are "singularly unimaginative . . . they are nearly always inclined to pick up the weapon that lies closest to hand, even if it is a broomstick or a mallet."[2] Carefully premeditated murders are rare. The fatal crimes are often improvised, occasionally involving bludgeoning, dismemberment, or mutilation, as in the "Headless Torso" murder of Hannah Brown detailed in numerous street ballads and as in Nancy's murder in *Oliver Twist*.

Murderers in these popular genres also share some form of remorse, rang-
ing from the singsong contrition of the ballads—"Come all you thoughtless
young men, a warning take by me, / And think upon my unhappy fate to be
hanged upon a tree"—to the proud, Byronic monologues of the title character
in Edward Bulwer-Lytton's *Eugene Aram*.[3] The kinds of remorse expressed
vary from genre to genre. In street literature, brutal killers save their moralizing
contrition for their last moments on earth, hoping to be forgiven by God and
exhibiting "great mental agony."[4] Murderers in melodrama tend to be somewhat more sympathetically presented, and guilt springs from the virtuous side
of their natures. Count Orloff in *The Twins of Warsaw* (1831) regrets his wickedness and tries to repent, but it is too late. Unlike many criminals from street
literature, Rushton in *The Factory Lad* (1832) is not "a fiend in human form"
but a former factory worker who is unbalanced through grief at his wife's
death. Both characters are distorted by their own natures and circumstances;
they are not monsters.

In fiction, murderers are presented in more complicated ways than in street
literature and even in melodrama, and their remorse reflects that complexity.
Their guilt is often all-encompassing, dooming them far more than any string
of evidence could. Sikes unconsciously longs for death to escape from the accusatory, haunting eyes of his victim in *Oliver Twist*. He causes his own accidental hanging. The inadvertent justice of the death is ironic and horrible.
The title character of William Thackeray's *Catherine* (1839–40) attempts to
poison her lover, but she is so overwhelmed by remorse that she confesses her
crime before the poison takes effect. She also hopes to murder her husband, yet
on the night of the crime she tries to warn him and prevent her accomplices
from going through with their attack. Years after his role in the murder of a dissolute upper-class lout, Bulwer-Lytton's Eugene Aram is so infused by his
sense of guilt that he brings about his own capture and execution. In Elizabeth
Gaskell's *Mary Barton* (1848), John Barton withdraws from society, his
friends, and his family after he kills the factory owner's son. Finally driven by
remorse and the desire to atone for his crime, he gives himself up to his victim's father.

In most of the popular literature of this period, suspense does not reside
in the discovery of the murderer's identity. In fact, knowing the murderer's
name and crime made people more eager to buy broadsides like "Trial, Sentence, and Execution of Robert Blakesley." Over two-and-a-half million people
bought ballads about the homicides of Rush and the Mannings because they
knew who the killers were and what crimes they committed.[5] Suspense in early
popular street literature develops through descriptions of the criminal's apprehension and demeanor at the sentencing and execution. In melodramas
featuring homicide, the crime occurs on stage. The audience is warned about
the murder either by ominous hints from minor characters or by the confidences

of the criminal. Harris, the agitator-villain of *The Factory Strike* (1838), kills the factory owner's son on stage, and we know all along that Warner, the passive hero, is innocent: the suspense lies in wondering whether and how he will be exonerated. In *Maria Martin* (1840) and *The String of Pearls* (1847), the perpetrators announce their plans at the beginning of the plays and proceed to carry them out. In criminal melodrama, the central interest is the villain's psychology and eventual capture, not detection.

Similarly, popular fiction featuring murder creates suspense by leading readers to anticipate the way murderers are revealed and punished. Those who read *Eugene Aram* were already familiar with the legend of the crime, and the narrator quickly enlightens those who were not. Thackeray teases the reader with what might happen to his sly heroine, but her homicidal nature is as clear as her choices are limited from the opening of the novel. Sikes's first appearance suggests his capacity for murderous rage, and during the course of the action, he threatens Oliver, Fagin, Nancy, and even his own dog with violent death. The brief question of the murderer's identity in *Mary Barton* is quickly resolved, and the reader becomes engaged in Mary's attempts to free her lover without implicating her father. Mystery and suspense in early Victorian popular fiction reside in character and the workings of justice.

Different genres treat motive and remorse in different ways because of their varying forms and purposes. The action and language of street ballads function within a narrow set of conventions. Murderers are "monsters" or "base seducers" who are apprehended and executed with the inevitable finality of Greek tragedy. Their laments and confessions are tonally and stylistically similar; their victims, if not always pillars of virtue, are usually pathetic. The accounts of apprehensions and executions have a ritual quality. The background and commission of the crime are heavily shadowed by the criminal's future execution. If gallows literature can be said to have a climax, it occurs when the criminal is "launched into eternity," and the ballads are structured to lead to this moment.

Melodrama has a greater variety of conventions. In melodrama, the passive good are usually rewarded and the evil-doers always punished; it is a rare play, such as *The Factory Lad,* that leaves situations unresolved. False murders abound, and the virtuous are apparently killed only to be resuscitated for the revelation and distribution of just deserts in the final act, as when Sweeney Todd's victim in *The String of Pearls* marches into the courtroom to terrify Todd into confessing. Supernatural or purportedly supernatural events are common in melodrama of this period, although not as central to the plot as in the Gothic and vampire plays of the preceding decades.[6] When the supernatural does appear, it is to move the play toward the triumph of its conventional morality. William Corder is haunted by his victim's spirit in *Maria Martin;* Mrs. Martin's prophetic dreams lead to the discovery of her daughter's murder.

Because novelists were not as restricted by conventions as were the authors of gallows literature and melodrama, images of murder in fiction are more various. Most writers choose to focus on the social causality of the murders they invent. In *Oliver Twist,* Charles Dickens exposes the seamy underside of London life while establishing the criminality of government, local officials, and an indifferent public. Sikes's behavior is both alien to his environment— he is abandoned by his horrified associates after he murders Nancy—and a natural outgrowth of it. Eugene Aram kills an upper-class man who seduces an innocent, working-class woman, driving her to suicide, and who has also, not incidentally, taunted Aram about his poverty. In killing him, Aram is nearly an avenging social presence, ridding the rural eighteenth-century countryside of upper-class corruption. The murder in *Mary Barton* is crucially connected to the social and political landscape defined by Gaskell. The victim has shamed and exploited members of the working class in a variety of ways: he has tried to seduce Mary, insulted Jem, Mary's honest suitor, and rejected and mocked the union negotiators. In *Catherine,* as in *Oliver Twist* and *Mary Barton,* murder is rooted in the social environment. Although the working classes of Thackeray's novel behave with loutish violence, the upper classes are even more loathsome. The feeble-witted Count, Catherine's first lover, is the real source of her criminal activity. Despite her crimes, Catherine is a sympathetic character because of her limited opportunities, her vulnerability to the Count, and her capacity for remorse. In each of these novels, murder is rooted in class, social, and economic systems.

For all their shared emphases on the psychology of the killer and the extreme violence of what one street patterer called "barbarious [sic] and horrible murder" (Mayhew I, 215), these forms of early Victorian popular literature present different reasons for the violence they describe. These dissimilarities suggest varying purposes and audiences for each genre. In Part I, I will discuss some of the conventions peculiar to street literature, melodrama, and fiction, and then I will consider the significance of their differing presentations of social setting and their contrasting estimates of the causes of violent murder.

# 1

# Street Literature, 1830–1850

*His throat they cut from ear to ear*
*His brains they punchèd in*
*His name was Mr. William Weare*
*Wot lived in Lyon's Inn*
English Street Ballad

So pungent and succinct is the verse account of William Weare's violent murder in 1824 that Robert Browning, himself a connoisseur of homicide, remembered it well into his old age (Altick, 28). This street ballad and others like it represent a uniquely Victorian genre whose topicality and brevity entertained, informed, and in many cases, horrified hundreds of thousands of English readers. Although street literature existed for roughly 350 years before it became extinct in the 1870s, only in the Victorian period did the contemporary political, religious, and sensational issues featured in the broadsides so accurately reflect the public's concerns.[1] Until the rise of the mass journalism that displaced street literature, nowhere else could working-class members enjoy such immediate and brief versions of—and responses to—current events and attitudes. Street literature "gave a very large number of people access to current events, trade customs, local legends and the cultural life around them."[2]

The subjects of street literature were as various as the interests of the audience. Street drolleries, broadsides about royalty and political figures and their activities, ballads on a particular subject or issue, and gallows literature are the main categories Michael Hughes provides; more recently, Martha Vicinus adds propaganda to this list.[3] Inexpensive copies of ballads were printed and sold quickly to capitalize on a recent event or idea. Street literature was almost "the only cultural form which lived beyond the moment of expression and which directly reflected the tastes and attitudes of ordinary people" (M. Hughes, 6). Unlike other genres of the period, street literature flourished "with few influences from above," and writers and publishers like the greatly successful Jeremy Catnach "seized upon events and followed them up in the way which, we can assume, reflected best the developing tastes of their working-class readers."[4]

If street literature acted as a barometer of public taste, then the public wanted to read about murder. "Cocks," or fictitious accounts which purported to be genuine, often featured homicides. "Imaginary murders, usually with a lurid love interest, seem to have been the most popular" of all subjects (Neuburg, 127). Gallows literature—accounts of condemned murderers who were publicly hanged—was the most popular form of street literature, outselling other kinds of broadsides by a wide margin (M. Hughes, 9). These ballads and accounts were based on actual crimes and executions; hangings were public until 1868 and provided a "spectacle-cum-holiday" for the crowds who gathered to see them (M. Hughes, 10). After a wife-murder in 1831, Catnach "sent his versifiers down to cover the trial just as a modern editor would send reporters. He sold half a million copies of what they came back with."[5] Homicide was good business, and the gallows functioned as a sporting event, a threat, and a vivid opportunity to see criminals meet their end.

Although actual trials and executions were sometimes covered by writers, gallows literature owes more to imagination and convention than to journalism. Many ballads purport to be the work of remorseful criminals themselves, who show a remarkable propensity for repentent, languishing letters from the death cell. "Genuine" confessions are concocted and embellished by writers and patterers. Richard Altick writes that James Rush was an inspiration to one intrepid patterer who decided to have Rush "confess to the murder fourteen years earlier of his old grandmother, whom he buried under the apple tree in the garden; and, more recently, to the murder of his wife" (Altick, 53). Many dying confessions were written the night before the hanging by frantic writers or later invented from rumors and newspaper articles "with as much artistry and disregard for the facts as any novel" (M. Hughes, 10).

As in melodrama and sporting events, there are conventions within street literature that function as an important part of the public's enjoyment. A vivid woodcut often accompanied the account, showing the killing or the execution itself. If the nature of the crime is particularly violent, as in the dismemberment and burning of Jane Jones by Daniel Good, the woodcut features the crime; this murder was worthy of two panels.[6] Blood spurts with accusatory emphasis from the victim's multiple wounds, splattering the murderers. Despite the patterer's promise that each picture captures the crucial moments of a particular criminal, many woodcuts are used again and again. Extraordinarily popular contemporary murders, like those of Thurtell, Rush, and the Mannings, occasioned new pictures (Altick, 50). Otherwise, a few woodcuts did the work for most ballads.

Two particularly popular illustrations show the hapless criminal hanging. In each one, the figure is faceless, his head conveniently bagged. The criminal in one woodcut hangs on the scaffold with a huge crowd extending from the foreground to the horizon. The last row of observers wear hats and shawls, but otherwise, they are as anonymous as the criminal. The scaffold is framed by a white churchlike structure on one side and a dark prison on the other; the effect of the whole is stark, anonymous, and bleak. There is no action, merely the conclusion of an action. This woodcut was used as early as "The Trial and Execution of Martin Clinch and Samuel Mackley" in 1797 and as late as "The Execution of John Gleeson Wilson" in 1849 (Hindley, 181, 197). Another popular woodcut shows a figure hanging sideways, bent from the rope, hands bound. There is no foreground, no crowd, and a white background. In both woodcuts, and others used during this period, the murderer is captured at the moment of his punishment; the woodcut itself is an apprehension. In other pictures, there are multiple hangings or murders "photographed" by the artist acting as a witness of justice.

Beneath the woodcut, if one appears, is usually a prose account of the murder, a description of the execution, sometimes a confession in the form of a ballad often supposedly by the criminal, and final words (Altick, 48). Sometimes a letter to a grieving, shamed wife or sweetheart is added. Accounts of the murder itself are full of details about the commission of the crime without much explicit enlightenment as to why it was committed. In "The Life, Trial, Confession, and Execution of James Greenacre," the writer gives the "long and connected chain of evidence" which accused Greenacre of the murder of Hannah Brown without any mention of why he killed her; the medical evidence is detailed and sometimes italicized (Hindley, 192). The reader learns that the bone of her neck was *"sawed nearly through"* while she *"was yet alive,"* and that this "part of the evidence produced a thrill of horror throughout the court" (Hindley, 192). In "The Execution of William Cogan," the motive for the murder is cited perfunctorily: "They both drank freely, and when they got home they quarrelled" (Hindley, 200).

Writers often assume that readers will already know the motives for murder or will be able to deduce them from a few quick details of the victim's social and sexual standing. In these cases, balladeers hasten to illustrate what is still mysterious. In the famous "Red Barn" murder of 1828, William Corder killed Maria Marten, his lover, because she wanted to marry him and threatened to tell people about the child they buried. His confession deals lightly with motive and emphasizes details of what actually happened:

> When we left her father's house, we began quarrelling about the burial of the child; she apprehended wherein it was deposited would be found out. The quarrel continued about three quarters of an hour upon this sad [*sic*] and about other subjects. A scuffle ensued. . . . (De-Sola Pinto, 189)

The scuffle describes Maria's blood, murder, and eventual burial with great care. Ordinary places and objects—a red barn, a hammer—provide a frisson of identifying horror.[7] Stephen Knight points out a similar inattention to motive and emphasis on detail when discussing the Newgate Calendar: "Geography, tools of trade and crime, and names and ages of criminals and victims are all given in crisp factual detail. This does not extend to a clear view of the individual and the causes of action."[8] Motive in street literature is underplayed, implied, or omitted.

Another common convention in street literature is the tendency of the criminal to present his or her own story as a moral fable. Daniel Good "recalls" the way he burned his victim until "this dark deed by Providence was brought to light" (Hindley, 195). In "The Life, Trial, Execution, Lamentation, and Letter written by the unfortunate man James Ward," the unfortunate man warns his readers about the inevitability of capture and punishment:

> I dragged the body from the stile to a ditch running by,
> I quite forgot there's One above with an all-seeing eye,
> Who always brings such deeds to light, as you so plainly see,
> I questioned was about it and took immediately. (Hindley, c)

Sometimes the murderer asks readers for their prayers, as in "The Trial, Sentence, Confession, and Execution of F. B. Courvoisier" (Hindley, 193). At other times, the nameless narrator concludes with a moral admonition or tag at the end of the ballad, usually in language much weaker than the full and energetic description of the murder that precedes it:

> He soon was found guilty and sentenced to die,
> The death of a murderer on the gallows high,
> The blood of the murder'd must not cry vain,
> An we hope that his like we shall ne'er see again. (Hindley, 195)

Moralizing confession and remorse became so crucial a part of successful gallows literature that one of Mayhew's informants was quite aggrieved by the seemingly perverse insistence of Maria Manning—who, with her husband, killed her former suitor—on withholding an appropriate statement from the hangman in her final moments.

> Every day I was anxiously looking for a confession from Mrs. Manning. All I wanted was for her to clear her conscience afore she left this here whale of tears (that's what I always calls it in the patter), and when I read in the papers . . . that her last words on the brink of heternity was, "I've nothing to say to you, Mr. Rowe, but to thank you for your kindness," I guv her up entirely—had completely done with her. . . . the public looks to us for the last words of all monsters in human form, and as for Mrs. Manning's, they were not worth the printing. (Mayhew I, 224)

The warnings and repentence helped to "fend off the persistent complaints of the pious that crime literature of the streets was morally poisonous" (Altick, 48). They were thus commercial obligations, sops to critics.

Yet these ritualized confessions and warnings were more than that. They were expected and valued by the public. Murderers' crimes make them "monsters in human form," and accounts of their executions were popular in part as public expressions of relief. Murder overturns the moral and social order, but execution, with its punitive finality, restores the community from potential chaos. Similarly, the remorse and contrition of many criminals provides a satisfying, religious symmetry for the reader. Atonement mends the moral fabric murder rips. In his study of death in nineteenth- and twentieth-century fiction, Garrett Stewart discusses the way "fictional dying . . . is bent on meaning. . . . Lives may bow to the random, the undreamed; story must be ruled by congruity."[9] Early street literature is rigorously bent on meaning. Readers must have been reassured by the hope that "fiends" and "monsters" could return to humanity by suffering from a belated recognition of their wickedness.

Last words and final attitudes of murderers become extremely significant in street ballads. Descriptions stress the physical suffering and emotional responses of killers to emphasize that criminals are always subdued by society. Murderers in gallows literature are at their ends tormented, prayerful, or at the very least, suffering greatly. Corder is "resigned" at his execution and "so weak" that he can not stand by himself (Hindley, 189). Rush is also in "agony" about his crime and, like many criminals, is haunted in his death cell the night before by his victim (James, *Popular Literature,* 257). At the scaffold, he has a "most melancholy and dejected appearance," first walking with a "firm, unwavering step," and then raising "his pinioned hands to his face" and "trembling violently" (Hindley, 196). Criminals who are reconciled with God tend to die quietly and with some amount of miserable dignity, but those who protest their innocence to the last shout accusations, struggle, and suffer violent death throes. Maria Manning, considered by the public and the patterers to be the evil mastermind of the two Mannings, had "a long struggle with death," while her husband died very quickly (Hindley, 198). Conversely, William G. Youngman prays with "evident fervency," clasping his hands in "unmistakeable devotion" (Hindley, 202). As the drowning mind is said to see impressions of a whole life in a moment, suggests Stewart, "so too the hanged man is thought to have time for the rehearsal of life" (32). The murderer's attitude toward the murder determines his or her style of dying. Repentant killers are rewarded with quiet deaths, while arrogant criminals are punished with vividly horrific suffering for their refusal to reshape their poses for the public.

Audience response to execution is an important characteristic of gallows literature. At the execution of Robert Blakesley, "for the first couple of minutes, the wretched man struggled very much, to the great gratification of the crowd, at the pain he was supposed to be suffering" (Hindley, 194). Rush's death was "greeted with loud applause by an immense crowd" (Hindley, 196).

One narrator observes of the George Gardner hanging that "the crowd contained a large proportion of women, but was orderly in the extreme" (Hindley, 201). At one hanging, "the upturned faces of the thousands of spectators presented a most extraordinary spectacle" (Hindley, 200). Sometimes the crowd is presented as a group of potentially weak and wicked people subdued by the example before them. At other times, they are a moral, if somewhat bloodthirsty, force relieved by the vivid elimination of a dangerous element in society.

Stylistically, the ballads tend to be fairly uniform. The repetition of certain lines from broadside to broadside suggests that the same authors wrote many ballads and that particular descriptions were expected by the audience. "For the sake of cursed gold" acts as a form of shorthand in some ballads; with a short phrase explaining the motivation, writers locate readers in the crime and move on to more lurid details.[10] Many of the ballads and prose accounts feature what seem at first to be strong anticlimaxes. The ballad of William Weare begins with a graphic description of his death and ends with a deflationary addition of his name and address. These prosaic details impart a veracity to the ballad that might not have been there otherwise. The following paragraph concludes the prose account of John Gleeson Wilson's hanging: "This terminated the life of one of the greatest criminals that ever disgraced the human family. Upwards of 100,000 persons were present, the railway running cheap trains from all available parts" (Hindley, 197). Yet approximations of the crowd's size, accounts of extra trains, and local addresses stress the spectacular, ritual quality of the execution. These anticlimaxes may, in fact, have been read as second climaxes attesting to the significance and grim reality of the events.

The moment of ultimate justice often occasioned violence greater than that of the original crime. James Walvin notes that two criminals were hanged on February 23, 1807, "but twenty-seven spectators died in the crush."[11] The awful irony questions the usefulness of public executions as deterrents to other criminals. The image of a huge and rambunctious crowd that was as violent, in its way, as the murderer it came to see hanged was a haunting one for middle-class citizens. Yet the "campaigns against the violent and bloody recreations of the poor were often led by men whose own recreations were equally cruel" (Walvin, *Leisure and Society,* 10). These details of crowd size and misbehavior suggest that the appeal of hangings was to some extent a sporting one, reminding us that "well on into the 19th century, the fight broadsheet remained popular" (Holloway, 680). Prize fights also attracted thousands of people who traveled to matches on specially scheduled trains, and "on the not infrequent occasions when a pugilist was slugged to death, his adversary was charged with homicide."[12] Watching criminals meet with justice was itself a kind of blood sport.

The stylistic conventions regarding the crowd enable us to "appreciate the complex subtle effects . . . which these hangings would have had in a society permeated by public executions" (M. Hughes, 111). Treating the event as a public exemplar made its legitimacy somewhat more plausible, and writing about the orderliness of the crowd helps to confirm the sense that moral and legal order has been reestablished. Even when observers faint or behave wildly, this too may be interpreted as appropriate behavior: they are, in the world of street literature, moved by the extremity of what they witness or will witness. Public execution restores the authority that the murder threatened, and the crowd enacts whatever response is suggested by the ballad.

Street literature of the 1830s and 1840s is thematically unified by the idea of betrayal. Murderers are guilty not only of killing, but also of failing to honor the most basic contracts implied within particular kinds of human relationships. These betrayals include those of master by servant and guest by host. Courvoisier, murderer of Lord William Russell, craves God's mercy for having severed the master-servant bond with violence:

> I've slain a master good and kind
> To me has been a friend.
>  .   .   .   .   .   .   .   .
> I robb'd him of property and life,
> And the poor man of a friend. (Hindley, 193)

Far from a symbol of oppressive aristocracy, Russell embodies the nobility of the upper class. His death shocks by exploding a relationship that is, for some Victorian readers, sacrosanct. The Mannings's homicidal exploits are especially vile because they "betrayed a friend and took his life" (Ashton, 370). The victim, O'Connor, is presented as Maria's innocent suitor who suffers from the pangs of courtly love. He is their guest, but "as they fondly did caress him, / They slew him" (Ashton, 368–70). The Mannings bury him in the kitchen, the site of his death, and the idea of the guest-host relationship being betrayed in this way is only somewhat less horrible than when Gloucester is blinded by his guests in *King Lear*. Creating and honoring contracts is a human activity; abandoning them with violence seems a fearful descent to the bestial.

By far the most common relationship betrayed by murder in street literature is that of sweethearts. Men kill their mistresses when they get pregnant or insist on marriage, thereby interfering with plans for more socially suitable mates. Sometimes women kill their sexual partners when the men refuse to marry them. Rush is a "base seducer" who refuses pregnant Emily Sandford when she "begged most pleadingly to be his wife" (Hindley, 196). After Rush kills four people, she testifies against him on the stand. His rejection transforms her into a prophetic, avenging presence. Good's crime echoes the theme of the "helpless woman" betrayed by her seducer (James, *Popular Literature*, 256). George Caddell murders Miss Price after she becomes pregnant and urges marriage. This was her mistake, points out the writer: "She . . . still thought herself an equal match for one of Mr. Caddell's rank of life" (Hindley, 2).

The social ambition of the seducer and his partner's determination not to lose position sometimes create a murderous tension. Miss Lucy Gurd commits "Cruel and Inhuman Murder" because Captain Lawson seduced her, broke his promise to marry her, and boasted about the way he "triumphed over her virtue" while courting a wealthier woman (Hindley, 6). When she threatens his reputation, he tries to retrieve his incriminating letters and, with particularly poor timing, to force his sexual attentions on her. Until she met him, she "bore a most excellent character," but he drags her down (Hindley, 6). She evokes more sympathy than most killers in street literature, but as for so many fallen women in Victorian popular writing, loss of virginity is linked to violent death. Like Maria Martin and Miss Price, Miss Lucy Gurd is doomed to be a victim and a killer because of her "indecent" desires for erotic love and social status.

The independence of women is presented ambivalently in gallows literature, often with an emphasis on sexuality and violence (Vicinus, *Industrial Muse*, 10). Women die violently as victims of homicide or justice. They are punished for sexual adventuring, poor judgment, and social aspirations. Sympathy for the pregnant single woman is often laced with the sense that she causes her own death. The murders by or of women also tend to function as a kind of displaced sexual energy, and their executions as a purgation of eroticism.

The primitive excess of the killings—bludgeonings, burnings, dismemberments—finds stylistic and thematic analogues in Victorian pornography. Peter Webb has observed that "rape and flagellation" are the sexual activities most frequently described in nineteenth-century pornography.[13] The characteristic desperation and frenzied repetition he discusses could as easily apply to the violence of sexual crimes in gallows literature. As in the treatment of murder, "sexual fulfillment . . . is sought by the male, usually at the expense of the female" (119). In *Sexual Fiction,* Maurice Charney says that sexuality for Walter in *My Secret Life* "is a form of conquest,"[14] a familiar theme in street literature, where women are punished for exercising their sexual power. Even the startling fountains of blood so common in woodcuts have their parallels in Victorian pornography: Walter and others are compulsively frank about the physics and variety of "sexual juices that stain sheets and clothing" (Charney, 71). The images of murdered women in gallows literature usually celebrate the pornography of violence.

The transformation of conscious or unconscious female sexuality into violence allows the reader to dismiss it—and the implications of women's sexuality—with relief, in much the same way that the "fiends in human form" are dispatched so satisfyingly. Femaleness itself may be the source of women's violence. Elaine and English Showalter quote one Victorian who writes of menstruation: "It is not improbable that instances of femine cruelty (which startle us as so inconsistent with the normal gentleness of the sex) are attributable to mental excitement caused by this periodical illness."[15] Nina Auerbach has identified particularly Victorian concerns about women, sexuality, power, and taboo,[16] and street literature often asks the same questions as Victorian fiction and art, although in simpler ways.

Maria Manning becomes a nightmarish distortion of the abuse of sexual power in early popular writing. Her "sad and fatal morning" is on the day she marries Frederick Manning, not the day she murders O'Connor (Ashton, 368). In one version of the crime, "The Bermondsey Tragedy," her husband plaintively says: "'Twas she who shot O'Connor and swore she would shoot me, / Unless I would assist her to bury his body" (Hindley, 198). As a result of sexual adventuring and an unseemly desire for power, women may turn into Lady Macbeth. The inability or refusal to recognize traditional female roles, including that of the demure companion who repels advances while repressing her own sexual nature, can have violent repercussions.

Even "virtuous" women become symbols of a provocative sexuality that may lead to murder. Sarah Kirby dies at the hand of George Gardner, a rejected suitor, who had "amused himself" by "watching her undress through a chink in the wall" (Hindley, 200). He claimed that she withheld beer from him. Clearly, however, Kirby's murder is sexually motivated. A woman who has such an erotic effect demands action, in Gardner's view, and if she refused sex, murder is his only alternative. Because she insists on making her own sexual choices, she causes her own death. Homicide or execution eliminates the dangerous enigma of female sexuality.

Punished for losing their virginity, for retaining it, for becoming pregnant, for insisting on marriage, for social aspirations coupled with erotic desires, women in street literature are murdered. The connection of sexuality and violence in gallows literature of the 1830s and 1840s, apparent in the presentation of female victims and murderers, indicates the tensions in male-female relations. More significantly, such connections suggest that ignoring or rejecting traditional authority is dangerously threatening. Although street literature of murder does not address social issues as explicitly as early Victorian melodramas and fiction do, the punishments inflicted in it upon women who are somehow dangerous is part of what seems to be its consistent social function. The frantic, chaotic murders and ritualized executions of street literature reflect a resounding determination to punish criminals with the violence that characterizes their attack on legal, sexual, and moral authority.

# Melodrama, 1830–1850

In *The Fortunes of Nigel; or, King James I and His Times* (1822) by Edward Fitzball, a watchmaker complains that his idle apprentices have deserted him "because forsooth here has been a cry of murder—nothing more—only a cry of murder."[1] The cry of murder attracted and troubled many in the audience as well as on the stage of the early Victorian theatre, and this general concern is reflected in melodrama, one of the most popular entertainments of the time. Once dismissed by scholars as noisy, conventional claptrap, the themes and purposes of melodrama now illuminate many studies of nineteenth-century popular literature.[2] In the nineteenth century, when drama "was for the last time in English history an entertainment for all classes of society, a truly popular drama in both senses of the word,"[3] melodrama did more than animate escapist fantasies. The strenuous subgenre,

> with all its crudities, fantasies, and dramatized dream-world of ideal love, justice, courage, and virtue, was not only thoroughly representative of its age but also socially and politically more advanced than other forms of nineteenth century theatre. (Booth, "Defence," 9–10)

As Robertson Davies suggests in *The Mirror of Nature,* melodrama is a particularly revealing way to explore "what was taken for granted, or feared, or fiercely desired" at the time.[4]

The "Theatre for the People,"[5] whether set in medieval Spain or Victorian England, providing social comment or nautical adventure, often presented murder. Two early Victorian melodramas of homicide, *Maria Martin; or, The Murder in the Red Barn* (1840) and *The String of Pearls; or, The Fiend of Fleet Street* (1847), were especially popular. Their appeal and significance can be better understood when they are set among the usual conventions and purposes of melodrama.

Melodrama did not become a recognizably separate theatrical form until the 1790s, coinciding with the rise of the Gothic novel, a genre with many melodramatic characteristics. A sweeping range of plays could be called melodramas—by the late Victorian period they included "Gothic, domestic, Scribeian and Sardouian, sensation, Robertsonian drama, romantic cloak-and-sword drama, and the problem play"[6]—but in every permutation, hectic plots dominate characterization. The good end happily, after surviving extreme misfortune, while the bad die miserably. Michael Booth says that melodrama shows "the world its audiences want but cannot get,"[7] and Davies concurs: audiences "did not mistake romance for reality, but . . . wanted romance to sweeten reality" (24). The predictable features and conventions of the genre enable the plays to conclude with a resonant and satisfying finality.

Plots take place at breakneck speed and include an unchanging trinity of characters: hero, heroine, and villain. The hero almost always takes a back seat to the heroine and her relationship to the villain, who is usually male. The passive hero flounders on the high seas, or struggles to escape from imprisonment, reacting rather than acting. It is the "villain's desire for the heroine" that usually animates the plot (Booth, *Melodrama,* 24). He is never a likely suitor, and the following passage of *The White Slave; or, The Flag of Freedom* (1849) typifies the heroine's reaction to her pursuer: "I fear not your threats and menaces. The blood that flows in my veins teaches me to despise fear. Become yours—your bride? Dog! Rather would I die a thousand deaths than submit to such bondage" (Booth, *Melodrama,* 29). Often as not the heroine's virtuous contempt only inflames the villain further. His menacing courtship—or his decision to murder rather than ravish—suggests the thematic relationship between sexuality and violence that is crucial in both criminal melodrama and street literature.

Audience sympathies reside with the endangered female character, but the focus of the play is on the villain. Dramatists knew, as Gilbert Cross observes, that "human nature was more interested in unrelieved vice than in unfailing virtue."[8] Melodramatic villains are both exuberantly evil and "remarkably purposeful" (Booth, *Melodrama,* 18). The Byronic antiheroes of Gothic melodrama often experience shattering remorse, but Victorian evil-doers tend to disdain repentence and die with criminal dignity intact (Cross, 155). The most common formula for the genre requires a male villain, but female villains appear on the Victorian stage with some frequency. They are often punished for their crimes with greater severity than their male counterparts (Cross, 215). In George Lillo's *The London Merchant* (1731), a didactic drama still popular in the Victorian period, seductive Millwood entangles the criminal hero in a net of illicit sex and murder from which he cannot escape. She induces him to kill his uncle and, almost worse, to rob his employer. Both perpetrators die on the gallows, but he repents while she is launched into eternity unreconciled to her fate. Forceful, aggressive villains are punished in melodrama; forceful, demanding women are punished with particular vigor.

Chaos threatens to erode the moral authority of the melodramatic hero and heroine. The greater the danger, however, the greater the relief and satisfaction at the cheerful symmetry of the conclusion. Temporary chaos is heightened by the repeated use of falsely accused heroes and real or faked supernatural events. In *The Factory Strike* (1838), Warner, a passively virtuous worker, is arrested for the murder of the factory owner's son. The crime was committed by Harris, the agitator-villain, and Warner is reprieved at the final moment. Similarly, in *Maurice, the Woodcutter* (1830), Maurice is sentenced to death for the murder of Baron Liebheim. The real killer is apprehended in time to save Maurice. Supernatural elements in melodrama also provide additional suspense before the play's heartening resolution. The murderer of *The Eddystone Elf* (1833) is a monster or fairy; in *Susan Hopley; or, Circumstantial Evidence* (1841), a ghost urges the heroine to wreak vengeance on the man who murdered her master. The supernatural, like the fortuitous last-minute rescues of innocent characters, causes justice to be reestablished in the world of the play. As in street literature, the antisocial, anarchic forces of violence are subdued with perfect symmetry and moral aptness. The natural disasters and man-made menaces titillate without deeply disturbing because they "are only a lengthy prelude to inevitable happiness and the apotheosis of virtue" (Booth, *English Melodrama*, 14). Having experienced agonies of suspense on behalf of the virtuous, audiences earn the pleasure of the villain's punishment at the play's conclusion. Villains get theirs with biblical swiftness and violence. As the frightening excess of gallows literature is resolved in graphic accounts of executions, so the catastrophes in melodrama are constant but temporary and ultimately satisfying.

Murder and violent death are significant among the catastrophes of Victorian melodrama and occur in a variety of contexts. Often homicides complete an inevitable cycle of action; people receive what they deserve. In *The Fortunes of Nigel* (1822), robbers kill a miser; indeed, he urges them to kill rather than rob him. Soldiers murder Count Orloff in *The Twins of Warsaw* (1831) after his murder of an informer. Sometimes violent death clarifies the values and purposes of the play, as in *Black-Ey'd Susan; or, All in the Downs* (1829), in which William, the sailor-hero, tells of a "little picaninny" who fell into the water and was in danger from a huge shark when another sailer named Tom dove in: "when Tom came up, all over blood with the corpse of the baby, in his hand, and the shark turned over dead on its side—my eyes! such a cheer. . . ."[9] In this nautical melodrama, human life, at least that of a picaninny, is less moving than the bravery of gallant tar.

Murder was an immensely popular subject for drama, reflecting the public interest in murder in general:

> The rapid growth of literacy and the rise of the mass circulation newspaper also enabled the people of the mid-nineteenth century to read about all kinds of crime and excitement and, not surprisingly, the most sensational and intriguing events of this kind made natural topics for melodrama.[10]

Allardyce Nicoll's index of nineteenth-century play titles lists fifty dramas beginning with the word "murder" (Booth, *English Melodrama*, 51). Many melodramas were based on actual crimes that had captured the public's attention. In his memoirs, *I'd Like To Do It Again* (1931), playwright Owen Davis recalls that "if a particularly horrible murder excited the public, we had it dramatized and on the stage before anyone knew who had been guilty of the crime" (Booth, *English Melodrama*, 51). Booth and Altick cite many plays that were based on murders sometimes "purely local in origin, such as *The Murder of St. George's Fields, Murder in Hoxton*, and *The Murder at Sadler's Wells*" (Booth, *English Melodrama*, 51).

Of all the sensational melodramas from the early Victorian period, and perhaps the century, the anonymous *Maria Martin; or, The Murder in the Red Barn* (1840) and George Dibdin Pitt's *The String of Pearls; or, The Fiend of Fleet Street* (1847) were the most popular. Booth calls *Maria Martin* the most famous criminal melodrama of the period, placing *The String of Pearls* second (*English Melodrama*, 139). Murdered by William Corder in 1828, the hapless Maria Marten, whose last name is misspelled in most of the plays based on her death, was the "progenitrix of one of the most celebrated melodrama figures of all time."[11] Plays based on her murder were produced even before Corder's execution in Norwich. "Tens of dozens" of versions were performed throughout the British Isles (Kilgarriff, 206). Sweeney Todd, the "demon barber of Fleet Street," also appeared in many genres and productions of the nineteenth century. The character first became familiar to English readers in a serial called "The String of Pearls" in *The People's Periodical* over the winter of 1846–47 (Haining, *Mystery*, 12). Once on stage in 1847, the story of the homicidal barber was popular enough to be adapted at the penny gaffs (Cross, 233). Pitt revised the play in 1848, and another version emerged in 1862. *The String of Pearls* and *Maria Martin* have been retold in many forms both during and after the Victorian period.

The popularity of the plays may be partly attributed to their relation to real crimes: *Maria Martin* was based on a contemporary murder, and *The String of Pearls* was touted as true.[12] Yet other nineteenth-century plays were based on local crimes and did not achieve more than a momentary notoriety. *Maria Martin* and *The String of Pearls* fascinated Victorian readers and audiences because of the themes and energies within the plays themselves.

*Maria Martin* opens with the title character waiting for William Corder, whom her brother calls a "nasty, mean, ugly, sulky fellow."[13] After arriving and sending Maria off to talk to her mother about their wedding, Corder boasts about his murderous intentions. He reaffirms his evil purpose while waiting for Maria at the barn. When she comes, she notices his "wild look" (224). He bursts out that ever since she threatened to turn him in for the murder or death of their child, he has been enraged. Although they "are linked together by blood," he tells her that she must abandon all hope of marriage or die (224).

She can not believe his duplicity and refuses to withdraw her hopes; after a protracted struggle, with its own musical accompaniment, he kills her.

Mrs. Martin has visions of Maria murdered at the red barn and calls for everyone to search it; off-stage, the body is discovered in the barn. Mr. Martin sees a vision of Maria urging him to avenge her death. Corder, who has moved and is planning to marry, soliloquizes on "a distressful, horrid dream" of Maria in white clothing looking toward the barn (231). He is arrested at his home. Chained in his death cell, Corder again dreams of Maria's spirit, who accuses and then forgives him. When he wakes in guilt and terror, he hands a confession to the Sheriff, hoping that his example will "secure thousands from future ruin" (235).

Some of the most significant features of *Maria Martin,* including the focus on the murderer and his psychology, the social motivations for the crime, and the presence and function of the supernatural, are also apparent in *The String of Pearls.* This play opens in the barber shop with a ferocious Sweeney Todd warning his apprentice, Tobias Ragg, to keep his mouth shut and not draw any conclusions about what he might see or hear. Tobias innocently unnerves Todd by vowing "may I be made into veal pies at Mrs. Lovett's" for speaking out of turn.[14] Mark Ingestrie enters for a shave, and Todd learns that he carries a valuable string of pearls. After sending Tobias out on a pretext, he pulls an off-stage switch: Mark sinks in the chair, and the chair rises, empty. Todd tries to sell the pearls to his next customer, Jean Parmine, who deals in precious stones, but Parmine becomes suspicious and threatens to go to the magistrate. Todd forces him into the barber's chair, touches a spring, and watches the chair sink again; Todd exclaims diabolically, "I've polished him off" (249).

Meanwhile, a "ragged wretch" named Jarvis Williams has agreed to work for Mrs. Lovett, whose bakehouse is adjacent to Todd's barber shop, despite her condition that once he is inside his workplace, he may never leave it (251). She shows him the bakehouse, "a gloomy cellar of vast extent and sepulchral appearance," making ominous remarks about the curious way that "everybody who relinquishes this situation goes to his old *friends, friends* that he has not seen for many years" (252–53). While Jarvis muses, alone, on her odd manner, he tries a pie, but finds a hair in it. When he tries another and finds a button, he is overwhelmed by disgust and fear. Parmine appears through a hole he made in the wall; somehow he survived Todd's attack, and he and Jarvis escape through the hole. Todd enters with malevolent plans for just about everybody, particularly Mrs. Lovett, whom he suspects may be growing "scrupulous and dissatisfied" (254). When she overhears him and demands her share of their money, he tries to charge her for nonexistent costs. She pulls a knife, but he shoots her and drags her body to the ovens.

In the equally busy second act, Tobias threatens to go to the magistrate with what he knows. Todd overpowers him, but as the barber raises his knife, the chair sinks, and Mark, the owner of the pearls, rises from it, bloodied and disheveled. Todd conquers his hysterical fear to consign Tobias ("pale and dejected") to a madhouse (257). After Todd leaves, promising the keeper that Tobias will die suddenly, Jarvis appears to rescue the youth. Colonel Jeffery, a friend of Mark's lover, meets Todd, who tricks him into taking the pearls and turns him over to the police. When the barber is about to testify against Jeffery, however, Mark appears in the court. Terrified, Todd cries, "'tis useless to deny my guilt; the very dead rise from the cerements to prove Sweeney Todd a murderer," and falls (262). Mark, alive after all, tells the astonished crowd that he was saved by a miracle to "confound the guilty and protect the innocent" (262).

Both *The String of Pearls* and *Maria Martin* focus on their energetic, purposeful villains, characters who illustrate the popular melodramatic themes of remorse and the fated man.[15] Corder exults in his wickedness. Similarly, Todd has designed a uniquely grotesque method of murder, and he is not above contemplating the death of almost every character in the play. The dreams of *Maria Martin* and the apparent ghost of *The String of Pearls* work to break down the villains and bring them to justice. Maria Martin's spirit directs people to her body, haunts Corder, and finally presides at his execution, having exacted a confession from him at the last moment. Mark Ingestrie terrifies Todd by his appearance in the barber's chair, and systematically erodes his "killer's" credibility and sanity on the witness stand. In this way, the victims triumph.

The plays, however, do not stress the vindication of the virtuous, but the suffering of the guilty. Corder, chained in his cell, scorns himself and his miserable crime: "This bosom is a waste, a wilderness, a blank in the creation. Sin hath blighted all, and left me desolate—a very wretched—fit prey to the unlettered hangman" (234). Although he shows no specific sorrow or regret for Maria's death, preferring to dwell on his own monumental suffering, he abandons his disdain for the moral fetters of society. The sleep he hopes will bring him serenity only brings further horror as Martin points to her wounds and calls him her murderer. He wakes distracted and undone, determined at last to release a confession: "Oh, Heaven, 'tis but the darkness of my soul doth haunt me thus! All—all—is but a dream! Guilt—guilt—I cannot hide thee" (235). He hands the confession to the Sheriff, crying: "Guilt—sin—crime—horror— all is there" (235). In further contrast to his early energetic wickedness, Corder falls to his knees, piously urging that we remember him as a bad example. Maria Martin's vengeance is secondary to the fall and Byronic torment her killer undergoes. Those who attack the stability of society must suffer for their anarchic malevolence.

Sweeney Todd, similarly, is focal in his madness. After Mark's first appearance in court, Todd begs the court's pardon for "a sudden giddiness" (261). Then, like Macbeth seeing Banquo, he is entirely unstrung: "Look, my Lord

Judge, Mark Ingestrie is by your side! Do not whisper to him. Your ermined robe is stained with blood! Ha, ha, ha" (261–62). Todd can not imitate sanity as he babbles to the court:

> Yes, it was a dark, foul deed; but heed not what you hear Lord Judge—the prisoner has bought his victim! What! do you still remain, and suffer such corruptness? I feared it would come to this, and through accursed gold—for which men sell their souls and barter their eternal salvation! (262)

At Mark's third appearance, Todd proclaims himself a murderer and falls to the ground. Without explaining why he has preferred to haunt Sweeney rather than accuse him forthrightly, Mark merely concludes the play by announcing his purpose to confound the guilty and protect the innocent. As in *Maria Martin,* our sympathies are with the innocent, but our attention is on the villainous; the murderers are punished at great length, while the victims make only brief appearances in bringing those murderers to justice.

*Maria Martin* and *The String of Pearls* share several characteristics that are not regular features of melodrama and may help to explain the special appeal of criminal or homicidal melodrama, or at least of these two unusually popular examples. The lack of mystery and the presence of messy, on-stage crime are the most immediately striking of these shared characteristics. Each villain declares his homicidal intentions at the start of the play. Alone, Corder gloats over his hypocrisy, declaring that conscience can only bother one after a deed is committed; it can not prevent the deed. After starting guiltily at Tobias's innocent reference to meat pies at Mrs. Lovett's, Todd decides to kill Mark, his first customer. While whetting the razor on his hand, he chuckles, "I shall have to polish him off," laughing so malevolently that Mark threatens to leave the shop if he does it again (237). Todd "kills" him and attacks his next victim in a matter of minutes. Suspense in the play builds as the audience waits for the murderer to be apprehended, not revealed. As most people who saw the plays would know the plot anyway, suspense also resided in waiting for the crime to be committed. The guilty were guilty from the moment the curtain rose, and the audience was never at a loss as to who would commit the crime and suffer horribly for it.

Each murder occurs on stage with messy violence. Maria Martin's death is the climax of the first act. When she refuses to "renounce all pretensions" of marrying Corder, she tries to escape, but he seizes her and throws her around (225). She falls on her knees, begging for mercy in the name of the child. This only serves to make him "thirst for blood" (225). Music covers the rest of the action: "She shrieks as he attempts to stab her" (225). He hesitates at the last moment but fears that her screams will bring help and finishes her off after her plaintive cries for mercy: "He again attempts to stab her. She clings round his neck. He dashes her to the earth, and stabs her. She shrieks and falls. He stands motionless till the curtain falls" (226).

The violence of Todd's murders is also extreme. Although Mark simply sinks through the floor and disappears, Parmine fights with Todd and is forced into the chair after "a fierce struggle" (249). After musing on "a little poison, skillfully administered" as the proper way to kill Mrs. Lovett, the barber abandons that idea in favor of an instant death (254). Mrs. Lovett is also violent and in her rage at his attempt to cheat her of her share of the money, she threatens him with a knife, only to have him draw a pistol and shoot her. He "opens the furnace door, a fierce flare lights the stage—he drags the body of Mrs. Lovett to the ovens as the act drop falls" (254). As in the street literature of the period, the dastardly deed must appear in its full horror not only because violence was presumably entertaining, but also so that the villain's extreme punishment may be seen as just. Because one's sense of relief at the resolution of the criminal melodrama is measured by the chaos and crime that precede it, the murders in *Maria Martin* and *The String of Pearls* must be visible and excessive. The frenzied nature of the homicide and the ensuing excess of the villain's retribution justify each other; seeing justice done at the play's conclusion becomes a cathartic pleasure.

The plays share an even greater emphasis on the murderer than most melodramas do on the villain. Psychology becomes focal. Corder is arrogant, evil, and hypocritical, but also himself fearful. The audience is drawn into intimacy with the murderer and his volatile concerns through the constant use of soliloquies. Each of Corder's conversations is preceded or followed by a soliloquy in which he discusses his plans and hopes. Like many heroic villains of the Victorian period, Corder is a Shakespearean shadow. As he prepares for the murder of Maria, he echoes Macbeth: "The deed were bloody, sure; but I will do it, and rid me of this hated plague" (216). Although he grapples with fearful hesitation several times, his struggle results in more evil. He emerges with satanic energy and speaks with hubristic exultation:

> Am I turned coward, or what is it makes me tremble thus? Have I not heart sufficient for the deed? or do I falter with remorse of conscience? No, by heaven and hell 'tis false! a moment, and I launch her soul into eternity's wide gulph, the fiends of hell work strong within me. 'Tis done! I'll drown my fears and slake my thirst for vengeance in her blood. (219)

His fear of discovery causes him to contemplate another death, that of Maria's brother George: "If I thought he overheard me, I'd strangle him" (219). As Maria approaches the barn, he calls on his allies, the "fiends of hell," to spur him to murder and help him "not to feel pity nor remorse" (223, 224). Corder and his plans dominate *Maria Martin* in part because we enter into his world and his psychology through soliloquies.

In a similar way, the psychology as well as the actions of Sweeney Todd are central to *The String of Pearls*. The barber is not only evil, like Corder, he is insane and takes far more pleasure in crime than Corder does. He laughs so repeatedly and unpleasantly in anticipation of Mark's murder and the acquisition of his pearls that even Mark, the most passively innocent of nautical heroes, is unnerved. Todd delights in the double meaning of "polishing him off." Where Corder is irredeemably wicked, aligning himself with the devil several times, Todd is psychotic as well. He threatens to kill Tobias—"I'll cut your throat from ear to ear"—at the start of the play and promises or attempts to kill practically everyone by the play's conclusion (246). Even more clearly associated with the devil than Corder, Todd is bathed in the fiery glow from the bakehouse furnace as he drags Mrs. Lovett to the ovens. When Jarvis hears the barber coming, proverb becomes prophecy: "Talk of the devil and he's at your elbow" (255). Designing and arrogant, Todd tells Mrs. Lovett: "Idiot! you should have known Sweeney Todd better, and learnt that he is a man to calculate his chances" (254). William Corder finally repents at the end of *Maria Martin,* although not before he has been thoroughly haunted. Sweeney Todd, in his furious, fearful insanity, wishes he had not become unhinged by Mark's "ghost," but he curses gold, not himself, and never seems to regret a life of homicide. The deviousness, arrogance, and dangerousness of the two murderers overshadow every other character on stage.

The crucial connection between sexuality and violence provides the basis for each murder. Often either the victims or causes of murder in melodrama, women are frequently both. In *Luke the Labourer* (1826), patient and virtuous Maria dies from starvation and a blow, both the doing of her indolent husband, Luke, who is ill-tempered and lazy. Similarly, in the temperance melodrama *Fifteen Years of a Drunkard's Life* (1828), Vernon, a gentleman, degenerates through alcoholism and recognizes his wife, Alicia, only after fatally wounding her in a desperate robbery attempt years after their separation. Count Orloff in *The Twins of Warsaw* (1831) murders women and orphans. Women in melodrama, helpless as orphans, often seem to inspire their own deaths merely by existing virtuously. The innocence of the often arbitrary victim emphasizes the murderer's malevolence.

There is an explicit connection between sexuality and violence in criminal melodrama that is recognizably Gothic. In *Frankenstein,* the doctor's fear of the monster is strangely linked to his apprehensive anticipation of his upcoming marriage to his cousin. The monster's ominous warning that he will be with the doctor on his wedding night has multiple meanings for Frankenstein. In many novels and melodramas of the Romantic period, the murderous and lustful impulses of villains are mixed; rapes and attempted rapes sometimes take place in crypts and graveyards.[16] Edda of the melodrama *Edda; or, The Hermit of Warksworth* (1820) is mad with misery after being seduced and abandoned; her madness and need for vengeance drive her to kill her seducer. Sexuality—especially women's sexuality—often results in or is connected to homicide. This is especially true in the numerous vampire plays of the early part of the century.

In Planché's *The Vampire* (1820), the vampire's victims are beautiful young maidens whom he first must marry. Ruthven, the vampire, courts Lady Margaret, who is stricken by the memory of a gory vision she had in which he appeared. When he seizes her hand, she murmurs, "Heavens! How strange a thrill runs through my frame. . . . a strange confusion, a wild emotion overpowers me."[17] Sexuality may have been submerged in violence on stage because of "the official censorship of the Lord Chamberlain's Office" and "the innate censorship of the time" (Bargainnier, 729). One critic writes that "the reading public went on a century-long debauch of printed sadism to replace the sex notoriously absent in Victorian literature."[18] Whether or not he would agree with that blunt analysis, Gilbert Cross observes that "conservatism toward displaying sex on stage" ran extremely high, and French plays were often cut and rewritten for the proprieties of the proper English stage (Cross, 210).

*Maria Martin* dealt with sexuality vigorously and explicitly at a time when love on stage was the "love of Aphrodite not Eros" (Cross, 209). The motivations and nature of the murder suggest that death is punishment for women who do not understand or respect social authority. Corder has several reasons for killing Maria: all have to do with her fallen state, her shocking hopes to marry him despite her fall, and her supposed infidelity with another man. Although the audience knew from the outset who was going to be killed, a foreign viewer could have guessed the victim's identity because of Maria's implied sexual passion, in and of itself a crime. Maria's brother is astonished at "how deeply and fondly my silly sister loves him" (216). He "doesn't like the look of him," and Maria's response reveals her faulty judgment: "Were you a young woman, my dear little brother, I think you'd . . . feel towards him as I do" (215). Her sexuality endangers her. Maria's very existence after illicit and mutually pleasurable sex is a motive to murder: "I loathe the banquet I have fed upon," says Corder (216). His own desires are now only hers and repulsive. "Your blood be upon your own head," he declares, and Maria is thus the cause of her own murder in several ways, all stemming from her sexual behavior. In the world of the play, her murder is an execution.

Sexual motives for murder in these criminal melodramas, like those in ballads, are inextricably related to social issues. Both Corder and Todd kill partly to fulfill their visions of rising in the community. Having ruined Maria's reputation, Corder kills her to protect his own; marrying her would abort his ambitions for a more suitable wife. When she declares her love for him, he questions her sincerity: "Nay, did you love me you would secure my fame" (225). Love can only be proved by a show of devotion to his status. Marriage would be her salvation but his undoing.

Her desperate hopes may have resonated beyond the stage into the audience. With the New Poor Law of 1834, "an unwed mother became solely responsible for the support of her bastard; there was no provision at all to help her get money from its father."[19] Sally Mitchell describes the way legislators saw pregnant women as potential extortionists and blackmailers, rather than as fallen angels (23). Audiences would have known that Maria had no recourse beyond threats and moral force. Corder is understandably amazed by her pleas: "Marry thee! You cannot think me so lost" (225). For him, sacrificing his ambitions would be as shocking as murder—perhaps more so. Before his arrest, he recites the progress he has made toward his goal:

> How strange is every action of my life. I met by chance a lady some time ago at Seaford, where I had been for the recovery of my health. From thence I came to London. Some time elapsed, and when passing on through Fleet Street, again did I accost her. We parted, and wonderful to say, this is the very woman who has answered my advertisement, and whom I have selected as the future partner of my life. (231)

Corder has won a lady, not a woman, a suitable "partner" in a business marriage that will help him to rise in society. As a fallen woman, Maria is a millstone that will keep Corder from his "proper" social level.

The sexual reasons for Maria's violent death are all connected to power. Corder suspects her of infidelity. Even though he bears her little love now, any mention of the child—which is sometimes referred to as theirs, sometimes as hers with another lover—increases his murderous rage because it symbolizes crime, lust, and guilty sexuality with another partner. Ultimately, Maria is killed because she knows enough about Corder to put him in danger. She assures him that she would never turn him over to the police as she once threatened in anger, but the possibility that she could is as damning to Corder as the certainty that she will. He can not tolerate her ascendancy in any part of their relationship. Her lack of submission is galling and dangerous: "And am I not in thy power? No—(*Pause*)—thou art in *mine,* and by Heaven I will keep thee so; ay, and for ever" (235). Maria dies for her refusal to abide by the authority of sexual tradition. Her knowledge of their crime is power, but so is her carnal knowledge, and Corder can not let her live with both.

Sweeney Todd's erotic feelings are totally submerged in the climactic pleasure he takes in murdering again and again. There are curious and significant differences in motivation for the "murder" of his male customers, who do not really die, and his actual killing of Mrs. Lovett. He tries to murder his customers due to his psychotic delight in violence coupled with the desire to improve his economic status. He kills Mrs. Lovett in a distorted and parodistic version of the same sexual and social motivations that cause Corder to kill Maria.

Greed and the desire to rise in society through wealth initiate his life of theft and murder. His account of his path to crime parodies the same social and economic values held by most upwardly mobile Victorians:

> When a boy, the thirst of avarice was first awakened by the fair gift of a farthing; that farthing soon became a pound; the pound a hundred—so to a thousand, till I said to myself, I will possess a hundred thousand. This string of pearls will complete the sum. (248)

This is a criminal version of the Victorian work ethic. He wants money and works as hard for it as any tailor or merchant. He invents the deadly and complicated barber chair, designs the practical, if grotesque, connection between his shop and Mrs. Lovett's, and pays scrupulous attention to the financial details of his business. His values mirror those of hard-working, ambitious businessmen around him. Interestingly, Todd blames his criminal activities on the gift of a farthing he got as a child, rather than on any personal characteristic or trauma; it is as if the desire to improve one's social and economic standing is succumbing to temptation, and there is no virtue in either. In an odd way, he is almost a criminal hero, as in the Newgate novels and plays. His crimes reflect the legal crimes around him, and he indignantly accuses Parmine of trying to cheat him of his "rightful" money for the string of pearls.[20]

The motivation for the actual murder in *The String of Pearls* is not explicitly sexual; the only talk of love, romantic or erotic, occurs in a farcical comic scene involving minor characters ("The fire of love rageth—it consumeth my very vitals") and Colonel Jeffery's sedate proposal to the woman who loves Mark (251). Although there is no romantic relation between Mrs. Lovett and Sweeney Todd, there are overtones of parodied love in their bakehouse confrontation. Todd uses the language of lover or husband, and strangely, Mrs. Lovett is killed for the same reason as Martin: she knows too much about Todd, and she is a partner in sin. Neither villain can stand the thought of being in a woman's power, and her existence becomes a threat. In a burst of paranoia, Todd broods:

> I have too many enemies to be safe. I will dispose of them one by one, till no evidence of my guilt remains. My first step must be to stop the babbling tongue of Tobias Ragg. Mrs. Lovett, too, grows scrupulous and dissatisfied; I've had my eye on her for some time, and fear she intends mischief. (254)

It is unclear whether he fears she will turn him in to the police, or that she merely wants to stop her own part in their crimes. Mrs. Lovett has not threatened him, as Martin threatened Corder, but she is an accomplice. Her wavering accuses and endangers Todd. Like Martin, she refuses to disappear quietly. She wants to be a full partner—to have a business marriage—an "equal share of the fruits of our mutual bloodshed" (254). Like Martin and Corder, the barber and the baker are murderously linked by their crimes.

Even in parody, sexually based relationships are inseparable from economic concerns. Todd pretends to go along with her demand for money, but then, in a bizarre impersonation of a husband, he decides to charge her for "support, lodging, and clothes," although she cries, "Why, I haven't had a new dress for these six months!" like any plaintive wife or mistress (254). "Besides," he adds, "am I to have nothing for your education? (*Draws finger significantly across his throat*) Yes, for some years you have been totally provided for by me" (254). Mrs. Lovett is treated like a demanding lover or a nagging, acquisitive wife who will not let her husband reasonably pursue his business ends. The only person the "friend of Fleet Street" really kills is a demanding and potentially powerful woman.

Both *Maria Martin* and *The String of Pearls*, then, feature female victims whose murders are centrally connected to their sexuality and demands for power. As in street literature of the gallows, the murder or violent death of women in melodrama is a result of social and economic ambition. In both street literature and melodrama, women are killed for wanting social and sexual parity with men. Those who neglect the traditional routes to status or who defy conventional moral codes are murdered. Men kill to protect their status from the embarrassing or designing attempts of guilty women who determine to share it. Although social environments in ballads and melodramas are not presented as explicitly as they are in early Victorian fiction, some of the implications of homicide in these two popular genres are clear. The tension between sexuality and an inordinate desire for social or economic status is often murderous, and those who flout authority do not go unpunished.

# 3

# Fiction, 1830–1850

Criminal fiction of the early Victorian period fueled critical debate. Although some readers rejected the Newgate novels that sprang up in the 1830s and 1840s, books such as Edward Bulwer-Lytton's *Paul Clifford* (1830) and Harrison Ainsworth's *Jack Sheppard* (1840) were immensely popular. Newgate novels chronicle the adventures and escapes of independent, courageous criminals, often legendary eighteenth-century robbers and highwaymen. Some have liberal, reforming emphases; in *Paul Clifford,* Bulwer-Lytton criticizes laws for making and punishing criminals instead of preventing crime.[1] Many people believed, however, that fiction featuring robbery and murder inspired rather than warned against crime by presenting wrongdoers sympathetically. The literary trend toward criminal heroes and their violent and illegal activities became so pronounced that Thackeray created *Catherine* (1839–40), an aggressive anti-Newgate novel, with "the greatest disgust for the characters he describes" and the hope that he would "cause the public also to hate them."[2] Like other critics of the genre, Thackeray worried that romanticized accounts of crime would inspire actual crime.[3] Despite Thackeray's "persistent and resourceful opposition to the sensational crime fiction" of the period, he was "an aficionado of crime" (Borowitz, "Thackeray," 15). He considered and enjoyed criminal cases, and, "like DeQuincey and Defoe before him, he wrote a criminal biography."[4]

This ambivalence characterizes many crime readers and writers of the early Victorian period, emerging in all forms of criminal fiction. I will discuss the treatment of murder in four different kinds of early Victorian novels: Bulwer-Lytton's *Eugene Aram* (1831), a romantic Newgate novel; Dickens's *Oliver Twist* (1837), a sensational melodramatic fiction; *Catherine* (1839–40), a parody; and Elizabeth Gaskell's *Mary Barton* (1848), a social-industrial novel.

In these four novels, murder is thematically central and influences or affects the characters' destinies. The circumstances of the murder itself, the psychology of the murderer, the killer's role in his or her own death, and the use of suspense or mystery are significant in each work. Although they share with contemporaneous ballads and melodramas an emphasis on the murderer, the novels are markedly different from these other genres in the variety of suspenseful situations and the relevance of social conditions to the crimes. All four of the novels show particular sympathy for the poor and working classes, especially working women; each employs the pattern of seduction and betrayal of a poor woman by a wealthy man. The place of the murder itself in early Victorian criminal fiction depends on the novel's subgenre and the author's purposes; how the murder is presented, in turn, affects our response to the criminal. *Eugene Aram, Catherine, Oliver Twist,* and *Mary Barton,* like many popular Victorian works, imply or make statements about society through their treatments of murder and murderers.

Bulwer-Lytton's *Eugene Aram,* a Newgate novel that romanticizes the criminal, was an immediate and overwhelming success with the reading public.[5] Nancy Tyson traces the lasting appeal of the story in *Eugene Aram: Literary History and Typology of the Scholar-Criminal,* noting that it was dramatized at least ten times in seventy years (118). In Bulwer-Lytton's version, Aram's intelligence blinds him to moral truth and becomes a tragic flaw. Critics were inflamed by the way the novel "elevates Aram's social status, omits the wife and seven children deserted by the actual Aram, and turns him into a High Tragic Hero."[6] Because the victim of *Eugene Aram* is completely repulsive, the scholar-criminal seems to commit "an act of heroism carried out in the service of a principle" (Tyson, 141). This vision of homicide caused such long-lived outrage that Bulwer-Lytton was forced to revise the book seventeen years after its first publication (Tyson, 87).

Bulwer-Lytton romanticizes both the criminal-hero and the eighteenth-century England in which he lives. The novel opens in idyllic Grassdale. Roland Lester, a widower "of an affectionate and warm heart," has retired to domestic activities and the appreciation of his two daughters.[7] Beautiful Madeline is "eminently thoughtful and high-wrought," while cheerful Ellinor possesses a good but "less elevated" character (8). Their cousin Walter hopes to marry Madeline but is thwarted by her fascination with Eugene Aram, a withdrawn, middle-aged scholar. When Madeline eventually causes "that vague sensation of delight which preludes love" in Aram's heart, Walter leaves Grassdale to see the world (22).

The novel's second plot, which converges with the first when Aram is accused, tried, and hanged for an old crime, begins when Walter discovers that his father led a dissolute life under the name of Daniel Clarke. He begins to suspect that Clarke died under Aram's hand. Meanwhile, a crude criminal named Houseman, Aram's cousin, arrives in Grassdale and blackmails the scholar over their past. Houseman later identifies Clarke's recently unearthed bones and, in Walter's presence, accuses Aram of the murder. Bent on justice and vengeance, Walter returns three hours before Madeline's wedding to have the groom arrested. At his trial, Aram speaks brilliantly but unconvincingly in his own defense, claiming that the bones were not proved to be Clarke's and that Houseman accused Aram to throw suspicion from himself. Madeline dies of shock and sorrow without ever losing her faith in Aram's innocence. In his death cell, the scholar writes a long autobiographical confession detailing the circumstances of the murder. He attempts suicide but is revived and brought to the gallows, where he dies before he can be hanged.

The murder is presented in a flashback from Aram's point of view. In their younger days, he and Houseman knew Clarke, and Aram was disgusted by him:

> To over-reach, to deceive, to elude, to shuffle, to fawn and to lie, were the arts to which he confessed with so naked and cold a grossness, that one perceived that in the long habits of debasement, he was unconscious of what was not debased. (258)

Aram brooded on the lack of justice that made Clarke wealthy while he was so poor. Then, he recalls bitterly, Clarke "taunted my poverty" (260). Seeing Aram's rage and frustration, Houseman invited him to kill Clarke. The scholar also learned that "a quiet, patient-looking gentle creature," a lacemaker, was enticed to Clarke's house and subjected to "the most brutal violence" (261). When the story leaked out, she killed herself in a "paroxysm of shame and despair" (261). Clarke and Houseman come to Aram's room, where the former speaks "with the utmost unconcern of a fraud he purposed, and with a heartlessness that made my veins boil, of the poor wretch his brutality had destroyed" (262). They leave the room for a walk some way out of town:

> We walked forth; the rest—why need I tell?—I cannot—O God, I cannot! Houseman lied in the court. I did not strike the blow—I never designed a murder. Crime enough in a robber's deed! He fell—he grasped my hand, raised not to strike but to shield him! Never more has the right hand cursed by that dying clasp been given in pledge of human faith and friendship. But the deed was done, and the robber's comrade, in the eyes of man and law, was the murderer's accomplice. (262)

Unsuspected, Aram buried his share of the money that he and Houseman stole from Clarke. The scholar moved, withdrew from society, and "never touched what I had murdered my *own* life to gain" (262).

Bulwer-Lytton performs authorial gymnastics to guarantee a partially sympathetic reception of his criminal hero; the grounds on which we understand Aram are constantly shifting, especially in the case of his crime. The murder occurs fourteen years before the action of the novel begins, but we do not learn about it until the penultimate chapter, when we have already formed an idea of Aram's elevated, though flawed, character and values. Secondly, we are spared the actual murder even in memory because of Aram's romantic tendency to emphasize the symbol—Clarke futilely grasping his hand—rather than the fact. The crime becomes a personal crisis of will for Aram, and he remembers it in this typically solipsistic fashion, not in a more graphic, factual way. Lastly, and most significantly, Aram did not actually murder Clarke; he was a morally guilty accomplice. This revelation, in a last-minute confession, is meant to be taken as truth, not evasion. It is peculiar and telling that Bulwer-Lytton, whose self-avowed purpose is to expose the sophistical reasonings that caused Aram to commit the crime, resorts to a sophistry of sorts in misleading us to think of the scholar as a murderer. Presenting Aram as a killer, not a robber, throughout the book raises the emotional stakes. By revealing at the last moment that Aram is not a murderer after all, Bulwer-Lytton softens Aram's actual crime. He also emphasizes Aram's arrogant character. Aram takes possession of the murderer's guilt while retaining the relative moral innocence of a passive bystander. His is not a minor crime but, typically, Aram intensifies his role and purpose in the murder itself.

In the context of the novel, Aram's real crime is neither robbery nor murder. He decided to play God by sentencing Clarke to death, and he did not stop the crime when struck by its actual horror. He is punished for his arrogance and detachment. Like Byronic heroes of the Romantic period, Aram cuts himself off from society and can only understand the external world through self-reference. He has abdicated his responsibilities as a member of the community. Although struck by the poverty and misfortune of Grassdale's working classes, Aram's sympathy is expressed through flowery rhetoric, not action. The reader is repelled by Aram's egotistic sensitivity and pride. However, as with Byron's heroes, the act of withdrawing from society is simultaneously presented as a courageous and dashing one. Aram's isolated pursuit of his studies earns him the respect of the community he shuns, and Madeline is intrigued and infatuated by his knowledge. His suffering, if limitlessly self-conscious, is genuinely noble. He grows more dignified after his arrest. The crime of which he is accused is itself a sympathetic one, as Clarke is clearly a threatening and evil presence in the community. Thus the reader feels ambivalent toward Aram, his crime, and his way of life. More significantly, becoming embroiled in the contradictions and subtleties of Aram's character distracts us from Clarke's violent death. We are asked to attend to Aram rather than to his crime.

In *Oliver Twist*, the crime and the psychology of the criminal are also focal, but the crime is murder and the criminal violent, not cerebral. The murder of Nancy is graphic and central to the killer's psychology and our response to him. In the principal action of the novel, the orphan Oliver passes between two opposing realms. The world of exploitative, murderous indifference is represented by the parish workhouse, Sowerberry's funeral establishment, and the criminality of Fagin and his associate Bill Sikes. When forced to participate in other people's crimes, Oliver meets the emissaries of the opposite world, that of care and benevolence. Being snatched or catapulted from one realm to the other, Oliver discovers that Nancy is the only caring force in the criminal world; she tries to protect him from Fagin and Sikes. She again tries to rescue Oliver by warning Rose Maylie that he is in danger, and Fagin incites Sikes to kill her for this betrayal.

Even more forcefully than Bulwer-Lytton, Dickens depicts a crime that requires the reader to consider the criminal's psychology. The murder of Nancy is more graphic than the crime for which Aram is partly responsible, and the aftermath of her brutal death is no less grim than the killing itself. Fagin goads Sikes to a murderous rage by implying that Nancy has betrayed them, describing her crime, then suggesting of another associate, "Suppose that lad . . . was to peach—to blow upon us all."[8] He slyly asks Sikes what he would do; Sikes replies, "I'd grind his skull under the iron heel of my boot into as many grains as there are hairs upon his head" (418). His reply to Fagin's next question— "What if *I* did it!"—evokes an even more homicidal response (419). Fagin then calls on Noah, his spy, to tell Sikes about Nancy's meeting with Oliver's virtuous friends. After this maddeningly deliberate revelation of her guilt, he hypocritically asks Sikes, "You won't be—too—violent, Bill?"

Sikes commits the crime itself at night: "There's light enough for wot I've got to do" (422). After realizing what Sikes intends, Nancy begs him to "spare my life for the love of Heaven, as I spared yours. . . . I will not loose my hold, you cannot throw me off. Bill, for dear God's sake . . . stop before you spill my blood" (423). Spoken in desperate loyalty, her words turn out to be prophetic; Sikes later discovers she "will not loose" her hold as she haunts him after the murder. Sikes takes out his pistol, but knows "even in the midst of his fury" that shooting her would be too dangerous for him, so "he beat it twice with all the force he could summon" across her face:

> She staggered and fell, nearly blinded with the blood that rained down from a deep gash in her forehead, but raising herself, with difficulty, on her knees, drew from her bosom a white handkerchief—Rose Maylie's own—and holding it up, in her folded hands, as high towards Heaven as her feeble strength would allow, breathed one prayer for mercy to her Maker.
>
> It was a ghastly figure to look upon. The murderer, staggering backward to the wall and shutting out the sight with his hand, seized a heavy club and struck her down. (423)

The horror of the deed infects even Sikes. The bloody details, combined with the heavily symbolic resonances of Nancy reaching toward Heaven with Rose's handkerchief, help to make this scene almost hypnotic in its effect.

Although Sikes's act is primitively evil and repugnant, his unexpected capacity for guilt and remorse humanizes him. Suddenly he is vulnerable. After leaving the scene of the crime, he panics when a blithe peddler draws attention to a mark on his hat: "Here is a stain upon the hat of a gentleman in company, that I'll take clean out before he can order me a pint of ale" (427). So terrified that he does not realize the accidental and playful nature of the remark, Sikes "with a hideous imprecation overthrew the table, and tearing the hat from him,

burst out of the house" (428). He can no longer use violence to control his circumstances because "there were twenty score of violent deaths" in his fear
(429). The once-tyrannical criminal is now subject to the dreadful personifica-
tion of his surroundings: "Every object before him, substance or shadow, still
or moving, took the semblance of some fearful thing" (429). Nancy's eyes, "so
lustreless and so glassy," haunt her killer, and his decision to return to London
for a hiding place is pathetic: "There's somebody to speak to there, at all
events" (430, 432). Never before has Sikes expressed so basic a human need.

Perversely, Sikes's humanity emerges only when he has cast himself from
every stratum of society. After a few days of terror and isolation, he is less
himself because he has become every man; his former companions are appalled
to see his "blanched face, sunken eyes, hollow cheeks, beard of three days'
growth, wasted flesh, short thick breath: it was the very ghost of Sikes" (448).
He "made as though he would shake hands" with Charley Bates, who cries,
"Don't come nearer me. . . . You monster" (449). Ironically, Sikes has never
been less a monster than in that small, tentative gesture. Sikes becomes a figure
with whom the reader can identify when he is being hunted down like an animal. When a demonic crowd pursues him, he is nameless because he has become, in some ways, everyone. We can not help but recall Oliver's panic
when, early in the novel, he is mistaken for a thief and chased through the
streets:

> There is a passion *for hunting something* deeply implanted in the human breast. One
> wretched breathless child, panting with exhaustion; terror in his looks, agony in his
> face . . . they hail his decreasing strength with still louder shouts, and whoop and scream
> with joy. "Stop thief!" Ay, stop him for God's sake, were it only in mercy! (99)

Sikes's panic is no different from Oliver's: "The man had shrunk down,
thoroughly quelled by the ferocity of the crowd and the impossibility of escape"
(453). Ironically, the murder of Nancy and its aftermath humanize the man
whose violence set the chase in motion.

Most sympathetic after he commits a horrible murder, Sikes and his sudden vulnerability force the reader to consider the nature of crime. Criminals
may behave like "fiends in human form," but even at their worst, they show
tender possibilities that work to enforce the connections Dickens has been making throughout the novel between the worlds of the criminal and the lawfully
respectable. Virtue and humanity exist in the underworld of Nancy and Sikes.
Conversely, violence animates the supposedly righteous mob pursuing Oliver,
and criminal neglect resides by legal fiat in the workhouse. The murder—its
course, violence, and aftermath—enables Dickens to complicate the seeming
simplicity of his moral design and to draw lines across the division between the
criminal and the respectable.

Thackeray also uses a violent crime to comment on the criminality of contemporary society in *Catherine,* his gory anti-Newgate novel published serially in *Fraser's* from 1839 to 1840. Thackeray hated Newgates—especially *Eugene Aram,* which he parodied in "George de Barnwell"—because they made crime romantic and criminals dashing.[9] He also despised their fakery: "Newgate novels . . . pretended to portray 'low life' but created only 'the sham low' which catered to the middle-class reader" by putting familiar ideas into the mouths of glorified murderers (Ferris, 13). With genial contempt, *Catherine*'s narrator promises that his characters will suit the "present fashionable style and taste," as they are "agreeably low, delightfully disgusting, and at the same time eminently pleasing and pathetic" (166).

Thackeray lampoons what he considers the vulgar and debasing taste for Newgate fiction, but he also burlesques the morally reprehensible desire to get rich and rise in society at any cost. That desire incites criminals in *Catherine* to cheat, dissemble, betray, even kill. Genteel, upwardly mobile ingenues or merchants are indicted alongside the grubby criminals they would disdain. By the way Thackeray presents the murder, however, and in his ambivalent response to his central character, he makes the criminal—if not the crime—more attractive than he intends.

Catherine is "a very smart, handsome, vain, giggling servant-girl" employed by her aunt at the Bugle Inn because her good looks attract business (175). Courted by John Hayes, she is infatuated with Count Galgenstein, who seduces her with tantalizing accounts of life among aristocrats and effusive compliments on her beauty. He is "a professional lady-killer, and therefore likely at some period to resume his profession" (202). After one violent quarrel between the lovers, the malicious Corporal Brock tells her, "He wants you off his hands; he's sick of you" (218). Catherine has a child by the Count and the baby is put out to nurse with the Billings family. When Brock robs Galgenstein after learning that he was going to have the Corporal dismissed from his regiment, Catherine is held responsible for the crime. She tries to return to her aunt's but is turned away. Catherine marries John Hayes, and the Count weds a wealthy aristocrat. After having "obtained a complete mastery over her lord and master," Catherine decides she wants her son back (291). Brock, now known as Major Wood, finds the child and returns him to his eager mother, telling Hayes that the child is Catherine's orphaned nephew.

Young Tom Billings grows into a surly thug and Brock, now the Rev. Dr. Wood, moves in with the menage. Hearing that the Count is in town, Catherine sends Tom to him. The meeting is inauspicious, although Galgenstein gives Tom money. Pathetically, Catherine loiters around the rooms of her former lover. Finally, at Marylebone Gardens, the Count is "amazingly stricken by the gait and ogling of the lady in the mask" (340). They renew their romance. She fights with the suspicious Hayes about it and attacks him with a knife. Afterward, she fantasizes about his death: "If I were free, Max would marry me; I know he would;—he said so yesterday" (362). Taunted and bullied by young Tom, Hayes fears for his life and plans to run away before Tom murders him.

One night, Brock and Tom encourage Hayes to drink eight bottles of mountain-wine and then lead him "up to bed, whither, in truth, he was unable to walk himself" (382). There is noise in the night, and "Mr. Hayes did not join the family the next day" (385). Catherine meets the Count in a churchyard, but while she wheedles and lies about the circumstances of her sudden freedom, the Count freezes with "the most dreadful surprise and agony" (388). He sees Hayes's head on a spike in the churchyard and goes mad on the spot. Here the narrative ends and Thackeray closes the novel by quoting descriptions of the crime on which the story was based. He concludes with a round dismissal of Newgate literature, saying that "it was necessary to administer some medicine that would produce a wholesome nausea, and afterwards bring about a more healthy habit" (303).

The murder in *Catherine*, lovingly prepared for from the beginning of the story, is presented briefly and obliquely within the narrative. Only the contemporaneous newspaper accounts Thackeray cites describe "the murder of Hayes, the dismemberment and disposal of his body, the apprehension of the murderesses, and Catherine's execution by burning at the stake."[10] After Hayes is taken to bed, the lodger comes down to ask what the noise is about. " 'Tis only Tom Billings making merry with some friends from the country," replies Catherine, and the lodger leaves (382). The house calms, and in an ominous one-sentence paragraph: "Some scuffling and stamping was heard about eleven o'clock" (383). Thackeray ironically describes the elimination of the body:

> After they had seen Mr. Hayes to bed, Billings remembered that he had a parcel to carry to some person in the neighborhood of the Strand; and, as the night was remarkably fine, he and Mr. Wood agreed to walk together, and set forth accordingly. (383)

Billings goes out on business on the following night, "old Wood good-naturedly resolved upon accompanying him; and forth they sallied together" (385). The narrative proper ends, and Thackeray then quotes the gory details of the actual crime from newspaper articles.

Thackeray may have raced through the murder in *Catherine* because the serial in *Fraser's* was rapidly reaching the end of its time or audience. But the impatience in the narrative voice during the description of Hayes's drunkenness on that night seems genuine:

> And now might we depict, with much accuracy, the course of Mr. Hayes's intoxication, as it rose from the meriment of the three-bottle point to the madness of the four—from the uproarious quarrelsomeness of the sixth bottle to the sickly stupidity of the seventh; but we are desirous of bringing this tale to a conclusion, and must pretermit all consideration of a subject so curious, so instructive, and so delightful. (382)

The author wishes to discredit his criminal subject and does not spare the reader's sensibilities in the attempt:

> Blue lights. Green lights. The whole strength of the Band. Catherine burning at the Stake! Billings hanged in the Background!! The three Screams of the Victim!!! The Executioner dashes her brains out with a billet. The Curtain falls to slow music. God save the Queen! No money returned. Children in arms encouraged, rather than otherwise.[11]

The abrupt and ironic presentation of the murder within the narrative is emblematic of Thackeray's disgust with his characters and the Newgate tradition of romanticizing crime. By hurrying past the murder as he does, Thackeray leaves the emphasis of the novel on the characters, much as Bulwer-Lytton does in *Eugene Aram*. Because like Bulwer-Lytton he fails to show the criminals during their most awful deeds, readers develop an affection for cunning Catherine. The criminals and their concerns evade Thackeray's ultimate control, and his elided presentation of the murder comes to have a power he did not intend.

The narrator, Ikey Solomons, Esq. Jr., uses the name of the famous London fence who was a model for Fagin, but he is "too much like Thackeray to be an independent narrator" (Cabot, 412). He develops a sneaking sympathy for Catherine that gives the book its unexpected, if occasional, power and pathos. Throughout the novel, Catherine is silly, self-absorbed, superficial, and dangerous; she is, however, also capable of remorse. She poisons the Count during their first liaison because he is courting a wealthy aristocrat. But then she tries to dissuade him from drinking more of the deadly punch than he has already taken. He replies with a blow:

> Mrs. Catherine fell on her knees, and clasping her hands, and looking pitifully in the Count's face, cried, "Oh, Count, forgive me, forgive me!"
>
> "Forgive you? What for? Because I slapped your face? Ha, ha! I'll forgive you again, if you don't mind."
>
> "Oh, no, no, no!" said she, wringing her hands. "It isn't that. Max, dear Max, will you forgive me? It isn't the blow—I don't mind that: It's—"
>
> "It's what, you—maudlin fool?"
>
> *"It's the punch!"*
>
> The Count, who was more than half-seas-over, here assumed an air of much tipsy gravity. "The punch! No I never will forgive you that last glass of punch. Of all the foul beastly drinks I ever tasted, that was the worst. No, I never will forgive you that punch."
>
> "Oh, it isn't that, it isn't that!" said she.
>
> "I tell you it is that,——you! That punch, I say that punch was no better than paw—paw—oison." And here the Count's head sank back, and he fell to snore.
>
> *"It was poison!"* said she.
>
> *"What!"* screamed he, waking up at once, and spurning her away from him. "What, you infernal murderess, have you killed me?"
>
> "Oh, Max!—don't kill me, Max! It was laudanum—indeed it was. . . ." (225)

Although this is certainly attempted murder, its effect is comic. The scene is amusing partly because the Count is a foolish bully and partly because the verbal contretemps delays Catherine's revelation. But it is mostly comic because Catherine is too soft-hearted to go through with the crime. As in *Oliver Twist,* crime devastates the criminal. Even when remorse is played for comedy, the reader becomes more sympathetic to the criminal.

Catherine's furious, retaliatory effort at revenge ends in her repentence; she displays similar humanity before the actual murder of John Hayes, despite her eagerness to be free of him. Brock and Billings exchange peculiar smiles as Hayes "began bragging of his great powers as a drinker," and Catherine's "eyes were turned towards the ground; but her face was deadly pale" (381). She tries to protect Hayes from the plot she invented, whispering to Brock:

> "No, no! for God's sake, not to-night!"
> "She means we are to have no more liquor," said Wood to Mr. Hayes, who heard this sentence, and seemed rather alarmed.
> "That's it,—no more liquor," said Catherine, eagerly; "you have had enough to-night. Go to bed, and lock your door, and sleep, Mr. Hayes."
> "But I say I've *not* had enough to drink!" screamed Hayes; "I'm good for five bottles more, and wager I will drink them too."
> "Done, for a guinea!" said Wood. (381)

Eager to kill Hayes so that she may marry the Count, Catherine nevertheless cannot commit a coldblooded murder. Her previous attempts on Hayes and the Count demonstrate that impulsive murder is not beyond her. But this premeditated crime is obliquely presented perhaps because Catherine has become a dangerously engaging character for Thackeray as well as for the reader. Whatever the reason, he does not bring himself to show the brutality of the murder in which Catherine is implicated.

The abrupt treatment of the murder followed by details from the actual crime also suggests Thackeray's ambivalence toward the genre itself. His purpose, as he explains repeatedly throughout the novel, is to create a Newgate fiction disgusting enough to discourage readers from reading similar novels in the future. Yet any parody must have enough knowledge of its target to be effective, and as Thackeray becomes engaged by his sly heroine, he also is drawn by the power of the murder. He satisfies the audience's taste for bloodshed even as he mocks it. By quoting popular accounts of the murder, he concedes their power. Just as he comes to like Catherine and the protean Brock while pointing up their immorality, he finally gives the reader lurid and horrific details of dismemberment and execution while disdaining public taste. Becoming involved with homicide and criminal characters, even for a virtuously didactic purpose, is risky. The energy of characters who are so ruthlessly on the make and the sensational appeal of violent murder take over and enunciate themselves in something like their own terms.

In *Catherine,* Thackeray comments on the criminality of a society that enjoys Newgate fiction. He burlesques middle- and upper-class characters who, like their counterparts in *Vanity Fair,* eagerly sink virtue and charity in their itch to get ahead. Their self-seeking impulses rehearse the unprincipled scramble for money and social position that Thackeray saw as consonant with the lack of taste that devoured Newgate fiction. Catherine's story forces recognition of the reader's "kinship with low scoundrels" (Ferris, 17). Like Dickens, Thackeray uses a violent murder to criticize the social environment from which homicide springs.

In *Mary Barton,* as in the other novels discussed, homicide focuses several issues and concerns simultaneously. One of many social and industrial novels of the late 1840s and early 1850s, *Mary Barton* expresses the frustration, hardship, and rage experienced by the Manchester workers whose community the novel details. Much more pointedly than Dickens or Thackeray, Gaskell turns her fiction into a social and political lesson. Where social concerns are significant in *Oliver Twist* and *Catherine,* they are in *Mary Barton* paramount. The treatment of homicide and response to the criminal work to state and enforce the novel's reforming emphasis.

In the novel, the Bartons and the Wilsons suffer great privation. Mrs. Barton's sister, Esther, disappeared after a quarrel with John Barton about her fancy clothes and late hours; Mrs. Barton herself is failing from worry and grief. Shortly afterward, she dies in labor. John Barton joins the trades union because he is angry at the way workers, not masters, suffer when trade is bad. He and his coworkers are fired from the mill. Unable to find other work, John grows even more bitter when his infant son dies of scarlet fever and hunger, and he stores "hoards of vengeance in his heart against the employers."[12] Meanwhile, Jem Wilson falls in love with John's daughter Mary, but she has upwardly mobile fantasies of marrying Harry Carson, the factory owner's son. As John Barton becomes more involved with the Chartists, he neglects Mary, and meets with men who "were all desperate members of Trades' Unions, ready for any thing; made ready by want" (162). Jem proposes to Mary, but she realizes that she loves him only after he has already left on the heel of her rejection. Mary determines to stop meeting Harry Carson, who decides she wants to back him into marriage. When he proposes, admitting he had hoped to seduce her, she turns him down indignantly.

Unaware of Mary's feelings for him, Jem harbors jealousy and rage: "Some one should die" (215). He confronts Harry, who hits him and hisses: "Mary shall fare no better for your insolent interference" (230). When Barton and other workers visit the masters to negotiate, they are cruelly rejected and vow to kill a master. Lots are drawn; no one except the selected murderer knows who has been chosen. When Harry is killed, his father swears vengeance on the murderer, and Jem is arrested for the crime. Mary learns that her father killed Carson, and she manages to save Jem without indicting John. After Mary recovers from an illness brought about by the events of the trial— she confessed her love for Jem on the witness stand—they all return home.

The sick and remorseful John Barton then confesses the murder to Mr. Carson. At first vengeful, Carson finds that he can not hate his son's killer and returns to forgive him. After hearing Carson's merciful words, Barton dies in his arms. Later, Jem tells Carson that Barton killed Harry because "he grew aggravated with the sorrows and suffering that he saw, and which he thought the masters might help if they would" (456). Carson protests that working men inflate the power of the masters to help, but Job Legh, a family friend, responds that it is "the want of inclination to try and help" that bothers people the most (456). Carson eventually improves working conditions. Jem and Mary marry and go to Canada with Mrs. Wilson.

Gaskell cleverly provides several convincing motives for the murder of Harry Carson, but the way she presents the crime and its aftermath insures the reader's sympathy with the murdered as well as the criminal. Harry is not a likable character. He is, like Arthur in *Adam Bede* or Harthouse in *Hard Times,* carelessly wealthy, self-indulgently immoral, almost the classic seducer. He hoped to seduce and abandon Mary, he treats the working men who come to negotiate with cruelty, and he cavalierly taunts and dismisses Jem. To some degree, Harry is killed because of his own careless and irresponsible behavior toward members of the working class. Yet because we learn of his death in his family's home, it is impossible to gloat. We are moved to see the human consequences of the murder. Pathetically, Mrs. Carson refuses to believe that Harry is dead:

> "I am glad you are come," she said, looking up at her husband and still smiling. "Harry is so full of fun, he always has something new to amuse us with; and now he pretends he is asleep, and that we can't waken him. Look! he is smiling now, he hears I have found him out. Look!"
> And, in truth, the lips, in the rest of death, did look at though they wore a smile, and the waving light of the unsnuffed candle almost made them seem to move. (264)

Harry's sisters are stricken by his death. Their superficial concerns about parties dissolve in the face of real tragedy. Harry's death is not an occasion for celebration, despite his cruelty and immorality. His murder causes genuine grief in his household, agonizes the Barton and Wilson families, and does not, immediately, improve the lot of the working person. Although Carson in some ways deserves his death, Gaskell emphasizes the uselessness of such violence.

Because *Mary Barton* focuses on the human consequences of social movements and political action, the murder is shown in terms of sorrow and loss, not as the temporary triumph of the working classes over the upper classes, or as a fitting come-uppance for a careless rake. Barton and Carson, separated throughout the novel by class and circumstance, unite in grief at the end. No longer master and worker, they are able to meet on equal grounds of sensibility and humanity.

Also crucial to Gaskell's presentation of the murder and to our response to the criminal is the way the killer is selected. Barton—broken and embittered by the loss of his wife, son, and job—does not murder Carson for revenge. His dangerously wrong decision is not to kill Carson, but to join the union. After that, his selection as murderer is strangely arbitrary. Anyone could have been chosen, and the method is relevant to the rest of the novel. The very randomness of choosing lots reflects the indifference of the system that drove the workers to violence. In an industrialized wasteland, what is no one's fault is everyone's fault. Barton thus takes responsibility for the act that he committed after "volunteering" so randomly. Elaine Jordan argues that his murder causes self-murder: Gaskell kills "the realistic John Barton" by making him "a spectre, a shadow, an automaton" after he chooses the lot of a criminal.[13] As in the worlds of *Eugene Aram, Oliver Twist,* and *Catherine,* violence victimizes its perpetrators. Evil in *Mary Barton* is not expressed by malice, but by indifference and misdirected passion. Impersonal institutions like factories, parliaments, and unions have no answers because they are depersonalized. When John Barton enters this faceless world, he seals his fate as well as Harry Carson's.

The reasons for the murder, like the consequences of the murder itself, also reflect Gaskell's emphasis on the effects of social and political indifference on individuals and their families. *Mary Barton*'s "extraordinary achievement," says Carol Lansbury, "is . . . Gaskell's ability to make a timorous middle-class reader share the life of working-class people and sympathize with their lot."[14] Unlike Bulwer-Lytton and Dickens, Gaskell plays down the violence of the murder to show that Harry's death is the consequence of larger social and political violence: the deaths that matter most are those of Barton's family. Similarly, murder becomes the cause of social reconciliation. Barton and Carson abandon their hatreds, and Carson eventually brings about improved working conditions because of his hard-won enlightenment.

There is slightly more suspense in the early Victorian criminal fiction discussed here than there is in melodramas and ballads of the period, although the mystery still does not revolve around the identity of the murderer. The amount and nature of suspense in each novel testifies to their differing purposes. Bulwer-Lytton wants to explore why the murder occurs; that question throws the emphasis on the psychology and character of the criminal. For Dickens, suspense lies in wondering who will get killed; this focus stresses the conditions which encourage crime. The atmosphere surrounding Fagin and Sikes is so malevolently charged with sudden violence that the reader knows someone will die.

When the question of the victim's identity is answered by Nancy's murder, we are forced to consider the single tapestry of good and evil and the vulnerability of human beings, Sikes as well as the woman he kills. For Thackeray, the central question is when, not who. Although he too emphasizes the conditions of criminality and its inevitability, Thackeray, unlike Dickens, is less concerned to show the complex intermingling of crime and respectability than he is to show how pervasive these conditions are. Lastly, Gaskell creates little suspense in *Mary Barton* because her interest is not in why the murder was committed, but why people treat each other so harmfully. The particular issues surrounding Harry Carson's death lead to larger, more distressing questions that emerge from social circumstances.

Early Victorian fiction highlights the murderer, but our feelings about the killers reflect the novels' social points. We respond to Aram as to a solipsistic, Byronic hero, without giving much consideration to the community in which he acts. John Barton, conversely, strikes us as almost entirely a creature of the social conditions in which he acts—and is acted upon. Although they resemble the "fiends in human form" of gallows literature, Sikes and Catherine embody impulses that are also observable in ordinary people, or at least in the normal operation of society. Sikes becomes the nightmare extension of a society that does not care for innocence, and Catherine emerges as the burlesque extension of a society eager to trim principle—and sink good taste—in order to get ahead.

Unlike the ballads and melodramas of the early Victorian period, the criminal fiction of the 1830s and 1840s tends to be set in a specific and detailed social context with more explicit implications. In *Eugene Aram,* the murderer-hero has virtually killed Clarke for several reasons, all relating to the class and economic system in which Aram felt himself unfairly trapped. Dissolute and indolent, Clarke abuses his rank and wealth. Aram is very poor and wants money to continue and enlarge his studies. Clarke offends the scholar by squandering his advantages thoughtlessly, advantages that Aram would use, he says, to infinite purpose. Goaded by Clarke's sneers on his poverty, Aram broods about Houseman's suggestions of murder without really considering the money he would gain. He allows the story of Clarke's brutality toward a working woman to anesthetize his conscience. Throughout the novel, Aram is cognizant of social injustice. He responds to a moving tale by a peasant by asking, "When will these hideous disparities be banished from the world?" (42) Clarke's rape seems the crowning abuse of rank and power to Aram: "And it is to such uses . . . that this man puts his gold" (261). Yet Aram's concerned sympathy for workers and peasants is not an inherent part the novel's import. The scholar does not symbolize eighteenth-century rural community, but isolated self-absorption.

*Eugene Aram* is almost a pastoral; Bulwer-Lytton describes the rolling hills and good-natured rustics with affection for bygone days and values. In the year the book was published, 1831, Bulwer-Lytton, "dedicated to the cause of reform,"[15] entered the House of Commons as M.P. for St. Ives. Aram mirrors Bulwer-Lytton's own sensitivity to poverty and the need for reform. Genuinely dedicated to the land and those who work the land, Aram, in some ways, has murdered Clarke to preserve a way of life. Yet the presentation of his social and political viewpoints—his dramatic outrage at injustice—is also a way to minimize his personal reasons for killing Clarke. Bulwer-Lytton's feeling for downtrodden workers is apparent in *Eugene Aram* but does not infuse or guide the novel. Aram participates in Clarke's death for a variety of personal and political reasons. The murder is thus both independent of and subject to its social environment.

In *Oliver Twist,* in which a criminal kills another criminal, murder is a possible destiny for almost every character. The homicide grows directly from its social context; physical violence springs from violent neglect and a criminal way of life. There is criminal indifference and malice at every level of society (except the fairy-tale world of Brownlow and the Maylies). Even Bumble's comic courtship and marriage underscore the hypocrisy and self-love of most of the people Oliver meets. Ironically, Oliver is labeled a criminal throughout the beginning of the novel. When he asks for more food, the "gentleman in the white waistcoat" affirms: "I never was more convinced of anything in my life, than I am that that boy will come to be hung" (37). After the orphan cries not to be apprenticed to the murderously careless chimneysweep, the same gentleman says "not only that Oliver would be hung, but that he would be drawn and quartered into the bargain" (46). Noah Claypole, churlish employee at the funeral parlor, tells Oliver that he will come to see him hanged (68). The whole place becomes a madhouse when Oliver strikes Noah for maligning his mother: "Charlotte! missis! Here's the new boy a murdering of me" (70). Charlotte hopes that this outrage will teach Mr. Sowerberry not to hire "these dreadful creatures, that are born to be murderers and robbers from their very cradle" (71). Noah ridiculously enacts his own murder for the astonished and enraged Bumble: "He tried to murder me, sir; and then he tried to murder Charlotte; and the missis. Oh! what dreadful pain it is! Such agony, please, sir" (73). This choric accusation of virtuous Oliver is comic in its incongruity.

Branding Oliver as a criminal, however, also illustrates that for all the care given to bringing up orphans, he might as well grow up to be a murderer. The poor and lowly are assumed to be criminal or potentially criminal, and this belief, coupled with immoral indifference to the concerns of the poor, becomes a self-fulfilling prophecy. When Nancy tries to see Rose Maylie, she must staunchly ignore the "very audible expressions of scorn, of which the chaste housemaids were very prolific" (355). In a society where "good" institutions mirror and cause criminality, murder is inevitable. Yet innate wickedness, social victimization, and the lack of alternatives do not doom Nancy to violent death. Her efforts to protect Oliver and her loyalty to Sikes cause her murder. Only through martyrdom or disappearance into a fairy-tale world can characters escape crime and fear. Dickens's novel indicts uncaring and dangerous social environments and the qualities of human nature that create them.

The presentation of Count Galgenstein in *Catherine* implies that the upper classes are completely corrupt and dangerous. His cruelly amoral treatment of Catherine insures the violence that follows. In the novel, Catherine's social class is gross and violent, but the upper classes earn deeply felt contempt. Thackeray warns us against social stereotyping:

> My dear sir, when you have well studied the world—how supremely great the meanest thing in this world is, and how infinitely mean the greatest—I am mistaken if you do not make a strange and proper a jumble of the sublime and the ridiculous, the lofty and the low. I have looked at the world, for my part, and come to the conclusion that I know not which is which. (353–54)

One critic makes the same point about the middle class that spawns John Hayes:

> The more minutely we examine the life of this seemingly respectable victim, the more unsympathetically we respond. . . . Catherine's actions are made understandable, and even justifiable, by Thackeray's controlled development of a cynical truth: in the matter of murder, the victim is often no better, and sometimes worse, than the villain. (Cabot, 413)

The social ambitions that inspire Catherine to kill Hayes comment ironically on the nonexistent moral distance between the classes. Except perhaps for Catherine, characters in the novel are not made wicked by their society; they display society's wickedness. Like Dickens, Thackeray locates greed, hypocrisy, and criminality in several social and economic classes. But whereas Dickens's faith in reform leavens his damning portrait of sweeping criminality and indifference, Thackeray's vision is bleaker. People in *Catherine* are so reliably self-interested and amoral that glimmers of virtuous feeling—Catherine's remorse, Tom's love for her—disappear in the general stampede toward money and status. We can reform only our reading taste, selecting didactic novels in which moral distinctions are never blurry.

Written at the time of social protest novels such as Disraeli's *Sybil* (1845) and Kingsley's *Alton Locke* (1850), *Mary Barton* comments explicitly on the relations between classes in her presentation of Harry's death. The Carsons, wealthy manufacturers, contemptuously exploit the working classes on every possible level. Captivated by Mary's beauty, Harry showers her with gifts that seem munificent to her; Harry gives them as a matter of course. Nowhere is that difference of perspective more poignantly expressed than when Jem arrives ostensibly to visit John, with a narcissus in his buttonhole, "hoping it would attract Mary's notice, so that he might have the delight of giving it her" (123). She is woefully indifferent to his prize: "In her little dingy bed-room, stood a white jug, filled with a luxuriant bunch of early spring roses, making the whole room fragrant and bright. They were the gift of her richer lover" (124). Although his father married a factory girl, Harry disdains to do the same. He is chillingly heedless of Mary's well-being:

> No, I do not mean to give her up, whatever you and she may please to think. I am more in love with her than ever; even for this charming capricious ebullition of hers. She'll come round, you may depend upon it. Women always do. . . . Mind! I don't say I shall offer her the same terms again. (185)

Working-class women are commodities for which you offer terms. Knowing what happens to those who prize themselves too lightly, Mary understandably wants a marriage license as a "proof of purchase" (Ferris, 17). Once "damaged goods," she loses her economic value.[16] Harry's heedless language of bargaining is more than metaphorical.

Working men are also commodities to be used and discarded. The murder and its aftermath sensitize the elder Carson. In *Mary Barton*, it is "the want of inclination to try and help the evils which come like blights at times over the manufacturing places" that causes masters to dehumanize and mistreat their workers. Gaskell's concern for the lack of communication and the hostility between classes is a direct response to and comment on "the hungry forties," about which the novel is written. The murder in *Mary Barton* springs from an individual's desperate response to miserable social conditions. Similarly, the killings in *Oliver Twist, Eugene Aram,* and *Catherine* comment explicitly on class relations, the criminal justice system, and general social conditions of the early Victorian period.

The emphasis on the murderer and the relation of murder to social values and circumstances are the most striking aspects of homicide in each of the forms of early Victorian popular literature here considered. Although the psychology and concerns of the criminal are focal in each genre, with the loosening of literary conventions, the presentation of the criminal grows more complex. Killers in street literature of the gallows are two-dimensional; the brevity and focus on action inherent in street ballads do not permit complex characterization. Criminals must of necessity function through extremes: extreme desire—for sex, for money, or for status—causes extreme violence and excessive remorse or agony when murderers do not repent. Ballads are perhaps closer to fairy tales or morality plays than to fiction; characters are static and clearly innocent or indubitably guilty. The reader may feel pity for a fallen and abandoned woman, but no sense of injustice. Once a woman has been seduced, or learned the power of her sexuality, she is doomed to violent death, either as a victim of her betrayer or as a victim of justice.

The melodramatic murderer is as violent and vocal as his counterpart in street literature. However, his initiative and energetic dedication to evil fascinate the reader or viewer. Because of the way he flouts social convention, the melodramatic murderer engages our interest and sometimes a brief thrill of identification. Yet because the criminal and his crime are not closely related to a particular social environment, we are not implicated or endangered by our enjoyment. Watching murder being committed on the stage is therefore not only frightening, but titillating; the forbidden pleasure of seeing the lurid crime enacted is untainted by any real suggestion that the murderer is like us or that social conditions for which we are partly responsible cause crime.

As fiction has a much wider variety of conventions to draw from, including those of street literature and melodrama, the characterizations of murderers are more complex and ambiguous. The presentation of the criminal depends on the purposes of the author and not merely on a limited set of conventions. Murderers in early Victorian fiction, unlike those of ballads and melodrama, engage some part of our sympathetic attention. A more complicated presentation of motivations, characters, and social environments enables us to understand the crime. Although fiction does not justify or advocate murder, it makes homicide understandable. Our response to the murderer is more complicated in fiction than in melodrama or street literature partly because of the relationship between the criminal and his or her social context.

The murderers of street literature are called "fiends" or "monsters," but their implied motives are all too recognizably connected to conventional social values. Murder in street ballads becomes a terrible betrayal of the contracts that keep people human: husband and wife, master and servant. Homicide also shatters the most basic contract between an individual and society. Victims and killers in ballads often become symbols of unrestrained sexuality. Their deaths are necessarily violent resolutions to their dangerous lack of discipline. But by violating community values, murder restores a community of outrage. Killers are aberrations. Once they are hanged, society is exorcised. Those who try to ignore or circumvent authority are punished with resounding force.

The social implications of murder in melodrama are similar to those of street literature. Although criminal motives are versions of ordinary social concerns, murderers are monstrously unlike their community, not extensions of it. In melodrama, however, villains demand our attention through their evil determination. Unlike other characters, murderers have a sense of mastery over their fates, albeit a temporary one. For a time they may indulge their desires for wealth, sex, or violence. Murders in melodrama are more overtly outgrowths, versions, or parodies of sexuality and sexual relations than those of street literature. Women are punished for wanting sexual, social, or financial parity with men. Like ballads, melodramas featuring murder provide coded instructions for the socially ambitious or sexually unrestrained. Audacious flouting of social conventions, especially when enjoyed by the offender, will be punished. The audience or reader of melodrama thus may participate vicariously in homicide without risk, because the criminal acts are committed by individuals who do not represent the society in which members of the audience must make their ways.

Criminals in early Victorian fiction are, on the other hand, in some way logical extensions of their community. The implications of the murder are usually more shocking than the murder itself, which often occurs in memory or is omitted from the action. Killers are not "fiends" or "monsters," but people whose crimes develop from a disturbing tension between individual characteristics and social ills. Evil does not exist in a social vacuum. Aram kills Clarke partly because the latter has committed a crime against the working-class community. The scholar, however, does not realize that he, too—in the crime and in his way of life—has put himself beyond community values and is as guilty as his victim. Catherine's foolishness, self-absorption, and murderous immorality represent the values and habits of every class in the novel. Her wicked crime is ultimately pathetic because of her illusion that the upper class represented by Galgenstein is somehow better than her own class. These illusions spring from the distance between social and economic groups and from the readiness of any individual from one group to exploit someone from another.

Sikes's violence is an outgrowth of the criminal world in which he lives, although its excess belongs to Sikes himself. Like Aram, Sikes becomes a transgressor of community values. Although the values of the underworld have in some way caused the crime, once it has been committed, Sikes is a social outcast. Tellingly, Charley Bates, one of Fagin's band, not a policeman, eventually turns Sikes over to the mob. Bates's act and eventual rehabilitation, Nancy's goodness, and Oliver's virtue are testaments to Dickens's belief that with correct and caring public attention, criminality could be limited, social conditions improved. Barton's crime also results from his desperate economic state. Unlike the criminals of street literature and melodrama, Barton is not demonic or psychotic. He is a productive member of the community who turns to murder from anguish and rage at social injustice. Without overweening ambition or greed, John Barton wants only self-respect and dignity as a laborer. Like Aram, Catherine, and Sikes, Barton becomes a murderer in part through his own character and partly because of social conditions.

Ballads and melodramas of the early Victorian period imply messages to the victims and killers and provide warnings for the public: restraint and self-control are necessary to successfully maintain or improve one's status. Sexuality—especially women's sexuality—endangers by posing a threat to self-restraint. Any inordinate desire risks loss of position. Once those guilty of insufficient self-mastery die violently, through murder or execution, society is healed. Their deaths are cathartic. In fiction, however, where murder occurs in part because of specific social ills, violent crime and violent justice do not provide such complete remedies. Threats to community are not quarantined within individuals who can then be eliminated. The danger of homicide—and the threat to moral authority it involves—lies more disturbingly in the neglect or cruelty of the whole community.

# Part II

# "A Skeleton in Every House"

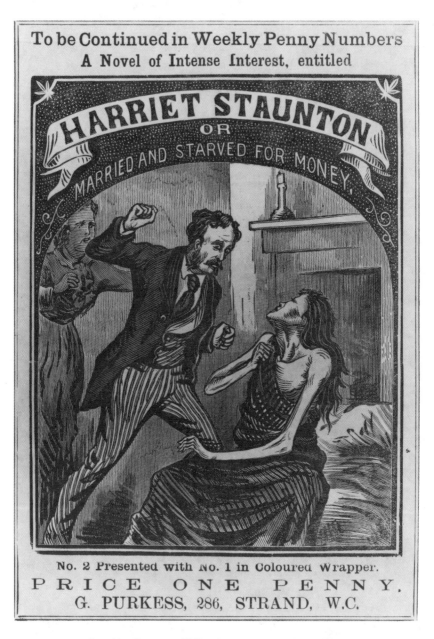

Pamphlet Cover, ca. 1860
Mid-Victorian writing featured extremes of womanly malice
and vulnerability.
*(Courtesy of the Michael Sadleir Collection, Lilly Library)*

# Introduction to Part II

"One strong feature of the times is the prevalence of atrocious crime," pronounced a writer for *Blackwood's Magazine* in 1818; "this is the common remark of every day."[1] Thirty-five years later, attitudes toward violent crime, particularly murder, were apt to be both more superficially optimistic and more tentative:

> Despite outbreaks of violent crime over the whole country between 1850 and 1853, Frederic Hill, a former Inspector of Prisons, could write in the later year that crimes were "taking a milder and milder form." Violent crimes continued to attract public attention on various occasions during the 1850s and 60s, particularly of course during the famous garrotting attacks in London in 1862. . . . They caused much public alarm—perhaps more acute because of the relative safety of recent years—but belief that there had been an improvement over earlier years persisted.[2]

Popular writing in the fifties and sixties reflects both an alarm over the frequency of violent crime and a hope that publicly or privately, justice will be done. Despite this belief in calmer crimes, the murders, especially those in street literature, are as violent as ever, raising numerous questions about whether the victim deserves his or her fate, whether the murderer will be caught, and even whether the killer deserves execution.

The famous murders that the English public read and talked about in the mid-Victorian period fell into two broad categories: they were either public and seemingly arbitrary or private and all too particular. Many of the public murders were unexpected because they occurred randomly. The garotting attacks of the sixties were the most fearful illustration of impersonal murders committed by virtually anonymous criminals who remained unknown to their victims. In a jocular, anonymous article in *Fraser's Magazine* called "The Moral Philosophy of Garotting," a supposed garotter extols his profession, boasting that "it treats the unknown victim as an abstraction."[3] In the "Railway Car" murder, Thomas Briggs, a solidly middle-class citizen, was killed by a stranger on a train headed to his home in the suburbs: "As the train prosaically puffed and clacked through the slum and factory district between Bow and Hackney

Wick, he [murderer Franz Muller] bludgeoned the elderly gentleman and took his watch and chain—overlooking £5 in his pocket—then dumped the body out of the window" (Altick, 201–2). The victim, apparently randomly selected, was murdered on a train full of people.

Another famous public crime that shocked the mid-Victorian public was the mystery of the man whose "remains were found in a carpet-bag on the pier of Waterloo-bridge in October, 1857."[4] Every aspect of this murder baffled readers and came to symbolize the volatile, inexplicable nature of contemporary violent crime. The victim was never identified, the murderer never apprehended, and for months articles detailed the desperate efforts of the police to extract useful information from a few scraps of frayed and blood-stained clothing. The crime haunted almost every discussion of murder at the time: the "Waterloo Bridge" murder provided incontrovertible proof that violent, public crimes can not be prevented or solved. Unlike murder reports in *The New York Daily-Times,* which "demonstrated that the judicial system successfully operated,"[5] mid-Victorian London journalism raises serious questions about the efficacy of British justice. The garotting attacks, the "Railway Car" murder, and the case of the Waterloo Bridge man demonstrated only that people can not be protected from random, impersonal violence. No one is safe when such murders are not followed by a ritual of trial and execution.

Murders committed among intimates or family members shocked general readers as much as public crimes did, emphasizing the impossibility of protecting oneself from a crime arising from domesticity and intimacy. In two famous cases, young women were arrested for murdering people they were supposed to have loved. Constance Kent, a sixteen-year-old girl from a middle-class family, was apprehended for the "Road" murder in 1857 of her four-year-old stepbrother, Francis. She was acquitted because of "the strong local sentiment in her favor," but five years later, she confessed to the crime and was sentenced to life imprisonment, "the judge's sobs being echoed by everyone in the courtroom" (Altick, 130). Local sentiment notwithstanding, the idea of a seemingly dutiful young woman harboring murderously cruel feelings toward a four-year-old touched a public nerve.[6] That she might have the desire and will to commit such a crime could not help but raise questions about other apparently innocent people.

In the same year Francis Kent died, Madeline Smith, daughter of a well-to-do Scottish architect, was arrested for poisoning her former lover, a French shipping clerk. As with Constance Kent, much local feeling in her support erupted; the victim fit "with fatal neatness into the British, and even more specifically Scottish, stereotype of the lubricious Frenchman on the loose in law-abiding, God-fearing society" (Altick, 179). Although she was also acquitted, the openness with which she bought large amounts of arsenic and the passionate explicitness of her love letters seemed like a betrayal of her sex. Murders committed by young, attractive, and demure women seemed much worse than many other killings because they were unexpected and grossly inappropriate for the gentler sex.

Poison became a particularly frightening symbol of concealed hatred. Unlike the bashing and dismemberment of public crimes, poison does not require any physical strength—even women can use it—and the victim has no warning. Most disquieting of all, poison can be administered during the normal round of domestic care, by people who serve dinner, raise children, and tend the sick. Three famous poisoners of the period, Drs. Palmer, Smethurst, and Pritchard, used their medical knowledge to murder inconvenient relatives and creditors.

These private murders of Kent, Smith, and the medical men shook traditional ideas of love and safety. One may be killed by one's sister or family doctor as easily as by an unhinged stranger. In *Adventure, Mystery, and Romance,* John Cawelti suggests that the midcentury detective stories of Edgar Allen Poe express perceived threats to the middle class, including "a new concern with psychological urges toward aggression and sexuality that were in sharp conflict with the ideal of the family circle."[7] Street ballads and journalism of the period also feature an unsettling "revolt from within" (Cawelti, 102). If random public killings make the heart of civilized London unsafe, private murders at the hands of someone trusted topple the final refuge of home and family. By the 1870s, public insecurity had become so prevalent that a pamphlet writer could say murders "are very easy of concealment, and that they are probably more frequent than anybody has hitherto believed. In a very material sense it is deemed possible that there may be, roughly speaking, a 'skeleton in every house'" (*Whitechapel Mystery,* 3).

Discussion of both public and private murder reflected the growing belief that the form and significance of murder was changing with the times, modernizing in some way. Violent deaths from blunt instruments still existed in popular street ballads, but the dismemberments and bashings were seen to have given way to a new kind of crime:

> Bill Sikes, too, with his knobbed stick and blackguardly appearance, was on the downgrade—outmoded as an efficient housebreaker by a more sophisticated and unobtrusive criminal who could return from cracking a crib in a second class railway compartment without exciting notice. . . . The old, riotous, reckless, openly menacing, Hogarthian underworld, so long a part of the English scene, was fast fading away.[8]

A realization that one is never safe from the threat of crime, even of murder perpetrated by criminals who look—and maybe are—just like the rest of us, exists in street literature, popular newspapers, and middle-class journals.

The discussion of these three groups of popular literature will emphasize the increase in mystery and overwhelming sense of insecurity generated by random and intimate crimes. In addition, these popular genres stress a changing depiction of women as murderers and victims, a growing concern with children's deaths, and the question of whether murder must out. Representations of murder at midcentury also support the contention that "by 1850 . . . the underworld itself is becoming Victorian" (Chesney, 369).

# 4

# Nonfiction, 1850–1870

The formal conventions of street literature in the 1850s and 1860s resemble those in earlier decades but feature significant differences in rhetoric and emphasis. Again, prose descriptions of the crime, trial, and execution precede a ballad of the crime that is directed toward readers who ought to learn from the experience: young girls, lovers, parents. Murderers suffer and often repent; the manner of the murderer and nature of this repentence is still a matter of great interest. In "The Execution of William Bull," the anonymous author notes that in jail, Bull "paid great attention to what the chaplain said" but seemed "to fall back at times into his usual sullen and morose manner." The crowd's size and behavior continue to interest midcentury readers. In "The Execution and Confession of Franz Muller, For the Murder of Mr. Briggs, November 14th, 1864" (Hindley, 212), people waited up all night to see the execution. At 5:00 a.m., a "heavy drenching rain set in, which had the effect of driving the majority of those who during the night had taken up positions, from their strongholds, and to hastily beat a retreat to the now open public-houses and coffee-shops, as well as to other places offering anything like shelter."

As in earlier ballads, a woodcut often accompanies the text. Many feature the criminal hanging on the gallows or being brought to execution. Some, however, present the victim before the murder. Many ballads tell the story of Maria Clausen, who is killed by her master's jealous son. In one woodcut, her dark hair is pulled beneath her chin with a ribbon. She wears a white apron over her long dress and holds a broom, looking pleasantly attentive, as though someone were speaking to her. Two pictures illustrate "The Reprieve and Sentence of the Penge Convicts," the story of Harriet Staunton, who was starved by her husband and his mistress. One picture shows a dignified woman in repose; the other shows a wraithlike creature in rags, wild-haired, beseeching with clasped hands the bearded man at her door. In another pamphlet about the crime, Mrs. Staunton is depicted as a well-dressed, pleasant woman wearing teardrop earrings and a feathered hat.

These sympathetic pictures of female victims, rather than lurid woodcuts of criminals caught in the act, suggest that shock stems from the incongruity of a Maria or Harriet getting murdered rather than from the act of murder itself. The imprisonment and starvation of a gentlewoman and the murder of a diligent working-class woman assault propriety. Woodcuts of the women when happily alive evoke grief and horror. The emotional emphasis has shifted from the just and final ends of the criminals to the shocking, unfair deaths of the victims. The early Victorian emphasis works to arouse fear of being a criminal, or doing something—as Maria does in *The Murder in the Red Barn*—that provokes a fatal attack. Those who do evil get punished. In later street ballads, the fear is of becoming a victim: those who do nothing also get killed.

Slight iconographic changes that appear in street ballads may be related to an increased rhetorical caution. The murderer-as-monster pattern exists in mid-Victorian as well as early Victorian street literature, but there is a greater sense of uncertainty or hesitance in the later ballads. Sometimes there are unanswered questions as to what has actually happened, whether the accused or obvious person did it, and whether the criminal will be discovered and convicted. In "The Wigan Murder: Examination and Confession of John Healey," the chorus runs: "Though justice strictly searched about, / They could not find the murderer out." Eventually, criminals are brought to justice by their own consciences, not by an avenging or coincidental discovery. Healey is made to say that the crime has "caused my very heart to bleed, / I could not sleep or take my rest, / I compelled was to confess." There is a growing sense that things may not be what they appear in several ballads on a murder at Eltham. One ballad runs:

> May God's finger soon point out the murderer
> And that we trust most speedily,
> And so clear up the dreadful mystery,
> Of the shocking Eltham tragedy.

Another on the same murder promises "if guilty found, he'll die for the deed." This tentativeness replaces the earlier convention in some street ballads of the criminal weeping contrite tears on the gallows. The guilt that drives Healey to confess and the trust that God will somehow cause the criminals to be discovered are part of the formula of eventual but indirect punishment that exists in much midcentury popular nonfiction.

Another significant change in the presentation of murder in street ballads occurs in the depiction of women victims and murders. One modern critic has written that "the classic English murder is not like the French for money, or like the American as a celebration of violence. It is par excellence the sexual murder."[1] Margaret Dalziel writes that the relationship between men and women is more fully presented than any other kind of personal relationship in cheap popular fiction, and the same is true of street literature, where murder regularly takes place between lovers.[2] Most midcentury street ballads of this type involve women killed by their lovers, husbands, or suitors. Unlike earlier ballads in which seduced or pregnant women are killed by socially ambitious men, mid-Victorian street literature features women who die at the hands of jealous or frustrated men.

Women who usurp male prerogatives or reject suitors threaten the authority of traditional sexual roles. Men murder women to control their sexuality by punishing or preventing other liaisons. In "Execution of Three Men," the victim is warned:

> She left with another man we hear
> Which filled his mind with jealous fear
> He quarreled with her as we see
> And said it's either you or me . . .

The ballad solemnly advises readers to avoid "cursed jealousy." In "Triple Execution at Gloucester," Charles Edward Butt had a loving companion in Selina Phipps, but he was "excessively jealous of her." At a small party of men and women outside on his lawn, Butt leaves with a gun; later, Phipps exclaims, "Edward is going to stab me." A man "rebuked Butt for using such threats." After Phipps disappears, a shot is heard. "But for his jealous mind" he would have been a married man. She refused to marry him because of his jealousy, "which preyed upon his mind." His violent possessiveness causes her refusal, which increases his jealous rage: love is expressed as desire for ownership, and death is the proprietor's only security. Other ballads tell such stories as that of "The Horrible Murder of a Young Woman, near Eltham," about a handsome woman whose "beauty captivated" her master's son; she too is eventually killed because of his jealousy.

Although these crimes have their analogues in earlier ballads, the emphasis now shifts. The murderers do not concern themselves with their social standing or ability to rise in the world. Women's sexuality is dangerous not because it can drag a man down, but because it may not be restricted or possessed. In this sense, murder becomes a form of sexual conquest. Even when the victim is presented sympathetically, jealousy can be considered a justification for killing a woman. In "Confession and Execution of Samuel Wright, for the Murder of Maria Green," events leading up to the crime are described somewhat mysteriously:

> He said he could not exactly say how the murder originated, but it was something in this way: That he was asleep in bed, and that the woman came and took him by the waistcoat and said he should not lay sleeping there. Some words ensued, and she threatened to leave him and go with some other man with whom she had previously cohabited. Upon that he jumped out of bed, and as the razor with which he had recently shaved himself was lying on the table he took it up and cut her throat. It was all the work of a moment. (Hindley, 207)

The woman's demands and willingness to use her sexuality insure the inevitability of her violent death. Public opinion was with Wright; most people thought that he did not deserve to die, and "not more than four or five thousand people came to the execution" (Hindley, 207).

A similar, though less extreme, sympathy with the man who kills through jealous rage exists in "Miles Weatherhill, The Young Weaver, and his Sweetheart, Sarah Bell" (Hindley, 214). Bell is the parson's servant; when she is forbidden to see Weatherhill, the weaver wounds the parson and kills a fellow servant of Bell's to "be revenged on Parson Plow." Although the "crimson blood on the flood did spill" as in earlier ballads, the writer does not warn young men or lovers as in an earlier ballad. Instead, there is general admonition: "Where true love is planted, there let it dwell." Weatherhill hangs, and his death has a romantic, nearly lyrical tone: "On the fatal drop, he cried, broken-hearted, / May we meet in heaven, my sweet Sarah Bell." A jealously possessive love turns to rage and frustration, and Weatherhill is presented as an avenger, a heartsick lover in righteous wrath. When women are seduced, as in earlier ballads, their sexuality eventually entraps. But when sex is parceled out sparingly, erratically—or worse, denied altogether—women are equally dangerous. Women who recognize this power and use it, like Maria Green, endanger their murderers most of all.

Overly powerful women in mid-Victorian street literature appear side by side with unusually vulnerable women. The victims in these ballads are extremely helpless either because of the number of people who attack them or because of their condition. Unlike the women who consciously or unconsciously use their sexual power, these women are almost martyrs. In "Horrid Outrage and Murder of a Female, at Cleveland," the mystery about the woman's attackers and their motives reflects a growing sense of insecurity and fearfulness that runs all through the nonfictional popular literature of the period; the victim's helplessness implies that only painfully vulnerable females can be considered "heroines" in street literature. A man discovers a woman's jacket hanging on a gate, which leads him to blood in the field, then signs of a "severe struggle";

> Each heart was filled with horror
>     As they gazed all around,
> But the victim of this fearful crime,
>     Was no where to be found.

Finally discovered "in a horrible condition" is "a female unknown, / Who to gain an honest livelihood / Round the country did roam." She is never identified further, and her murderers are only described as "five young men, all apparently under 21," who "sore ill-used" her. Like the case of the Waterloo Bridge man, this crime deeply disturbs because of its mystery. Because so many men "outraged" and murdered her, she is even more pitiable than most murder victims in street literature; her anonymity is pathetic and fearful. Similarly, in "Horrible Cruelty to a Servant Girl at Slough," a "gentleman farmer" and his wife repeatedly wound their seventeen-year-old nurse. The nurse does not die even after drunken Mrs. Morris, who is far more violent than her spouse, beats her with a cane, runs scissors through her hand until "they went out on the other side," cut her head several times with a poker, and hit her with a shovel. With comparative generosity, Morris only kicks her up and down stairs. "No doubt they would have killed her," mourns the ballad. Like the unknown woman at Cleveland, the nurse is much more vulnerable than most murder victims in street literature, especially those who die as a result of their own uninhibited or forbidden sexuality.

In "The Execution of James Clitheroe of St. Helen's, for the Murder of Mary Woods, this day," the murder's circumstances are "of a somewhat peculiar description." A married man who sleeps with "a poor paralytic woman" named Mary Woods, the murderer was "twitted" by his neighbors

> in the intensely acrimonious manner peculiar to vulgar and uneducated people, as to "the poor cripple Mary Woods" being *enceinte* by him. This seems to have annoyed Clitheroe very much, and his mortification and chagrin acting upon a morbid temperament prompted him to murder.

After sleeping with her one night, he cut her throat and concocted a feeble story of a suicide pact. Woods, like the woman at Cleveland, evokes sympathy and pity in part because she is so helpless. Neither woman is an accomplice in her own murder; nor was Harriet Staunton, a middle-class, weak-minded woman who is starved and ill-treated by her husband and his mistress:

> Alas! she was helpless, and weak as a child.
> So easily led, and so easily beguiled;
> No one to mind her, or for her to care,
> No food to eat, no clothes to wear. (Ballad, "Harriet Staunton," 3)

That Mrs. Staunton is compared to a child is significant in light of the fact that innocent, helpless children are also common victims of murder in mid-Victorian street literature. Perhaps only when women share the vulnerability of children can wholehearted sympathy be elicited. Those women who show any degree of independence or desire to control their lives—who wish to exercise the right to reject a suitor or to throw someone out of bed—are more clearly the source of their own violent deaths.

Although women are more often victims than murderers in mid-Victorian street literature, when they do kill, their crimes make the reading public shudder. Like Mrs. Manning, Constance Kent, and Madeline Smith, women who kill become powerful symbols of deceit and vice: "Though there were proportionately far fewer women criminals than men, they were said to be worse than most of the men—Cesar Lombroso, a leading criminologist of the nineteenth century later reached the same conclusion" (Tobias, 93). They were often seen as "far worse than most of the men" because they are part of "the popular iconography of the fallen women," which "fuels with forbidden love a drive for power Victorian society taboos in women."[3] "The Shocking Tragedy at Bayswater" is one of the juicier ballads in which a fallen woman commits murder. Flora Newington, while passing herself off as a Mrs. Davey, murdered "the respected Francis Moon," who had been entrapped by her good looks and amoral sexuality. A woman who will sell herself, suggests the ballad, is capable of anything:

> She would scruple not to toy we see,
> And sell her charms for gold,
> Beneath a cloak, such infamy
> Is sickening to behold.

Her beauty invites people to believe that she is virtuous. In the context of the ballad, a beautiful woman's deception is almost more shocking than her murder of Moon: "Beneath her fair face venom lays." Women murderers are almost always insidious rather than impulsive. Their cunning causes alarm. What might be lurking within one's family circle of seemingly innocent women? Coupled with an openly manipulative sexuality, their duplicity is powerfully disturbing. Many street ballads of the 1850s and 1860s indicate a strong fear of being assaulted from within the community or family and of sexually active or assertive women.

Children in "gallows" street literature, unlike women, are always innocent, virtuous, and sweet. Shockingly removed from the violence that ends their lives, children are killed in both public and private crimes. The motives of strangers are opaque; those of their intimates—usally mother or father—are all too clear.

When strangers murder children, ballads seek explanations but find none. In "Dreadful Murder of a Boy at Heaversham, in Buckinghamshire," a child is "found dead with his throat cut in a pea-field." Most of the ballad emphasizes the horror and irrationality of the crime itself. Rhetorical questions abound:

> Oh, what could tempt the monster
> To murder and destroy,
> Without a cause, a pretty little
> Smiling innocent boy?

The question returns later in the ballad:

> What motive had the murderer,
> To take his life away,
> What could possess the monster
> The little boy to slay . . .

The ballad concludes somberly, before the trial, that the murderer must "answer for that dreadful crime," yet the motive is an unasked question. The questions in the text become cumulatively more disturbing than they are perhaps intended to be. The unarticulated sexual nature of the child's murder looms over the grim conclusion. Lewis Carroll and John Ruskin certainly were not the only Victorians who saw "in young girls the objects of sexual curiosity and fascination."[4] James Walvin notes that "until 1871 the age of sexual consent was only twelve" (*A Child's World,* 144). As with the murders of innocent women, children do not provoke attacks, sexual or otherwise, and protecting oneself or one's child from assault seems impossible.

Ballads like "Execution of Frederick Baker" read like grotesque cautionary tales for children, except that the children never do anything wrong and so can not be seen as bad examples. Little Fanny Adams is happily playing in her garden with other children when "that monster Baker" approaches and gives them halfpence to leave him alone with Fanny (Hindley, 205). He lifts her in his arms while she protests: "Oh do not take me, my mother wants me, / I must go home again, good sir." Her cries are useless, of course, and Baker kills her. Why he singles her out from the other children and then murders her remains completely mysterious. Many ballads cite the child's age and innocence repeatedly to convey the impossibility of the murder being somehow appropriate. In "Sentence of William Fish, The Blackburn Murderer," Fish dismembers his victim, a seven-year-old girl, and then suffers terribly in the jail cell after "his cowardly heart gave way." But the reader never comes close to understanding the crime or the criminal.

In a particularly horrific ballad called "Lamentation and Execution of James Longhurst . . . for the wilful murder of Jane Sax, a little Girl seven years old," the killer tells his own story. He confesses that he "shamefully did her mistreat," and then "coward-like," killed her. While her dying cries bring witnesses, although too late to save her life, he "a guilty wretch did stand, / And licked her blood from off my hand." The child haunts Longhurst as he suffers in his jail cell: "Poor Jane was always in my sight." The implication that he has sexually abused the child and the weirdly feral image of licking her blood away renders the ballad almost unapproachable. The "monsters" of the thirties and forties ballads always have motives, although they usually do not articulate them, and the execution's finality abates the horror of their crimes. But murderers in mid-Victorian street literature do not always make it to the gallows: the ballads often end before the killers die or are found out. These verses are dominated by a horror which cannot be justly punished even by execution, like the image of the cornered, baffled Longhurst licking his victim's blood.

Equally unsettling are the ballads in which children die at the hands of those closest to them. Far from being motiveless, these crimes are transparently purposeful. Children become expensive burdens who prevent their parents from earning a living or going their own way. In "Life, Trial, Character, Confession, and Execution of Stephen Forward, for the Horrid Murder of Three Children near Holborn," the murderer lives with a married woman and kills three of her four children (Hindley, 216). Although no one says so, the children are inconvenient or costly. Perhaps they are killed to punish their mother. In "Cruel and Inhuman Murder of a little Boy, by his Father," each parent lived with a new mate. Their son, an "unusually intelligent and nice-looking boy," is taken from his grandmother's house, where he had been staying, and hanged by the father (Hindley, 224).

Mothers are no less eager to eliminate their noisy responsibilities. In "Barbarous Murder of a Child by a Schoolmistress," a mother hits her offspring on the head with a flint and then, bizarrely, cuts out its accusatory tongue and wraps it up in a drawer (Hindley, 219). This ballad is another example of the mid-Victorian need to have murderers who for a time "get away with it" somehow incriminate themselves and suffer horribly as a result. She saves the tongue only to have it discovered. Even while tentative about her guilt, the writer imagines her torment:

> And if she is found guilty,
>   How sad will be her case.
> If she has a woman's feelings,
>   She surely will go wild,
> She in such a barbarous manner killed
>   Her tender infant child.

The writer does not seem to have the same faith in the triumph of justice that his predecessors possessed. Nevertheless, the killer's guilt and wretchedness is in question. This anguish is the writer's, not the mother's, and the ballad is haunted by a fear that she will not be found guilty.

The schoolmistress's infant may have been killed through cruelty or her desire to be free of the child; the motive is not as clear as in other similar ballads. Only in "Trial and Sentence of Constance Kent" does a private or family crime have a public sense of randomness. Kent asks, "Why did I kill my little brother dear?" and her tortured question, like those of other killers or narrators, remains pointedly unanswered. Her account is chillingly incomplete:

> My little brother, a darling sweet,
> That fatal morning did soundly sleep,
> I was perplexed. I invented strife,
> Fully determined to take his life.

She kills him through boredom, perversity, or temporary madness.

Despite the horror of infanticide, some of the ballads on the subject seem to be perhaps unintentionally sympathetic to the murderers. Mothers kill children for survival when their own situations are desperate. In "Execution of Mary Cotton At Durham, for the West Aukland Poisonings," a forty-year-old nurse kills her seven-year-old stepson after her husband dies. When taking care of him—an "irksome and burdensome" chore, suggests the author—she was unable to earn her living as a nurse. The financial urgency surrounding that crime is painfully realistic: "She had tried to get him admitted to the workhouse and complained of the hardship of having to keep him, and on being refused replied. Perhaps it don't matter, as I shan't be troubled with him long." Although she is called a "demon" who may have committed other murders, Mary Cotton is a somewhat sympathetic, or at least comprehensible, figure because of the circumstances of her crime. Unlike the demented dismemberments of children by strangers, this crime is almost poignant; with pathetic obviousness, she has the child insured "in a club" before the murder.

"Murder of a Child near Neasham" tells the story of a woman who drowns her six-year-old child. The woman's situation is similar to that of Mary Cotton and as disturbingly realistic. When arrested she asks:

> What could I do? and began to cry. . . . Mr. Ward what could I do with the child? My aunt had run away, and left it at Ashby. I went over to try and get it into the workhouse but could not, and I wanted one or two women to take the child, but they could not; they had got enough of their own. I did not know what to do with it. My husband did not know that I had had this before I was married. I dare not tell him. I did not know what to do with it, so I threw it into the water, I have been miserable ever since.

As the grimly pathetic tale unfolds, the woman emerges not as a demon, but as a destitute and driven mother. Poverty and need make people into things: she calls her child "it" and "this." She is ashamed of her premarital sexual activity and terrified by its possible consequences. She kills to protect herself and her way of life:

> To Measham I did repair,
> With Nelly by my side,
> And I threw her in the river there,
> And there the darling died.

She suffers greatly in her jail cell and warns others to "walk in virtue's ways." Yet this admonition, like those of earlier street ballads, seems weak after her description of the circumstances that led to the murder. Even though the crime is horrible and imprisonment an appropriate punishment in context for someone who has broken several moral laws, the reader feels pity for the hapless mother.

In some ballads where parents kill children, the social implications are clear and pointed. At the time, unmarried women in poverty "looked to any desperate solution" to the problem of motherhood, often entrusting "their children to vicious and sometimes criminal women who looked after them for a fee" (Walvin, *A Child's World,* 161). Bernd Weisbrod discusses the humiliations visited upon unmarried women who tried to put their children up for adoption.[5] Since "murder verdicts were hardly ever returned in cases of overlaying or suffocating children in bed" (Weisbrod, 206), little wonder that penniless mothers or "baby-farmers" killed infants. Until the compulsory registration of births and deaths in 1874, it was possible for a newborn child to disappear without notice (Walvin, *A Child's World,* 162). Many street ballads come close to blaming desperate social conditions for the criminality of impoverished parents.

Perhaps one of the most famous and pathetic ballads about parents killing offspring is "The Esher Tragedy—story of Mary Brough who killed her six children on 9 June 1854, and afterwards attempted suicide" (M. Hughes, 11; Hindley, 199). The crime was famous because the killer once "nursed the blooming prince of Wales" and because there were multiple deaths (Hindley, 199). The ballad itself follows the conventions, including virtuous and beautiful child-victims, rhetorical questions about possible motives, and surmises about the prisoner's dreadful anguish in her cell. But the prose confession slices through the standard conventions:

> On Friday last, I was bad all day; I wanted to see Mr. Izod, and waited all day. I wanted him to give me some medicine. In the evening I walked about, and afterwards put the children to bed, and wanted to go to sleep in a chair.—About nine o'clock, Georgy . . . kept calling me to bed. I came up to bed, and they kept calling me to bring them some barley water, and they kept calling me till nearly twelve o'clock. I had one candle lit on the chair— I went and got another, but could not see, there was something like a cloud, and I thought I would go down and get a knife and cut my throat, but could not see. I groped about master's room for a razor—I could not find one—at last I found his keys, and then found his razor. I went up to Georgy, and cut her first; I did not look at her. I then came to Carry, and cut her. Then to Harry—he said, "don't mother." I said, "I must" and did cut him. Then I went to Bill. He was fast asleep. I turned him over. He never awoke, and I served him the same. . . . The two children here, Harriet and George were awake. They made no resistance at all. I then lay down myself. (Hindley, 199)

Though the ballad asks "what on earth could urge it on," the answer is embedded in her confession: exhaustion, illness, despair. The prose account, in its bleak realism, subverts the ballad, and the reader, strangely, feels more sympathetic to the murderer than a bald description of the crime might suggest is possible. Ballads like this imply social messages. Rather than victims of nearly supernatural, inexplicable evil, children are, perhaps more frighteningly, sacrifices that must be made for their parents' physical and emotional survival.

The emphasis on the death of children in mid-Victorian street literature may stem from a changing sense of what a child is and can do. Children's criminality and sexuality were commonly disturbing subjects for journalism. In the early half of the century, "generation after generation of youngsters flooded to the growing towns, and in many cases entered the ranks of the criminals" (Tobias, 41). Until the middle of the century, children who committed crimes—some little more than "youthful pranks" (Walvin, *A Child's World*, 57)—were treated with severity. Not until 1853 did transportation for juvenile offenders stop, and it is sobering to consider that as late as "1847, 1,272 children under the age of twelve were imprisoned" (Walvin, *A Child's World*, 150).

In the fifties, legislation regarding "criminal" children began to relax and "there was a marked drop in juvenile crime and in the number of juvenile criminals" (Tobias, 127). Images of underage criminals may still have haunted ballad readers of the period. With a general sense of juvenile crime decreasing, however, children can once again become symbolic martyr-victims of renewed innocence and virtue. Significantly, as women and their sexuality grow more suspect, images of children become safer. Four- and seven-year-olds may, in ballads, be punished for potential criminality, but they earn reader sympathy in ways that women do not, because Constance Kent, Flora Newington, and others are such familiar figures of criminality and carnality.

Street literature of the fifties and sixties, then, retains many of the conventions of earlier ballads: violent crimes, repentent murderers, sentimental warnings for readers. There are, however, significant changes that indicate a growing insecurity about the nature of public and private life. Many murders convey a threatening sense of an urban crowd, a peculiarly new anxiety about the city and its violence.[6] With the complexity of modern life, murder is no longer treated as the inevitable punishment for a misdeed. One can be killed suddenly by a stranger on a bridge or a railway car; leading a good life is no protection against mysterious criminals. Also, violent death can come from anywhere—in the garden, in the alley—for no reason. The community and home can not shelter potential victims. Trusted intimates—lover, parent, family doctor—may be harboring murderous resentment or rage. Women in particular can be deceitful and dangerous, especially when they have the power of determining their own sexual lives. The social conditions of life in the city may themselves drive mothers to the unnatural murder of their children. Random killers, family members, the very conditions of our lives: all may turn on us to make us victims—or murderers. Certainties about safety and who one can trust begin to crumble in the street literature of the fifties and sixties.

Newspapers like *The World We Live In* and *Cassell's Illustrated Family Paper* are directed toward a different, although sometimes overlapping, audience from that of street ballads. People who bought *Cassell's* were interested in subjects other than contemporary crimes and political events; *Cassell's* regularly featured articles on history and geography, as well as household hints, puzzles, and jokes. *The World We Live In,* unlike *Cassell's,* specialized in crime and punishment, but its scope was wider than that of street literature. Foreign crimes received much horrified attention, while street ballads featured local or national crimes. Several features in each newspaper address issues familiar to those who bought street ballads: insecurity about private and public crimes, the need to believe that the murderer suffers greatly, although not invariably at the hands of British justice, and the fearful suspicion of women's will and sexuality.

In a dispiriting 1867 sample issue of *The World We Live In,* murder occurs in every imaginable corner of private and family life. A regular reader might conclude that one is never safe from homicidal intentions while in the company of relatives and acquaintances. Children, wives, husbands, and lovers are killed. In one brief account, a woman is separated from her husband and lives with her lover and her (or their) children. She kills one child by hitting her on the head with a rolling pin or poker; the child contracts tetanus and dies (8). The child abuse had a history: "It is almost impossible to realize the brutality she suffered for many years past" (8). In other accounts, husbands kill their wives, protesting innocence and offering accidental death or suicide as explanation. One woman is killed because of jealousy, but in most briefly cited cases, motive is not discussed.

This litany of unexpected and fatal violence is fearful, but because the cases most fully discussed take place in foreign countries, the reader is permitted some distance from them. Fear of and fascination with foreigners and their customs suggest that barbaric non-Britons are capable of almost anything. Crucially, however, the circumstances surrounding each murder parallel English conditions. The distance from Turkey or France to England provides a safe way to examine and talk about what is also shocking about British crimes. Each of the three lengthy articles on crime, for example, reflects the public interest in and fear of women's sexuality and determination.

In "Parricide with Complicity," a son is goaded to kill his father by his mother. Although the husband was "a brutal drunkard" who "ill-used his wife," the article describes the woman like a French Maria Manning:

> The mother was the soul of the plot aimed at her husband's life. Of a violent and vindictive temperament, she by the ascendancy of an energetic will, incited her son to commit a crime which, while gratifying their mutual hatred

would get them the father's money, which he only "grudgingly" doled out (3). Although condemning the father's behavior, the article focuses on the mother's role as the murderer's evil genius. Her violent nature and her energetic will seem crime enough, regardless of the provocation. As in the story of Flora Newington, her real crime is power over a man.

Fear of the sexual power and explosiveness of women coincides with a dread of foreign savagery in an article called "Fratricide," in which an eighteen-year-old Arab girl slays her twelve-year-old sister. The elder, a prostitute, had been married twice. The sisters were very close; the younger slept in the same room as her sister and her sister's lover. When the elder becomes jealous of the two, she strangles her beloved sibling. The author primly notes that this tale is in part evidence that an Arab marriage "demoralises the wife," while a "Christian" marriage elevates her (5). But the article's most significant implications deal not with marriage but with the reader's perception of female sexuality. Sexual jealousy is so overpowering that it can dissolve lifelong bonds of friendship and love between sisters. Although the setting is different, this article indicates a fear of woman's sexuality and determination that mirrors similar themes in street literature.

"Wholesale Destruction of Children in France" addresses child murder and womanly evil. Julien Hippolyte is a thirty-year-old cabinet maker whose wife is more than five years older than he (3). She manipulates him into taking part in a murderous baby-farming scheme where children are deliberately and fatally neglected: "The probability is that she . . . suggested the destruction of the child to the unfortunate mother, for this latter agreed to pay the remainder of the sum agreed upon. . . . When the child was 'educated,' the word really standing for death" (3). Eventually, "no less than thirteen mothers admitted putting children to nurse" with the deadly pair. Much of the article reviles the wife's dominance over her husband:

> The history of the woman creates no other feelings than those of abhorrence, while for that of the man the thinking reader will experience something of a pity for the man will be found to be one of those men of weak intellect who, once giving themselves up to female influence, are utterly controlled, whether for good or bad by the woman with whom their fate is linked. (3)

He submits, like many a repentant murderer of street literature, while she savagely rules. At their trial, her "audacity was in singular contrast with the abject silence and condition of the male prisoner" (3). Both are found guilty; he is recommended for mercy while she is to be beheaded, although her sentence will be remitted to life imprisonment.

The most obvious horror in "Wholesale Destruction of Children" is the mass murder of children with the implied permission of their wretched parents. Another is the disastrous example of what happens when a man makes the mistake of "giving himself up to female influence" (3). Allowing a woman to take control is a grotesque inversion of acceptable authority, especially shocking because of the implication that her power is based in part on sexual dominance or allure. Lastly, there is a titillating and disturbing emphasis on "foreign" crimes; readers may have tried to allay their daily fears with fantastic horrors of supposedly uncivilized cultures. "Remember that we are English," a shocked Henry Tilney cautions the heroine of *Northanger Abbey* as she imagines a lurid murder, "that we are Christians."[7] Yet being English and Christian provided no protection against the crimes described in *The World We Live In*. Poor people in England did sleep three and more to a room; women who married young did turn to prostitution; indigent parents kept and patronized baby farms where children were criminally neglected. From the supposed seraglios of Turkey to London slums was not an immense distance; the kinds of murders that took place in the former occurred publicly and privately in mid-Victorian England.

*Cassell's Illustrated Family Paper* is a tamer and more domesticated periodical for the working-class and lower-middle-class reader. Its purposes are to educate and to entertain. Articles on geography, history, and current events appear beside those entitled "Why a Ship is Feminine" and "Unfashionable Clothes." *Cassell's* has a more explicit set of moral values than *The World We Live In*. As one historian of fiction in popular magazines puts it: "Criticism of the established order is avoided . . . all emphasis is laid on the necessity of reforming not institutions but individuals" (Dalziel, 94). Occasionally, as in *The World We Live In,* a short item gives an account of a strange or violent event such as "Poison in Flounces," in which five French working women are "afflicted" while sewing a green gauze ball dress because the material is full of "arsenical dust." Articles on murder are few and far between, but one entitled "Murder Will Out" is significant in the way it addresses the issue of murder and suggests the readers' need for reassurance.

A serial article, "Murder Will Out" addresses the disturbing contemporary mysteries on everyone's mind:

> In the full meridian splendour of the boasted enlightenment of the nineteenth century, murder is committed and the murderer is not detected. Who killed the little child at Road? Who slew the man whose mutilated remains were discovered at Waterloo Bridge? An apparently impenetrable mystery envelopes both these awful crimes, although no exertions have been spared to detect the murderers.[8]

Yet instead of attacking the police or discussing the effects of mysterious violence on people's lives, the author moves to a lengthy discussion of old myths about the discovery of murderers. The story of Eugene Aram is cited, as is the belief that when a corpse was touched by its murderer, the wound would bleed once more. Sometimes the supernatural—or nearly supernatural—coincidence helps to punish the killer: "Some apparently trifling circumstance, some overcaution on the part of the murderer, some sense of guilt on the culprit's own part, make the blood to cry . . . for punishment."[9] The cases of Thurtell, Corder, Greenacre, and the Mannings "show that the crime of murder seldom, if ever escapes detection" (nos. 165, 140). Aram's story proves that "the hand of justice, though sometimes slow, is sure to strike at last."[10] The collection of myths and actual cases is meant to prove that "long hidden or immediately detected, the awful crime of murder is brought to light in nearly every instance" (nos. 165, 140). The author energetically attacks the subversive fear that murderers go happily free and heinous crimes are unavenged or undiscovered. Yet the "nearlys" and "almosts," along with the haunting references to the Road case and the Waterloo Bridge mystery, suggest that the struggle to suppress distressing uncertainties about murder and justice is not wholly successful. Along with the emphasis on motiveless or unexpected crime in street literature, both *Cassell's Family Paper* and *The World We Live In* illustrate the concerns and insecurities of mid-Victorian readers who were beginning to believe they were no longer safe in their community or in their families.

The journals addressing a more prosperous audience, such as *Blackwood's Magazine, Household Words,* and *Cornhill Magazine,* share many perceptions about murder with working-class and street literatures but include a wider variety of concerns on the subject and discuss the issues in a vastly different style and tone. *Fraser's Magazine* and *All the Year Round,* along with other periodicals, tend to discuss murder in a general way instead of focusing on particular contemporary crimes. The articles are often occasioned by individual crimes, however, and include references to recent murders that the reading audience would recognize. Rhetorically more formal than their working-class counterparts, the journals are burdened with instruction—sometimes admonition—on how to feel and what to think about recent crimes. Where street literature exhorts, middle-class periodicals tend to guide the reader's response toward what the writers consider to be rational behavior. These journals discuss poisoning—usually in the context of secret murders in the midst of the family—and the question of whether or not murderers are caught and punished. Unlike street literature and working-class newspapers, middle-class journals indicate a growing sense of the police and the criminals as professionals, rather than as individuals accidentally discovering a body or becoming monstrously violent on impulse. Lastly, a growing consciousness of a particularly English kind of murder emerges.

Middle-class journals make explicit the social causes of particular crimes in a way that street literature can only imply. An article on capital punishment in *Fraser's* argues that infanticide should not be considered as serious a crime as the murder of an adult. The article, full of pity for mothers who are driven to murder through poverty or shame, is much less sentimental about children than the street literature that asks how anyone could commit such a gruesomely unfair crime. The writer suggests that infanticide will not be discouraged by capital punishment because the circumstances are always so desperate:

> As to infanticide, there can be no doubt that the temptation is so strong, the power of resisting it, under the circumstances, so weak, and it must fairly be owned the mischief done is much less, that there is no use in calling it by the same name as the deliberate destruction of a grown-up person.[11]

Really "more like procuring abortion than murder" ("Capital Punishments," 758) these murders evoke pity for the mothers. Unlike children in street ballads, these victims are not infant saints. They are, instead, unfortunate burdens who exist because of poverty and ignorance rather than vice.

The emphasis on poisoning in mid-Victorian middle-class journals illustrates the general fear of danger from within. Private murders are more fearful and, as a result, more commonly discussed than public crimes. Doctors, because of their access to drugs and their medical knowledge, and women, because of the positions of love and trust which define their lives, are the most suspect. In "A Criminal Trial," an article on Dr. Palmer's trial in *Household Words*, the author is concerned to explain the calm and collected demeanor of the murderer that so astounded the general public. Palmer was supposed by "the most conservative modern authorities" to have killed twelve people (Altick, 154), including his wife, mother-in-law, brother, and an illegitimate child of his own. His infuriating final words on the gallows—"I am innocent of poisoning Cook by strychnia" (Altick, 159)—ominously suggested secret Frankenstein-like medical knowledge that people feared. The premeditated murder is chilling; the writer argues that the "complete self-possession of his constant coolness, of his profound composure" everyone remarks on is "of a piece with his misdeeds; and that it is not likely that he ever could have committed the crimes for which he is to suffer, if he had not this demeanour to present, in standing publicly to answer for them."[12] Disgusted that people might interpret this gall as innocence, the writer assumes Palmer's voice to refute the ideal: "I poison my friend in his drink, and I poison my friend in his bed, and I poison my wife, and I poison her memory, and do you look to ME, at the end of such a career as MINE, for sensibility?" (325) The three famous mid-Victorian trials of doctors who poisoned people supported those who "raged against the helplessness of patients in the hands of the profession"[13] and bolstered the public fear of private murders, those committed by trusted associates or relatives.

Paranoia about poison also focuses on women, in part because poison requires no physical strength to be effective and in part because female poisoners like Madeline Smith were receiving a lot of journalistic attention. A nightmare figure for the mid-Victorian reader, the woman poisoner is abetted by her good looks:

> It is amazing the variety and amiability of character that is worn for years, to cover the foul fiend within. For long periods these female vampyres live in the heart of a family circle, wearing the most life-like masks of goodness and kindness, of personal attraction and spiritual gifts; caressed, feted, honoured as the very pride of their sex, while they are all the time calculating on the lives and the purses of those nearest and who should be dearest to them.[14]

Suspicion of women's sexuality mingles with the fear of being murdered by a loved one while she pretends to nurse and care: "May no such tigress smooth our pillow; smile blandly on us in our pains . . . and mix with taper fingers the opiate of our repose" ("Ursinus," 176). The hysterical prose style responds to the notion that women can and will poison those close to them. Victims cannot anticipate the crime or protect themselves.

Whether murder will out is discussed in *Cornhill* with the same intensity of concern as it is in *Cassell's,* concluding with a more sophisticated version of the same hopeful idea that murderers punish or reveal themselves. Although people want to think that murderers are always found out, writes the author of "Criminal Law," "experience daily proves that this is not the case; and few instances have proved it more clearly than the comments made and the attention excited by the murder at Road."[15] The writer sneers at the weak-minded whose belief that homicide always comes to light "surrounds murder with a sort of romantic interest. It is looked upon as something which falls under the jurisdiction of special providences—a gloomy, awful, Byronic transaction, mysteriously committed, and miraculously avenged" ("Criminal Law," 701). Not so: homicide is usually "a clumsy piece of bloody and stupid brutality, perpetrated by some wretched creature" who is difficult to track down "not because he has shown any particular skill," but because it is difficult to discover what happens in secret, and no one is paid to do so. The author has nothing but contempt for those who think "that it is possible to find out who murdered Master Kent by producing loose suggestions—that four months after he was murdered a lady was seen to comb her hair in one of Mr. Kent's bedrooms" ("Criminal Law," 702).

Yet after quelling "desultory and idle curiosity," the writer goes on to advance a theory that is little more than an elevated version of the inevitable repentance and suffering murderers experience in street literature. Whether or not the murderer is apprehended does not matter because he or she—struggling with overwhelming remorse—will never kill again. The Road killer "must have suffered, and must be suffering, torments of terror, compared with which the gallows would be a relief. Who would not prefer being hanged at once to the constant dread of detection?" ("Criminal Law," 707) Presumably, the icy Palmer, as well as countless other murderers, would choose the "dread of detection." Imposing a haunted, wracking guilt on the unknown murderer and deciding that this remorse would prevent the person from committing future crimes wraps the reader in a protective layer of myth and comfort. A happy killer is intolerable, while a hunted, tormented murderer is acceptable. Murder will not necessarily be found out, but that hardly matters because the murderers, like Sikes or Aram, provide their own punishment.

Middle-class journals, unlike street literature and working-class periodical newspapers, feature police and criminals as professionals. Very impressed with the new detective police force, Dickens includes several articles on detectives.

He is taken with their systematic successes and sharp wits. It is impossible to describe "the high amount of skill, intelligence, and knowledge, concentrated in the character of a clever Detective Policeman," asserts the author of "The Modern Science of Thief Taking."[16] When *The Times* reports on the Waterloo Bridge case, police are praised for their "vigilance" and "indefatigable efforts" (17 October 1857). Criticism is offered very delicately: "We would, however, beg with the utmost deference to suggest that the police are not exactly pursuing that course which is most likely to lead to the dress being identified" (14 October 1857). Although an individual policeman is sometimes named in street literature or in *The World We Live In,* only middle-class journals feature policemen as a class of effective professionals.

There is a parallel sense of criminals who commit murder and theft professionally, rather than on impulse. "The Predatory Art" in *Household Words* discusses thieves as a group in some detail, while the author of "Injured Innocents" insists that readers face reality: "The habitual criminal is an actual living fact."[17] In an article by a supposed garotter, the writer dismisses the proverb that murder will out, which is only true because "murder is mostly undertaken by unskilled amateurs, induced by personal vengeance or special temptation" ("Garotting," 260). The article is humorous but its subject and implications are not. "I declared war on society," states the writer, and he symbolizes the perception of a new kind of criminal who coldbloodedly plans an arbitrary crime. To believe that there is a class of criminals who steal and kill repeatedly means that murder can be a profitable way of life, that the public is unprotected.

Finally, in middle-class journals, there is a growing consciousness of a characteristically British kind of homicide linked to the mid-Victorian style of life. Murders are either random, like the garottings or child-murders by strangers, or particular, from within the circle of the victim. To hear a multiple murderer like Palmer described at his trial as a man who has "a good character, and is much respected at Rugeley" is to redefine crime and criminals (*The Times,* 15 March 1856). Murder can be committed in the alley, the bedroom, and the garden by people the victim has never seen—or has daily seen. The most popular crime in England, writes someone for *Blackwood's,* does not occur in "mountain isolation," like many Swiss crimes. Famous and fascinating English crimes

> are those perpetrated in the very heart of the pressure of modern life. A London man of business is disposed of, in a crowded train, returning to his home in the suburbs; a medical practitioner poisons his relations under the eyes of the Glasgow doctors; a child is found mysteriously dead in the bosom of a respectable family; a young lady buys arsenic, and her lover dies . . . .[18]

There is a "skeleton in every house," and leading a virtuous life is no longer a protection from violent death. No one is safe when homicides are committed "in the press of civilisation, under the noses of policemen, amid the snort of steam-engines, or with the murmur of city life rolling around" ("Switzerland," 493). Sophistication, technological advancement, the trappings of tradition and authority, even personal bonds do not preclude murder. Popular nonfictional literature of the 1850s and 1860s reveals a realization that one is more endangered in a place of supposed safety than anywhere else. Middle-class magazines, unlike street literature, reflect on the causes of crime by tracing murder back to its social roots. But ultimately that reflectiveness does not matter. Both working-class and middle-class popular genres portray a dangerous world in which a threat that is peculiarly domestic and English undermines authority.

# 5

# Melodrama, 1850–1870

Like their predecessors in the thirties and forties, mid-Victorian melodramas on crime found large and devoted audiences. So many versions of *Sweeney Todd* were performed at The Royal Victoria that patrons called the theatre "The Bleedin' Vic."[1] Plays like *The Scamps of London* (1843) and *London by Night* (1868) appealed partly because of their commitment to realistic presentations of the seamy, unromantic world of modern crime. These melodramas feature a "riff-raff cast of railway porters, ruined roués, drunkards, cadgers, shoe-blacks, vagabonds, bill-discounters and policemen" who "speak a racy Cockney slang, and play out exciting scenes of metropolitan depravity in hotel rooms and railway stations, garrets, gaudy pleasure gardens, miserable dives and brickfields close to Battersea" (Smith, xx). Yet middle-class audiences in the fifties and sixties were also beginning to see their own concerns reflected in "cup and saucer" drama, so called because the actors used real crockery on stage and because scenes occurred in kitchens or dining rooms. Murder and crime were also often part of the action in these plays, patronized by audiences drawn from more affluent and respectable classes. Whether theatrical crime took place in the professional underworld or the middle and aristocratic classes, the nature of the crimes themselves represented a movement away from the lurid excess of early Victorian melodrama.

Mid-Victorian melodrama of crime shares many characteristics with street literature and nonfiction of the same period. Instead of the protracted, bloody crimes of *The String of Pearls* and *The Murder in the Red Barn,* midcentury crimes are secret and shameful, desperate, not demoniac. Stealth and deceit mark criminal behavior. Murders and robberies spring from a specific social context, not from psychosis or vindictive malice. Crimes committed to improve social status eventually create a subgenre of plays about the man or woman with a past. In C. H. Hazlewood's *Lady Audley's Secret* (1863), the central character is a villain whose bigamy must be concealed at all costs. In *The Ticket-of-Leave Man* (1863) by Tom Taylor, the hero's time in prison is hidden from his employer to protect his job. By the end of the century, "women with a past" plays by Henry Arthur Jones, Arthur Wing Pinero, Oscar Wilde, and others present more complicated and sympathetic responses to women with compromising sexual histories. *Lady Audley's Secret,* however, betrays little sympathy for its murderous, ambitious central character, emphasizing instead the criminality of her sexual and social frauds.[2] Like many murderers and victims in mid-Victorian street literature and periodicals, Lady Audley evokes a fear of women's independence and sexuality.

Melodrama of the fifties and sixties also indicates a developing recognition that criminals and police are distinct professional classes. As a character, the detective becomes as interesting as the murderer. The detective figure in *The Ticket-of-Leave Man* and the growing number of detectives in the melodrama and fiction of the rest of the century suggest increased ambivalence and anxiety about the belief that murder may not out, so professionals must bring criminals to justice. The relation of crime to social pressures and values is also more explicit in mid-Victorian than in earlier melodrama; there is a parallel increase in the use of imagery such as masks and ladders as social metaphors. Lastly, the resolutions of these plays imply greater insecurity on the subjects of crime and punishment. Plots conclude as neatly and coincidentally as in all melodramas, but underlying the sudden revelations and convenient last-moment confessions in plays like Hazlewood's and Taylor's is the growing suspicion that crime is all around, that criminals might not be discovered until it is too late.

*Lady Audley's Secret* and *The Ticket-of-Leave Man* were among the most popular melodramas of the fifties and sixties. Elizabeth Braddon's 1862 novel was adapted by many authors and performed for years after its publication.[3] The most famous version, by George Roberts, was never published (Rowell, *Victorian Theatre,* ix). An adaptation by the prolific C. H. Hazlewood was first produced at The Royal Victoria Theatre in May 1862, three months after the debut of Roberts's version (Rowell, *Victorian Theatre,* 236). The substitution of an aristocratic setting—the country estate of Sir Michael Audley—for the docks and shops of *Black-Ey'd Susan* (1829) and *The String of Pearls* "suggests a corresponding change in the composition of its audience," a reversal of the "exodus of polite Society from the theatre" (Rowell, *Victorian Theatre,* ix, viii). The "out-and-out female villainy" of Lady Audley in such a genteel rural setting attracted a large audience and may explain why the novel was "dramatized three times in 1863" alone.[4] After repeated appearances of the red-haired, hypocritical Lady Audley, "villainesses proliferated" and became an "integral part" of sensation drama, domestic drama, and melodrama (Booth, *English Melodrama,* 157). For a short period after the success of Hazlewood's version, "red hair marked the adventuress"; later, the female villains of melodrama returned to their traditional "raven black" tresses.[5] In 1913, *Lady Audley's Secret* became a film, and the play, like *Ten Nights in a Bar Room* (1858), is still occasionally revived as a comedy.

Tom Taylor, longtime contributor to *Punch,* was famous as a farceur; he wrote the popular comedy *Our American Cousin,* which Lincoln watched on his last night. It is, however, "in the humbler sphere of petty larceny" that Taylor's most lasting achievement was set (Rowell, *Victorian Theatre,* 59). The play has several sources. Adapted from the story *Le Retour de Melun* by Brisbarre and Nus, it was published in *Les Drames de la Vie* and later dramatized by the authors as *Leonard.*[6] Taylor's melodrama is "a direct descendant of Fitzball's *Jonathan Bradford,*" which focused on an innocent man accused of a crime (Rowell, *Victorian Theatre,* 59). "One of the forerunners of modern social drama in England," the play was also notable at the time for its realistic dialogue and settings (Rowell, Introduction to *Nineteenth-Century Plays,* viii). *The Ticket-of-Leave Man* opens "in a public tea-garden with parties at tables drinking and eating, waiters moving around taking and delivering orders, shrubs, trees, statues, and all the paraphernalia of a busy restaurant" (Booth, *English Melodrama,* 158). The idiomatic exchanges of the police and the criminals fairly crackled with authenticity, especially when contrasted with the more traditional dialogue of the young lovers. Lastly, audiences were thrilled by "the introduction of a stage detective, the protean Hawkshaw, whose facility for make-up fired a string of successors to more and more impenetrable disguises" (Rowell, *Victorian Theatre,* 59). Eventually, Taylor's play was filmed, one year after Hazlewood's came to the screen (Booth, *English Melodrama,* 182).

In *Lady Audley's Secret,* the curtain rises on Phoebe, Lady Audley's maid, wrangling with her cousin and fiancé, Luke, "a drunken Gamekeeper."[7] She is helping to prepare for elderly Sir Michael's birthday celebration. Luke suggests that Lady Audley, the estate's former governess, is not as genuinely fond of her husband as she appears. Lady Audley enters with Sir Michael and behaves charmingly to him and her stepdaughter, Alicia. Alicia is nevertheless suspicious and jealous of her young "mother-in-law" and impatiently awaits the arrival of her cousin and fiancé, Robert. He turns up with his friend George, whose wife died while he was in India. He is shocked to recognize the face of his wife in Alicia's miniature of her stepmother and vows: "If I have been deceived by her, woe to the traitress—woe—woe, and punishment" (244). In the garden, Lady Audley confesses her bigamy to the audience. She is eager "to taste the sweets of wealth and power" that she could never have enjoyed while married to her "fool of a first husband" (245). George overhears her boasts and threatens to expose her crime; after attempting bribery and bullying, Lady Audley tricks him into going to the well. As he stoops to get her water, she pushes him down the well, crying: "Dead men tell no tales!" (248). But canny Luke has secretly observed the murder.

When Lady Audley suffers from "abject fears and whisperings of conscience" in act 2, she quells them: "I am Lady Audley, powerful, rich, and unsuspected, with not one living witness to rise up against me" (251). At this moment, Luke appears, "flushed with drink," to extort money from the horrified Lady Audley (251). She agrees to meet him at his house later. Robert also suspects her, and after a cat-and-mouse exchange, he accuses her of killing his friend and her first husband. She persuades him to keep silent for Sir Michael's sake; he agrees only if she leaves the estate forever. Duplicitously, Lady Audley tells the family that Robert has become "too agreeable" toward her (255), and Sir Michael orders him from the house. When Robert visits Luke to try and learn the reason for Lady Audley's intended meeting, she sets fire to the house, hoping to rid herself of Luke and Robert at the same time. Robert survives the fire, however, and brings the dying gamekeeper to accuse Lady Audley. Yet once again he reconsiders: "It will be better not to cast a stain upon my uncle's name" (266). Luke "falls back in the arms of the Peasants," and Alicia arrives with timely news of Sir Michael's death. Lady Audley still hopes to evade further accusation, but Luke revives before dying and George accuses her. His account of having been "an invalid for months" as a result of her attack falls on uncomprehending ears. When she sees him, she goes mad on the spot and dies. The other characters form a "tableau of sympathy" over her body (266).

Lady Audley's cunning bigamy and eventual murder represent the mid-Victorian fear of the wicked woman whose manipulative sexuality allows her to pursue dreams of wealth, social status, and power. She displays the disruptive and transformational energies described in Nina Auerbach's *Woman and the Demon*.[8] It is likely that Sir Michael's estate would eventually prove an inadequate sphere for a woman of Lady Audley's wickedness and determination; she would "soon bid adieu to a country life," her maid suspects, after becoming a widow (246). "You are a traitress, madam!" accuses George (246), and his wife is a lively symbol of the "tigress" attacked in articles about female poisoners. Like Mrs. Lovett, Lady Audley uses her power consciously. Only Alicia has pointed suspicions:

> I don't believe she's sincere in her regards. She smiles and coaxes you, it's true; but I sometimes fancy her looks are like the sunbeams on a river, which make us forget the dark depths which lie hidden beneath the surface. (249–50)

Married to a man three times her age, Lady Audley would raise anyone's eyebrows, yet she successfully ensnares Sir Michael and very nearly achieves her ambitions. Who is safe when the most ruthless conniver insinuates herself into the aristocracy? What hypocrisies might ordinary wives and mothers conceal? Lady Audley flirts with the truth when talking to her guileless second husband:

> LADY AUDLEY:  Ah, my dear, we may read *faces* but not *hearts*.
> SIR MICHAEL:  And could I read yours, I'm sure I should see—
> LADY AUDLEY:  That which would change your opinion of me perhaps.
> SIR MICHAEL:  Not it, I warrant, for if ever the face was an index of the mind, I believe yours to be that countenance.

LADY AUDLEY:  (*Aside*) We may have two faces. (*Aloud*) Bless you! bless you for your confidence! (241)

"Of all things in the world," declares Lady Audley blithely, "I hate hypocrisy the most" (256). The rapidity with which she is capable of changing roles is her strength; when Robert enters to question her about his friend's disappearance, she hurries to "resume the mask, which not only imposes on him, but on all the world" (252).

Other melodramas of the period also emphasize the ever-potential danger of women's sexuality. Even innocent female characters could inspire murderous jealousy. In a strange tropical revision of *Othello*, the melodrama *The Island of St. Tropez* (1860) by Montague Williams, a middle-aged sailor is poisoned by his Iago-like friend, who also poisons his mind against his new young wife. Amelie had loved another man but married Henri through gratitude. The sailor dies after learning of Amelie's innocence. In *The Deserted Mill; or, The Soldier's Widow* (1855) by Edward Fitzball, a man attempts to murder his rival for his fiancée's affections, although she has remained faithful to him; "if not for me to bloom," he malevolently declares, "for him you wither!" As in the mid-Victorian street ballads, ingenuous women are victimized by the effect their unconscious sexuality has on others. When they use their allure consciously to manipulate men, results are often lethal for others as well as for them.

As in Hazlewood's play, Taylor's *The Ticket-of-Leave Man* focuses on private rather than public crime, commenting on the relation of crime to social pressures and the sense of police and criminals as distinct professional classes. Hawkshaw and a fellow detective meet in the Bellevue Tea Gardens to watch the criminal activities of Dalton and Moss. Bob Brierly, a good-hearted associate of the confidence men, worries about his lack of money and his heavy drinking. Hawkshaw, in disguise, warns Brierly about the dangers of alcohol, to no avail. When May Edwards is refused a job as a singer at the Gardens, Bob takes pity on the starving girl. Dalton pays a bill with counterfeit money, and the police catch Bob while Dalton escapes. Bob and May correspond during his prison term. When released, he pretends to be recently discharged from "Her Majesty's Service," and he is hired as an accountant by a friend of May's, Mr. Gibson.[9]

Hawkshaw appears at Gibson's office on the day May and Bob are to marry. The detective has been called in about forgery, and although he recognizes Brierly, he compassionately does not tell Gibson that he employs a "ticket-of-leave man," or former convict. Dalton enters dressed as "a respectable elderly commercial man" (313). Hawkshaw does not recognize him and tells his plans to revenge himself on Jem Dalton for causing the death of a good detective who was Hawkshaw's close friend. Brierly is appalled to discover Dalton in the office; when they are alone, the thief blackmails Bob into keeping silent about Dalton's larcenous intentions. But Moss informs on Bob to Gibson, who fires him.

The final act of four opens in a working-man's pub where Dalton and Moss discuss the way they have hounded Brierly from job to job, preventing him from leading a virtuous life by informing his employers about his prison record; they hope he will become a permanent member of their gang. When hapless Bob enters and shows an innocent card player how Dalton and Moss have cheated him, the criminals are infuriated. Hawkshaw, disguised as a "navvy," looks on while they tell Bob's coworkers of his past. "Who knows, lads," suggests Hawkshaw gamely, "perhaps he's repented," but the workers reject and abandon the "jail-bird" (334). Bob finally pretends to go along with the plan to rob Gibson's office, but writes a warning note to his former employer. Convinced of Bob's sincerity, Hawkshaw reveals his identity and promises to help him. The thieves are caught red-handed. Bob suffers from "a clip on the head," but knows the satisfaction of having at last proven himself innocent (342).

*The Ticket-of-Leave Man* shares with street literature and nonfiction one of their central themes: the consciousness of police and criminals as distinct professional classes. This contrasts sharply with earlier ballads and street literature in which murderers kill because they are psychotic (Todd) or for personal advancement (Corder), not because they are professional criminals. Similarly, Hawkshaw does not accidentally or providentially observe and discover crimes. He is paid to do so. The first stage detective was the title character of Jerrold's *Vidocq, The French Police Spy* (1829), whose adventures had thrilled readers. Yet "the detective did not appear as a . . . stage character" with any regularity until "the establishment of a regular police force" (Booth, *English Melodrama*, 162). Like the detectives in *All the Year Round*, Hawkshaw is a formidable and canny adversary. His professional routine and acuity is suggested by his first appearance, when he "strolls carelessly to the Detectives' table, then in an undertone and without looking at them" demands that they "report" (271). Like Dalton, whom he pursues, Hawkshaw has endless disguises and aliases; he later enters disguised as a navvy "flustered with drink . . . and assuming a country dialect" (325). Cleverly, he induces Dalton to reveal his guilt time and time again, although he postpones his arrest until he catches the criminal in the middle of a robbery. Dalton starts at the detective's provocative remarks about forgery and counterfeiting; when Hawkshaw, still disguised, warns Bob about his "thieving companion here," meaning alcohol, Dalton jumps: "Eh? what do you mean by that?" (276) Hawkshaw's presence as professional detective is comforting and omniscient. Yet the need for detectives suggests growing anxiety about whether crimes will be revealed. Detectives are hired—and police forces established—when we can no longer assume that justice will be done providentially.

As professional criminals, the characters in *The Ticket-of-Leave Man* also have their own language, tools, habits, and pseudoethical codes, as well as their own adeptness at disguise; crime is now a game for very accomplished players. When Moss fails to recognize his disguised companion, Dalton says, "What, don't twig me? Then it is a good get up" (272). There is a "peculiar grip" by which criminals recognize each other or bind deals: "There!" cries Dalton. "Tip us the cracksman's crook—so!" (335). Crime is an occupation, not an impulse. Moss automatically evaluates the restaurant's flatware: "Uncommon neat article—might take in a good many people—plated, though, plated" (272). After crowing over his narrow escape at Gibson's office, Dalton says, "Come—I've my wax handy—never travel without my tools" (318). The ethics of professional criminals parody and unravel standards of law-abiding people: when Dalton bids low for forged bills, Moss exclaims, "Only fifteen—it's robbery" (274). He exits grumbling about having to "deal with people that have no consciences" (274). Moss vengefully gives Brierly away in public because he has exposed his cheating at cards: "I owe you one—I always pay my debts" (334).

Perhaps most disturbing and pervasive amidst the jargon, routines, and codes of the professional criminal is the implication that initiation into the world of crime is irreversible. Just as Fagin's gang pursues Oliver to his haven at Mr. Brownlow's, the fraternity of robbers and murderers in Taylor's play is relentless. "Hang me, if I haven't often thought of turning respectable," claims Dalton (273). Yet it would be impossible:

> DALTON:   Ah! nobody likes the Portland mark. I know that—I've tried the honest dodge, too.
> MOSS:   It don't answer.
> DALTON:   It didn't with me. I had a friend, like you, always after me. Whatever I tried, I was blown as a convict, and hunted out from honest men. . . .
> MOSS:   I never drop a friend.
> DALTON:   No, till the hangman takes your place at his side. (325)

The underworld of the play is a sinister collection of criminals who can not live honestly or trust each other. In Hawkshaw's opinion, "they can't leave London. Like the moths, they turn and turn about the candle till they burn their wings" (316). Drawn to the urban mire, like Sikes who escapes from the law only to return to his death in London, criminals are doomed to their profession.

The traditional melodramatic coincidences are given a twist in *The Ticket-of-Leave Man* because of Hawkshaw's professional determination to bring Dalton to justice. Fortunately for Brierly, Hawkshaw is everywhere. He has business at Gibson's, where he recognizes Brierly but withholds knowledge about his criminal past: "Poor devil, he's paid his debt at Portland" (312). Later, disguised as a sailor, Hawkshaw gives Brierly a job and tries to prevent his comrades from turning on the former convict once they discover his record. He is also there to take Brierly's note about the robbery to Gibson and rescues the outnumbered man from his dangerous associates. By his timely appearances, Hawkshaw saves Bob and avenges his friend's death simultaneously. Like the police of Dickens's admiring articles in *Household Words,* Hawkshaw is almost preternaturally efficient.

Although unique in some ways, *Lady Audley's Secret* and *The Ticket-of-Leave Man* were greatly popular in part through their successful use of traditional melodramatic conventions. Like Corder and Todd, Lady Audley is dangerous because of her arrogant ambition. Although she is a more sympathetic character than Corder in some ways, she shares his hypocrisy and energy. When declaring war on her first husband, she chooses words worthy of any melodramatic villain:

> Fool! why do you wage war with me—why do you make me your enemy? Tremble, if I am; for, if we are foes, I *must* triumph over you. Do you hear? *must*—for victory yields me safety—defeat, death! (254–55)

Like her predecessors, Lady Audley possesses a genius for action; she has Todd's improvisational skill in violence. When her first husband swears he will battle her to the death, she immediately reaches a literal conclusion, determining—in an aside—to murder him: "'Death! death!' Aye that is the word—that is the only way of escape" (247). Alicia is foolishly jealous of her betrothed, and her stepmother finds a way to turn suspicion to advantage: "A good idea. I'll work upon it" (255). She turns to Alicia to say: "Come with me, and I'll tell you such things about him, that will I'm sure prevent you ever again speaking to him" (255). Similarly, her maid innocently suggests the means of Luke's death, confiding: "I'm afraid to leave Luke when he's in drink: he may set the house on fire." In an urgent aside, Lady Audley muses, "'house on fire!' A good idea" (262). Like Corder, she aligns herself symbolically with the devil: "I have but one terrible agent to aid me, and that is fire" (262).

Coincidence, a crucial melodramatic convention, rules *Lady Audley's Secret.* Lady Audley is constantly being overheard or seen by the last person she would wish. George hears her gloat over his gullibility and leaps out to accuse her. Luke sees her push George down the well; when she triumphantly cries that "no one was a witness to the deed," Luke responds in an ominous aside: "Except me" (248). Luke dies by inches, reviving twice to relay and postpone crucial information. Sir Michael also dies conveniently—"struck down by a terrible fit"—so that Lady Audley may be accused without concern for his feelings (263). Like Todd, Lady Audley dies in a state of vigorously unrepentent insanity at the sight of her supposed victim: "But I do not heed. I have a rich husband. They told me he was dead—but no, they lied—see— see, he stands there! Your arm—your arm, Sir Michael" (266). Only after her madness heralds certain death can there be any sympathy for her. Pathetically and eerily she exhorts: "Do not touch me—do not come near me—let me claim your silence—your pity—and let the grave, the cold grave, close over Lady Audley and her Secret" (266). As in *The Murder in the Red Barn* and *The Factory Lad,* the curtain falls on a poignant "tableau."

Melodramatic conventions are also hard at work in *The Ticket-of-Leave Man.* The hero and heroine suffer passively and virtuously. An acquiescent and pathetic girl with a "sweet voice," May must try and find work in public because of her lowly circumstances (282). She supports herself by sewing and singing, managing to set money aside for her beloved Bob, who is too proud to accept it. She even apologizes for her virtue; when Bob says, "Thou's too soft for this life o' thine," she replies, "It's the fever, I think, sir—I usen't to mind unkind looks and words much once" (283). Although in desperate straits, May values her reputation and respectability before everything else. When Bob yearns to talk to May, she is hesitant: "But where I live, sir, it's a very poor place, and I'm by myself, and—" (284). Her room is "humbly but neatly furnished" (285). Her sympathy and compassion for the troubles of everyone she knows are limitless, her brave encouragement to Brierly after he is fired indomitable.

Bob is also connected to the stock melodramatic hero whose sensibility and moral strength outweigh his intelligence. Far from embittered by the time he spent in prison for a crime he did not commit, Bob uses the four years in jail as training in courage and respectability. When admiring May's room after his release, he reminisces: "As neat as the cell I've just left. But it wasn't hard to keep *that* in order—I had only a stool, a basin, and a hammock. Didn't I polish the hammock-hooks neither. One must have a pride in something—you know" (292). He is almost grateful for his incarceration: "I worked away; in school, in the quarry-gang first, and in the office afterwards, as if I had to stay there for ever—I wasn't unhappy either—all were good to me" (293). Bob anonymously repays May's landlady the money his associates stole from her, even though he had no complicity in the crime. He accuses Moss and Dalton of cheating her grandson, precocious Sam Willoughby, at cards, even though his honesty costs him his job so that "his last hope is gone" (334). In his desperate state, he still feels a responsibility to turn Sam from wicked ways and implores the boy to "hearken" to his message:

> A bad beginning makes a bad end, and you're beginning badly; the road you're on leads downwards, and once in the slough at the bottom o't—oh! trust one who knows it—there's no working clear again. You may hold out your hand—you may cry for help—you may struggle hard—but the quicksands are under your foot—and you sink down, down, till they close over your head. (332)

Although the other "navvies" laugh, Bob urges Sam to return to his grandmother, to be sober and steady; "you'll mayhap remember this day, and be thankful you took the advice of poor hunted-down, broken-hearted Bob Brierly" (333).

Clearly linked to the traditions and conventions of earlier melodrama, *The Ticket-of-Leave Man* and *Lady Audley's Secret* are also closely connected to the characteristic mid-Victorian themes of street literature and journalistic accounts of real crimes. Crimes in these plays are concealed, secret. Like the murders committed by respected doctors and trusted ladies, the crimes in *Lady Audley's Secret* and *The Ticket-of-Leave Man* shock because of their unexpectedness. The "secret" of Lady Audley turns out to be her bigamy, not her murder and attempted murder. Lady Audley, like the poisoners feared by writers of non-fiction, is insidiously hypocritical as she fawns on her elderly husband and suspicious stepdaughter. Luke and Alicia seem to be on to her from the play's start: "One can't always be smiles and honey like you are, my dear mother-in-law," Alicia retorts. "It's better to let one's temper come out at once, than brood over unpleasant things in secret" (240). Despite Alicia's wariness, Lady Audley nearly accomplishes her goals. Her major sin is the cunning she used to deceive George and gain Sir Michael's affections. Women who use their charm calculatingly are more threatening than impassioned murderers. George determines to bring her to justice because she is a criminally bad wife. He will, he says, be "the avenger of my wrongs—the punisher of a heartless deceitful wife" (247). Although she has committed bigamy rather than adultery, the warning could have been clear to potential domestic criminals. Like her bigamy, there is also something secretive and hidden about her crimes of violence. Rather than being hacked to pieces, George is confined to a well. Luke is imprisoned within a burning house and dies, eventually, from suffocation and burning. Similarly, although Lady Audley is improvisationally brilliant, her bigamy—like her arson-murder—is calculated. Even her assault on George results from a rational decision. The nature of Lady Audley's crimes—bigamy, murder, and assault—reflect a general fear of intimate and buried violence, suggesting a growing anxiety about being threatened from within.

The crimes in *The Ticket-of-Leave Man* are also calculated, not impulsive. Frustratingly, Dalton's indirect murder of Hawkshaw's detective friend, Joe, occurs in such a way that the law can not touch the criminal. Some murderers fall into a legal hole: they are morally guilty of the crime, but they can not be punished officially. Dalton's assault becomes murder, but it can not be punished. Hawkshaw broods on this injustice:

> Not to say murdered him right out. But he spoiled him—gave him a clip on the head with a neddy—a life-preserver. He was never his own man afterwards. He left the force on a pension, but he grew sort of paralysed, and then got queer in his head. . . . "Jack," he says, "I lay my death at the Tiger's door"—that was the name we had for Dalton in the force. "You'll look after him, Jack," he says, "for the sake of an old comrade." . . . I promised him to be even with Jem Dalton, and I'll keep my word. (317)

Dalton and Moss are also guilty of the secret crimes of counterfeiting and forgery. Brierly's past as a prisoner becomes his crime; he must conceal it to survive. Although he is innocent of forgery, his jail record proves him guilty, and the revelation that he has done time condemns him as surely and swiftly as a murder would have done. Gibson is only the first person to repulse him because of his "ticket-of-leave." Even the humble navvies in the working-man's pub reject Bob because of his past. Throughout the play, Bob suffers be-cause of his damning deception regarding the four years at Portland. Society forces him to lie; he does not overcome his secret crime until proving his hon-esty by turning the real criminals over to Gibson and Hawkshaw. The extreme and sensational nature of the crimes in a song performed by a minor character, Emily St. Evremond, contrasts ironically with the insinuating misdeeds in the rest of the play. Emily sings plaintively of "an interesting lunatic—with lucid intervals. She has just murdered her husband . . . and her three children, and is supposed to be remonstrating with one of the lunacy commissioners on the cruelty of her confinement" (324). Indirect and sly crimes like "accidental" murder, forgery, and counterfeiting are more threatening than fictive lunatics in murderous rages. Bob learns, to his grief, that even the smallest crimes of con-cealment make innocence look like guilt.

When considered in light of the hidden nature of the crime committed, the emphases on dangerous female sexuality and on professionalism of police and criminals in these plays have clear social implications. The appearance of Hawkshaw and later detective figures, and the professionalism and confrater-nity of criminals, suggest the recognition of crime as a significant problem that can not be solved by ordinary citizens. Organized crime was not peculiar to Victorian popular fiction, having appeared in earlier works as well. The need for a detective, however, is new and telling. In the street literature of the thir-ties and forties, murderers are caught in the act or soon afterward, incriminated by their own actions or by key witnesses. Mrs. Martin's dream exposes William Corder as her daughter's killer. Todd is revealed by his own sloppy workmanship—incompletely murdered; Mark lives to be revenged upon his would-be killer—and the paranoia that causes him to attack nearly everyone. By the fifties and sixties, however, criminal bunglings and supernatural clues can not be relied on to accuse and capture melodramatic malefactors. No longer semiromantic highwaymen or indigent workers driven to crime, killers calcu-late their misdeeds, and clever criminals require clever detectives.

In *Lady Audley's Secret,* Robert "has paid detectives, and advertised in every paper" to find George (249). Not until six months have passed does the amateur detective confront his prey with the miniature of George's first wife and the letter from Helen Talboys—Lady Audley's first identity—in her hand-writing. Robert's appropriation of the craft of professional detective work is necessary to expose the bigamous imposter. Even though Robert is a friend of the family and emotionally involved in the case, he craftily cross-examines Lady Audley to discover inconsistency in her testimony using the clues and interrogative techniques of the police.

Taylor's Hawkshaw became a household word for a shrewd, ratiocinative detective, and his line "I know you, Jack Dalton" became famous.[10] Through his long experience as a detective, he protects Brierly from a criminal life. As Robert seeks the truth about his friend's "death," so Hawkshaw pursues Dalton to avenge Joe's death. Yet this involvement serves to heighten his professional commitment to the case; it does not distract or dissuade him. The presentation of detectives and police as central characters in crime melodrama acknowledges the need for extraordinary and methodical measures to apprehend criminals. Murder will not come to light unless steps are taken to guarantee its discovery.

The relation of crime to social status and values is also more explicit in mid-Victorian melodrama than in its predecessors, featuring a curious ambivalence toward the aristocracy. Aristocrats may be criminally cruel, but boundaries of class remain enforced in most melodramas. *The Deserted Mill; or, The Soldier's Widow* (1855) shows the hero restored to his title as Count. In *The Day of Reckoning* (1851) by Planché, however, a heartless and conniving Count is killed by a noble working-class man whose father was ruined by the Count's refusal to pay him a large debt. Yet the man's son is killed in the same duel, living long enough to claim the deed so that the Countess's suitor is not implicated. Although the Count is wicked, the hero can not sully his hands by killing him. In *Marco Spada* (1853) by J. Palgrave Simpson, the brigand who has passed as the Baron Di Torrida reveals when dying that the heroine is not his daughter, but the offspring of an honorable man he once killed. She is thus able to marry the Prince.

Marriages between people of supposedly removed stations take place only after the ordinary person turns out to be noble or royal. *The Lady of Lyons* (1838) by Bulwer-Lytton is rare because its working-class hero, Claude Melnotte, proves that nobility of spirit is more significant than actual rank. Nevertheless, he married Pauline while disguised as a Prince; and when he reveals his true identity, eventually winning her love, his trickery has won him the daughter of a merchant, not a Duke. Not until T. W. Robertson's daring comedy *Caste* (1867) is the marriage of a gentleman to a working-class woman presented as a sensible and courageous choice. "Caste is a good thing if it's not carried too far," argues the hero; "it should open the door very wide for exceptional merit."[11]

In *Lady Audley's Secret*, aristocrats are not dangerous; those who intrude into higher social classes are. Because she has committed a social crime—she has married her titled former employer—Lady Audley is suspect from the start. This inappropriate coupling is emphasized by the grotesque difference in their ages. Her bigamy and murder spring partly from the ever-present need to maintain and improve social status. The play opens with a semicomic scene that underlines these social necessities; Luke wants to benefit from his sweetheart's improved status.

> You've been rising in servitude o'late; first you were housemaid, then parlour-maid, now you be lady's maid, at the top o' the servant's tree like; so as that be the case, I, as your sweetheart, ought to reap some of the fruits. I wants some money. (237)

Luke's request brings the financial advantages of social status to center stage prior to Lady Audley's first appearance; she has, he observes enviously, "played her cards well" (237). Even loyal Phoebe is astonished by her mistress's rapid rise in station: "What a change this marriage has made in her prospects, from a poor governess she has become the mistress of Audley Court" (241). Lady Audley's crimes are born of the desire to rise that prevails in the servant's quarters and at every point in the social hierarchy. Her temporary success and the extent of her ambition guarantee her gaudy downfall.

Bob Brierly's predicament also springs from his social context. Gibson admits that Brierly has been "steady and industrious," but concludes: "I must think of my own credit and character. If it was buzzed about that I kept a ticket-of-leave man in my employment—" (320). Dalton's success as a con artist rests in his ability to feign respectability. Bob's trials occur when he determines to make his way up the social ladder of righteous hard work despite his prison record. Even the comic subplot underlines relentless social realities. Emily St. Evremond must disassociate herself from her husband when she is a singer and he a trotter salesman: "Bye-bye, dear, till after the concert—you know I can't be seen speaking to you while you carry that basket" (324). He suffers comically because of their temporary class differences: "True—in the humble trotter-man who would suspect the husband of the brilliant St. Evremond! There's something romantic in it—I hover around the room—I hear you universally admired—visibly applauded—audibly adored—Oh, agony" (324). His dramatic tribulations keep the difficulties of social values and the necessity for improving one's status uppermost in the audience's mind. Respectability comes with money; wealth confers status. Emily recognizes the significant connection when she denies that Brierly's offices are boring: "Yes they are dull, but *so* respectable—look so like money, you know" (306). Money confers intelligence as well as status: "No man's a fool with £500 in his pocket," St. Evremond's husband observes.

Masks and ladders dominate the imagery that characterizes the process of social ascent. Lady Audley refers to herself as two-faced, and Alicia tries to show her father that her stepmother is "a perfect wax doll, as regards complexion; fair as the day when in a good temper, but black as night if she can't rule anybody as she likes" (243–44). Dalton pretends to be an honest businessman, and Bob is masked as a man with an unsullied past. Hawkshaw dons many disguises throughout the play, dramatically illustrating how people can pass as other characters in various classes. Brierly uses many images of rising on a ladder or rope: "I must begin lower down, and when I've got a character, then I may reach a step higher, and so creep back little by little to the level of honest men" (294). He learns how difficult it is to escape his past: "It's hard for a poor chap that's fought clear of the mud, to let go the rope he's holding to and slide back again" (305). Forces drag down the person who has made a "bad beginning" (332). The urgency of ascent and occasional necessity for disguise mark social crime.

In *Lady Audley's Secret,* crimes logically emerge from an environment in which social status is valued above everything. Lady Audley, however, is ultimately responsible for her bigamy and murder because of her cunning, arrogance, and ambitious use of her sexuality. In *The Ticket-of-Leave Man,* social circumstances drive would-be innocent people to crime. The play "represents a shrewd piece of social criticism," suggesting concern about the kind of society that "allows Bob Brierly to be wrongly convicted and, when he has served his sentence, refuses him the right to an honest living" (Rowell, Introduction to *Nineteenth-Century Plays,* viii, 61). Bob sees his prison past as a "cloud that stands like a dark wall between me and honest labour" (328). The play suggests that criminals want not only to bilk honest people, but also to corrupt them: "You see, when a man's in the mud himself and can't get out of it," explains Dalton, "he don't like to see another fight clear" (335). Significantly, Bob has *not* committed a crime; the play does not focus on an actual forger or murderer who repents and wants to live honestly. It would be more difficult to empathize so thoroughly with someone who was guilty, yet the way Bob is hounded as a former convict from job to job creates a certain amount of sympathy for the criminal who wants to start over.

Although they differ somewhat in their conservative or lightly reformist ideas about the way society is responsible for crime and the treatment of criminals, *The Ticket-of-Leave Man* and *Lady Audley's Secret* share the mid-Victorian fear that murder may remain hidden. Hawkshaw and the criminals he pursues are professionals; Robert hires professionals and acts as a detective himself to unearth Lady Audley's guilt. In Hazlewood's play, crime is intractable because it is so interwoven with what society values and approves—being pretty and engaging, and moving up through marriage to a higher social position. In *The Ticket-of-Leave Man,* crime is problematic because of society's own doubtful attitude toward reform and because crimes are not simple; the murder that is not legally murder means that Hawkshaw can not arrest the culpable Dalton for his friend's death. Similarly, there is ambiguity in the likeness of police and criminals in their jargon, disguises, and professionalism.

As in ballads, criminals are haunted by their misdeeds. Lady Audley suffers after pushing George down the well: "I wish I could banish the remembrance of the fatal meeting from my mind, but I cannot. By day I think of it, and at night I can fancy he is before me in the solitude of my chamber, when sleep should be sealing my eyelids and rest bring me repose—" (250–51). Even Robert, a well-intentioned rather than brilliant sleuth, notices the change in her; she has been "very *ill* at ease" (253). He tells her: "Your eyes are not half so bright as they were when I first came here—still I grant you they may be as sharp. Your manner is more anxious—you fall into deep reflection, and sometimes do not answer until you have been twice spoken to . . ." (253–54). When George appears, alive, at the play's climax, Lady Audley hardly needs to be formally accused of attempted murder. She is driven mad by the seemingly supernatural vision of her first husband. At first psychological, her punishment becomes physical: her guilt and George's "ghost" frighten her to death.

Even Brierly, whose crime is not stronger than falling in with bad companions and drinking too much, is racked with guilt and remorse:

> If I could only sleep. (*Earnestly.*) Oh, man—can't you help a chap to a good night's rest? I used to sleep like a top down at Glossop. But in this great big place, since I've been enjoying myself, seeing life—I don't know. . . . I get no rest—and when I do, it's worse than none—there's great black crawling things about me. . . . I say, Downy; do you know how a chap feels when he's going mad? (275)

He pathetically begs Dalton not to leave him alone for too long (277). Even the villain of the play has tried to live honestly only to be dragged down by associates, and the gallows is not far from his mind; when he "presses his elbows to his side in the attitude of a man pinioned," Moss urges, "don't be disagreeable, my dear—you give me a cold shiver" (325). By playing on the guilty feelings of the incipient criminal, Sam Willoughby, Bob is able to persuade him to mend his ways.

Although in these two plays criminals suffer for their misdeeds and are punished by capture or madness and death, disturbing questions about discovering and punishing criminals linger after the curtains drop. Lady Audley and Luke represent the crafty servant whose superficial amiability conceals conniving ambitions. She triumphs over justice for some time before her first husband comes on the scene. Even after her supposedly fatal attack on George, she lives for six months in relative freedom. Her crimes are successfully concealed by her charm and cunning. With the cases of Madeline Smith, Constance Kent, and Dr. Palmer in recent memory, audiences would have been quick to recognize the threat of the intimate crime committed by a trusted family member or respected scion of the community. Lady Audley and Luke are handily taken care of, but their real-life counterparts might not be identified and punished so neatly.

In *The Ticket-of-Leave Man*, criminals like Dalton and Moss successfully feign respectability, implicate honest Bob, and benefit financially from their crimes. With their tools, jargon, and disguises, police and criminals are strangely similar in the world of the play. Although Brierly is eventually exonerated, his four years in prison cloud the finale. Joe is avenged, but his indirect murder is disturbing: he did nothing to deserve it and only Hawkshaw's acuity brings Dalton to justice. The establishment of a professional police force is only partly comforting. Even Hawkshaw is unable to prevent a fatal accident, and killers do not inevitably suffer just deserts. As in mid-Victorian street literature and nonfiction, crime in the melodrama of the fifties and sixties is chilling because of the implication that dishonesty and violence surround innocent people. A veneer of virtue coats ambitious conniving at respectability. *Lady Audley's Secret* and *The Ticket-of-Leave Man* conclude with the melodramatic triumph of good over evil, but at the same time suggest unsettlingly that this victory occurs so satisfyingly only in melodrama.

# 6

# Fiction, 1850–1870

Sensation fiction came to replace Newgate novels as targets of critical scorn and distress. In some ways a domestication of the Newgate, sensation novels by popular authors like Elizabeth Braddon and Mrs. Henry Wood were both disturbing and titillating because they showed crime drifting from working-class streets to middle-class parlors and aristocratic ballrooms. More significantly, as Michael Wheeler points out in *English Fiction of the Victorian Period,* the "sensations" in these novels "provide a context . . . in which assumptions about the 'ordinary' are questioned or undermined."[1] The authors of *Corrupt Relations* suggest that in the sensational novels of Charles Dickens and Wilkie Collins, "plots intertwine the respectable and the criminal worlds," implying that "an elaborate criminal intrigue is the truest analogue to respectable social relations."[2] This energetic subgenre aroused moral and literary concern by showing the way bigamous wives or murderous cousins can be more threatening than highwaymen. In works by Braddon, Wood, Dickens, and others, moral disasters fester in the nicest families. Although Wilkie Collins is credited with "having introduced into fiction those most mysterious of mysteries, the mysteries which are at our own doors,"[3] many writers grappled with the same themes. In their emphasis on private, intimate crimes and dangerous women, sensation novels reflect a more general trend in popular mid-Victorian fiction, melodrama, and nonfiction.

Several kinds of fiction written in the fifties and sixties indicate a growing fear of criminal attack from within the community or family circle. The development of sustained narrative suspense and the treatment of police and criminals as professional classes illustrate a sense of vulnerability. As in nonfiction and melodrama, these novels directly or indirectly address social paranoia about infiltrators, a fear sometimes linked to that of independent, ruthless women. Similarly, novels of this period widen the schism between the virtuous, helpless heroine and the malevolent female villain. Significantly, in both female criminals and victims, sexuality and violence are causally connected. Contemporary criticism quoted by Winifred Hughes in *The Maniac in the Cellar,* a study of sensation fiction, expresses the belief that murder is wholesome "in comparison with the vaguer, weaker, less legally punishable sins of the flesh."[4] The "distaste for female passion and sexuality" that pervades sensation novels appears in other novels as well and often results in fatal violence (Hughes, *Maniac,* 29).

In this chapter, I will explore these themes by discussing two mid-Victorian romances, Sheridan LeFanu's *Uncle Silas* (1864–65) and Ouida's *Strathmore* (1865); two contrasting social documentaries, Dickens's *Bleak House* (1853) and Charles Reade's *Hard Cash* (1863); and the sensation novel that is said to have introduced the modern detective story, Collins's *The Moonstone* (1868). Although extremely different in form and purpose, these five novels share an emphasis on professional detectives and criminals, designing women, suspense, and fear of betrayal from within. The formal and narrative excesses of these novels suggest, among other things, an inability to satisfactorily resolve the issue of whether crimes can be punished and prevented.

Both *Uncle Silas* and *Strathmore* are peculiarly gripping romances with Gothic affinities. Critics called "the enigma novel" in which readers clamor to solve a mystery "all plot and little else,"[5] but the actions in LeFanu's tale, while thrilling, are also complex. Like works of the 1790s, *Uncle Silas* endows buildings and landscapes with strong emotional associations. The heroine's sensibilities are extreme: Maud Ruthyn is plagued by blushing, fainting, and fits of hysteria. Like many a Radcliffe character, she is highly sensitive to the sublime in vista and atmosphere: "Feverish and frightened I felt that night," she confesses. "It was a sympathy, I fancy, with the weather."[6] The murky religious convictions of Silas Ruthyn recall those of Catholic villains in earlier novels. LeFanu, however, has domesticated the Gothic, creating a strange hybrid: a Gothic romance that reflects mid-Victorian English values. The action takes place in two British country houses, not the spooky abbeys and monasteries of medieval Spain or Italy. The desperate, hectic traveling that the heroine undergoes—often involuntarily—in the Gothic novel, sometimes spanning continents, is reversed in *Uncle Silas;* Maud's freedom is more and more restricted, the action of the novel increasingly claustrophobic, until she is, at the climax, hidden in a corner of a jailroom in her uncle's house.[7] Sometimes physically threatened, Maud also suffers from tortures that are mostly psychological. As in LeFanu's short stories, "no one seems to be safe from the touch of the terrible, and there seems no way in which one might protect himself."[8]

*Uncle Silas* shares with other mid-Victorian popular writing the themes of dangerous, hypocritical women and of threats from within the family circle and respected community. Maud unconsciously "causes" at least some of the novel's violence: her beauty arouses the desire of her loutish cousin, who assaults his rival. Maud's wicked French governess—like the nearly demoniac female baby farmer in *The World We Live In*—is cruel and hypocritical. Her secret drinking and veiled remarks imply other hidden sins. Like Sir Michael, fooled most thoroughly by the woman closest to him—although not fooled to the same extent—Maud is in great danger from her supposedly benevolent instructor. Her terror of the Frenchwoman, in contrast to Sir Michael's happy ignorance, does not help avert her near-murder. Maud's own uncle proves to be the most significant threat to her welfare. Because of her early fascination with him and her sense of duty to her father's brother, she is slow to understand the nature of her danger. The murders and circumstances surrounding them are extreme, as *Uncle Silas* is a romance, a sensational enigma novel. However, its setting, psychological realism, themes regarding women and betrayal, and social implications root it firmly in the popular fiction of the fifties and sixties that made the familiar terrible, and the terrible inescapable.

Ouida's *Strathmore* is closer to the romances of G. M. Reynolds than to those of Ann Radcliffe. As in *Mysteries of the Court of London,* the plot provides a breathless and often horrifying glimpse of life in the passionate, morally imperiled upper classes. Her characters teeter between thrilling decadence and abysmal ruin; their glittering masquerades and personal intrigues enthrall the capitals of Europe. Private lives have political repurcussions; the hero is quick to cause his romantic rival and blackmailer to be arrested as a state prisoner when the happiness of his own bride-to-be is threatened. Unfettered by financial concerns or professional obligations, Ouida's characters freely pursue social and political power with all their energies. Their passions are larger than life; their punishment and repentances seem divinely ordained.

Yet *Strathmore,* for all its exoticism and excess, addresses many of the same themes as grittier, more determinedly realistic novels such as *Bleak House* and *Hard Cash.* Murder is focal, and suspense is heightened by effective if predictable narrative secrecy. At times, the characters know more than the reader, as when Strathmore whispers the name "Marion St. Maur" to his former lover and watches her quail before him. At other times, the reader has an advantage over the characters—as when the innocent heroine accidentally meets a beggar woman we know was her wicked predecessor—and the suspense resides in our anticipation of the character's enlightenment. Like the criminally wicked or lustful women of *Uncle Silas, Bleak House,* and *Hard Cash,* Lady Marion Vavasour in *Strathmore* is another version of Lady Audley and her peers. Her ruthless and terrible pursuit of power through the use of her eroticism results in her downfall and raises disturbing questions about female sexuality and desire for control over men. As in *Uncle Silas,* virtuous characters are betrayed by social imposters who pretend to be of the same class, or of a respectable character, but who are genuinely dangerous. *Strathmore* and *Uncle Silas* are wildly fanciful stories that domesticate terror by raising disturbingly realistic questions about violence, sexuality, and the near-impossibility of safety.

Ouida's novels have traditionally been greeted by critical disdain. *Strathmore* was "an instantaneous success"[9] because "nobody cared for the reviewers, and everybody, from peers to pantry-maids, read Ouida."[10] Part of *Strathmore*'s appeal was that it provided a look at the "more emancipated" lives of aristocrats (Bigland, 34). The characters in *Strathmore* have the weaknesses of every class but far more exotic opportunities to indulge them. Although women adore Strathmore, a ruthless aristocrat, he behaves with cool indifference until falling under the spell of beautiful, dangerous Lady Marion Vavasour, the toast of Europe. She is as ruthless as her prey: "Ah! It is Power! None wider, none surer on earth, while it lasts!"[11] Her passionate pursuit of power leads her to induce Strathmore to shoot his friend Bertie Erroll in a duel by telling him that Bertie attempted to seduce her. Although duels were supposedly the result of honorable quarrels, it is ironically the least honorable motive that drives Strathmore to kill his friend. Bertie dies with dignity, but Strathmore has no pity at his friend's death: he "stood by to see the shudder convulse the rigid limbs, and count each lingering pang—calm, pitiless, unmoved, his face so serene in its chill indifference" (226). Strathmore's extreme and horrible satisfaction at Bertie's death insures his extreme, nearly psychotic pursuit of revenge against Marion Vavasour once he discovers that she lied to him about Bertie's supposed seduction.

After years pass, the murderer falls in love with his victim's daughter, angelic Lucille. Her suitor, Valdor, is selfishly vengeful, but decides not to tell Lucille that Strathmore killed Bertie because "his remorse is holy—it is not for me to touch it" (510). Yet Valdor's threat to inform Lucille causes Strathmore to have him arrested. Strathmore cruelly pursues and torments Marion throughout most of the novel, but both characters are eventually capable of repentance. Strathmore forgives Marion in "the supreme expiation of his life" (604). Marion had determined to kill Lucille, but on hearing the young woman's prayer—"God is love"—she finally embraces virtue (604). The former Lady Vavasour becomes "a woman in the Order of St. Vincent de Paul" who "lives ever among the poor, the suffering, the criminal, the shameless . . . and leaves them saved but sore afraid" (607).

Suspense is integral to the success of *Strathmore* and to the reader's engagement with excessive, dangerous characters. Although the reader always knows the murderer's identity and motives, the narrative depends heavily on anticipation and apprehension. Ouida never surprises her readers; instead, she contrives to make them impatient for what they know will occur. When envious friends chide Strathmore about his indifference to feminine charms, readers begin to anticipate who his captivator will be; when he meets a beautiful and mysterious woman, they wonder when he will learn she is Lady Marion Vavasour. And finally, the slow and carefully described progress of their affair toward consummation awakens a less-than-virtuous eagerness for their immoral union to take place; readers know that Marion is married, although they learn that she is only masquerading as a wife. The consequences of this affair will be dire, and the reader wonders what form these consequences will take. Who will die? How will Strathmore achieve revenge? The lurid excesses of these characters and their passions fascinate readers because they threaten people like them—the innocuous, virtuous Bertie, tender Lucille. Strathmore is also capable of becoming virtuously ordinary through atonement. Only when daring arrogance is finally quelled by a spiritual rebirth, does the suspense—after having revealed *Strathmore*'s thematic as well as narrative purpose—conclude.

In *Uncle Silas*, LeFanu creates his own version of Ouida's Lucille and places her in the forefront of the action. Imaginative and impressionable seventeen-year-old Maud Ruthyn, the novel's narrator, is innocent but curious about her mysterious and rarely mentioned Uncle Silas. After being orphaned, she is sent to live with her uncle as his ward at Bartram-Haugh, his estate. As trusting as Lucille, Maud tries to believe the best of her malevolent relative, even though she is frightened by his sudden fits and a rumor that he unethically cuts down oak trees on his land so that he may sell the bark. She determines to be loyal to her dangerous uncle: "I would not avow to myself a suspicion of Uncle Silas. Any falsehood there opened an abyss beneath my feet into which I dared not look" (270).

As Valdor's desire, Strathmore's criminal past, and Vavasour's bitter jealousy threaten Lucille, so do treacherous, peculiar characters surround Maud once she is helplessly isolated. Silas's son Dudley, a "horrid bumpkin," she recognizes as one of a group of strangers who had earlier accosted her (253). His crude advances frighten and disgust Maud. When a rival suitor appears to visit her, Dudley assaults him. Madame de la Rougierre, a coarse, cruel Frenchwoman who had teased and terrified Maud as her governess, arrives at Bartram-Haugh to the girl's great dismay. Silas himself is the most fearful and eccentric of those that threaten Maud's happiness and her life. Like the hypocritical villains of mid-Victorian melodrama, Silas fawns on his prey before eventually revealing his true nature. He does not permit Maud visits from her kindly cousin Lady Monica Knollys, and he urges his niece to accept Dudley's marriage proposal; Silas sees his son as "a rough but romantic young fool, who talks according to his folly and his pain" (317). At Maud's persistent refusal, her uncle grows furious; when it turns out that Dudley is already married, she is relieved to learn that he is headed for Australia in disgrace. But Dudley remains hidden by Silas on the grounds, and Maud later learns that her uncle instigated the gatekeeper's refusal to let her leave the estate. Silas turns on her "in a voice of thunder" after she tries to bribe a servant to take a message to Lady Monica (384). The story she had heard about Silas having murdered a man in his youth returns to haunt her after she is confined to a barred room and guarded by Mme. de la Rougierre.

*Uncle Silas*'s strong Gothic affinities are accompanied by a complicated presentation of mid-Victorian themes of betrayal and women's complicity in violence. Uncle Silas and the governess pretend that Maud is going to visit her friend, Milly, Dudley's cheerful sister, in France. A ludicrous journey to Dover is really a night trip in a circle, and Maud discovers she is a prisoner at Bartram-Haugh. Like a terrified Radcliffe heroine, Maud "sees" her own murder when Dudley breaks into her room and attacks the drugged Mme. de la Rougierre, thinking she is Maud. Maud watches from her corner as Dudley strikes the sleeping woman again and again in the dark. It is strangely fitting that the governess is the victim: she is the only woman who helps to trap Maud, and her duplicity and violence seem worse than those of the men. A Gothic hero never appears. Maud's rescuers are the women who have befriended her: Meg, the peasant girl who warns her not to eat or drink what she is given, helps Maud escape to Lady Monica. Lady Monica and Milly offer support and encouragement to Maud as long as they are able. The way that "ordinary" people rescue Maud—like Maud herself—suggests that the heroine is more like us than not. Significantly, Maud learns that Silas and Dudley wanted her inheritance, but knowledge of more profound concerns eludes her. Mysteries of character remain mysterious, and we conclude that what happens to her—as extreme and impossible as it is—might happen to other innocent people outside the fictional world of *Uncle Silas*.

Full of mysteries, *Uncle Silas* undermines the reader's belief in the possibility of security in the home and social circle. While Maud is clearly a less than reliable narrator—her romantic attachment to a portrait of Silas lends credence to Lady Monica's sensible plain-speaking—her mysteries are often the readers'. She is in a constant state of bafflement and apprehension. Her worst fears are inevitably realized. She has no control over her life or any people in it and can only wonder fearfully why her father hires Mme. de la Rougierre, why he keeps her on after Maud protests, why Lady Monica distrusts Silas, why Silas promotes Dudley's courtship.

Yet the greatest mysteries in the novel are those of character and personality, not events. Baffling and terrifyingly enigmatic to Maud, Madame alternates between "graver moods" and "a sort of hilarity" (20). Maud finds these erratic changes fearful and incomprehensible. She does not understand her austere father or his attachment to Swedenborgianism. Her naiveté prevents her from realizing that Silas acts from calculating and cruel self-interest. The suspense comes to a crashing climax when Maud watches Madame's terrible death, but mysteries of character are never fully resolved. In the final chapter, Maud speculates unprofitably about her uncle's truest character: "Of my wretched uncle's religion what am I to say? Was it utter hypocrisy, or had it at any time a vein of sincerity in it? I cannot say. . . . Perhaps he was a sceptic" (433). Although Maud learns that Silas acted from financial motives, his greed does not begin to explain his cruelty to Dudley and Milly, his addiction to the laudanum that eventually kills him, or his wicked victimization of Maud. People in *Uncle Silas* remain, by and large, mysterious. LeFanu's characters are usually left in the dark: not darkness in the sense

> that they have necessarily succumbed to evil, but darkness in the sense that they remain unable to see their way through existence. The education of the protagonists of LeFanu would seem to go on indefinitely, never attaining to a surety of meaning or purpose. (Begnal, 78)

At the novel's conclusion, Maud is a happily married wife and mother for whom safe contentment must substitute for understanding or growth, and the mysteries that engage the reader throughout the story unnerve because they lack resolution.

The manner and import of the murders in *Strathmore* and *Uncle Silas* are central to each work. In Ouida's novel, one aristocrat kills another in a supposedly noble duel. But Strathmore's cruel delight at Bertie's death undermines the ideal of the duel as an honorable way of settling differences: he watches "with the dark glitter of a triumphant vengeance, the last agony of the man whom he had loved" (226). Pathetic and dignified, Bertie's death befits the rank of the participants and accords with the victim's maligned virtue: "Oh God!" cries Bertie, "I forgive—I forgive. He did not know—" (226). The ritualistic duel suggests religious sacrifice that demands a formal repentance. Strathmore rejects the adage "a life for a life" in refusing to strangle Marion after he learns of her deception. Instead, he tries to honor Bertie by caring for his infant daughter, Lucille. Nearly martyred by his brave rescue of six drowning people during a storm at sea, Strathmore nevertheless loses the opportunity for genuine repentance when he deliberately refuses to save Marion. Lucille— all that remains of her innocent father—must be saved twice: once from the knowledge of her guardian's murder, the second time from Marion's vengeful killing. Bertie can not be brought back to life, but once Strathmore and Marion repent and forgive each other, justice is done. The ritual that began with the duel has been completed.

The two murders in *Uncle Silas* are also a crucial part of the story's action. As a young rogue, Silas incurs debts and traps his creditor in a second-story room of his house at Bartram-Haugh, where he is killed in a mysterious locked-room crime. Like the duel in *Strathmore,* the death is exotic, removed from the ordinary reader. Yet the implications of the second murder are not remote. Maud watches Mme. de la Rougierre die in the same room she is to have died in, the room that witnessed the death of Silas's creditor years earlier. Murder is cyclical, repetitive; crime has far-flung and unanticipated consequences.

The excess of the second murder is also disturbing. Madame's death is a wild, nightmare vision in which the worst of Maud's fears come true. As Dudley stabs Mme. de la Rougierre in a frenzy of sexual violence, Maud watches, mute and horrified. This is a primal scene with clearly erotic associations (Brantlinger, "The Sensation Novel," 26). Only during the murder does Maud possess complete knowledge, but her knowledge can neither help nor enlighten. The wickedness of her uncle's world—her world—is briefly illuminated as if by lightning, but Maud experiences shock without insight.

Although the murders in both romances are in some ways too exotic and removed from the reader to be genuinely unnerving, they share certain unsettling social and sexual emphases with mid-Victorian street literature and melodrama. Significantly, Mme. de la Rougierre is the only character in the "present" action of *Uncle Silas* who is punished in such a violent way, one with such grim sexual associations. The other criminal characters bring about their own punishments. Dudley is self-exiled to Australia; Meg's father, another accomplice, is arrested on an earlier charge. Silas dies through an overdose of laudanum. Madame drinks the drugged claret intended for Maud, claret that causes her to drink too deeply. She is, in that way, murdered because of her indulgence in wine (characteristically French, the narrative implies).

Mme. de la Rougierre must be killed as a punishment for her betrayal of her sex and of the Victorian womanly ideal. The novel's other women are sisterly and try to help each other whenever possible. The virtuous men in the novel—Dr. Bryerly, the gruff and sensible Swedenborgian friend of Maud's father, and Lord Ilbury, eventually Maud's husband—are kind but inaccessible or uninvolved. Maud meets and likes Milly, Silas's untutored but good-natured daughter, at her arrival. Milly's "odd swaggering walk" and "boisterous laugh" are singular but appealing (188). When Milly is sent to a French school and Madame comes to Bartram-Haugh, a benevolent and comforting angel seems to have been replaced with an evil spirit. Meg, daughter of Silas's accomplice, warns Maud to stay away from Dudley, and Maud tries in turn to protect her from her vicious father. Meg manages to slip into Maud's jailroom to tell her not to eat what she is given. She and her fiancée help Maud escape after Mme. de la Rougierre's murder. Lady Monica, a level-headed, kindly woman, cares for Maud at her father's death and remonstrates with Silas at his isolation of her cousin. Mary Quince, Maud's servant, loyal and affectionate, has her mistress's best interests at heart. As the novel unfolds, Maud is gradually divested of her female entourage of helpers and friends, but Lady Monica, Milly, Meg, and Mary—whose alliterative names harmoniously suggest their connection— provide information and succor throughout the novel. They also provide an eloquent contrast to Mme. de la Rougierre, who consistently torments and conspires against her charge. Her sexual innuendos, her propensity to drink, her sadistic treatment of Maud all guarantee that she, like the women in popular nonfiction about murderers, will be killed in an obscenely violent manner as punishment for her betrayal of the feminine values embraced by the other women in the book.

As in the street literature and melodrama of the period, dangerous, sexually aggressive women represent a threat to virtuous society that must be met with violence. Marion in *Strathmore* is a lush and ruthless example of the powerfully erotic woman whose independence and immorality have fatal consequences. Voluptuously beautiful, Marion is described repeatedly to emphasize her nearly hypnotic effect on the men in the novel. She and Strathmore are well matched in their lust for power. He pursues it in the halls of the titled and influential, however, and she can only wield it from the bedroom. She enjoys power for the sheer pleasure of knowing that she can make men do what she wishes. Marion is simply willful; when she meets Strathmore, she determines to make him a conquest because of his indifference. She has him sacrifice his career and his friend for no other reason than to show she can do it. "Love me!" cries Strathmore desperately, "and I throw away for you honor, fame, life—what you will" (167). Marion takes him at his word, forcing him to sacrifice everything he values.

Lady Vavasour must be punished for her social as well as sexual crimes. Like Lady Audley, she is an interloper. Early in the novel, Strathmore says that a woman is "a dish like mushrooms, dainty but dangerous; with the beau sexe as with the fungi, it's fifty to ten one lights on a false one, and pays penalty for one's appetite" (86). Marion is false as a lover and as Lady Vavasour. Unmarried to the man she had been "cuckolding," Marion betrays the nobility, which has as profound an effect on them as her other deceptions have on Strathmore. When someone asks why Marion was cut so publicly, one socialite retorts:

> Pardon, madame! Lady Vavasour? Oh, I pray you drop that subject; society has been grossly outraged, foully insulted, Have you not heard? Indeed! Why, the marriage was fictitious—she was never his wife. The world has been deceived, and we—we have received the Marquis's mistress. (299)

Her crime, then, is threefold. She lures men on to their doom—reputedly having ruined countless others before she met Strathmore—she incites him to kill Bertie, and she has masqueraded for years as a titled aristocrat when she is really a courtesan. Like Lady Audley and women in street ballads of the period, Marion has transgressed against social and sexual authority and must be punished.

*Uncle Silas* explores the schism between extremely virtuous and unbelievably wicked women in much the same way that Ouida opposes Lucille and Marion as Strathmore's good and evil angels. In *Strathmore*, however, the focus is on the siren, while *Uncle Silas* emphasizes the Gothic heroine and narrator. Like the crippled and starved women of street literature, Maud is outrageously vulnerable. She is only seventeen and younger than her years because of the isolation in which she has been raised. Like many heroines of Jane

Austen's novels, she is motherless. She comes to be surrounded by people who want to do her harm. Her own imagination and constitution threaten her as well, making her even more vulnerable. Her delicacy causes fits and spells. Even before her father dies, she is too nervous and sensitive for her own good; she undermines her credibility when complaining about her governess by presenting her case tearfully, childishly, and incoherently. Even her blushing causes her trouble: friends and enemies alike may read her thoughts, although, in Dudley's case, they do not always do so correctly. Often in the course of the action, Maud is in "a sort of agony" (143). Her ignorance terrifies her. She cries "like a frightened child—and indeed in experience of the world I was no more" (130). Nor is knowledge comforting, since her most complete enlightenment occurs when Dudley kills Madame.

Maud's innocence and vulnerability contrast sharply with the cruelty of her governess. Mme. de la Rougierre, like Marion, sometimes creates mayhem for the joy of doing so; there is no other reason to tell Maud ghost stories and inform her that she likes to be with dead people than to scare her half to death. Closeted in the jailroom at Bartram-Haugh, she steals Maud's gypsy pin just out of cruelty. Like Lady Vavasour betrays men and society through her deceptions, Mme. de la Rougierre betrays women and is punished accordingly. The contrast between the heroine and female villain in *Uncle Silas,* even more than in *Strathmore,* creates one of the central tensions of the narrative.

Imaginative and gripping romances, *Strathmore* and *Uncle Silas* nevertheless address some of the significant mid-Victorian concerns about crime. Each crime—social, sexual, violent—takes place in the heart of family or community. Lady Vavasour dupes the highest and most envied people in Europe; like Becky Sharp, she uses what she has to grapple her way to the loftiest branches of society. Men who know the way she discarded others are still captivated by her; even brilliant Strathmore is taken in. The murder she contrives is only nominally disguised as a duel. She has Bertie killed on a kind of ruthless whim, and the murder is legal, if not moral.

Maud's ordeal in *Uncle Silas* also represents a characteristic mid-Victorian fear of being attacked by those most familiar. Her nightmare experience is that of a paranoid girl who is nevertheless right: her governess, cousin, and uncle *are* all trying to kill her. The movement of the novel symbolically presents the fear of murder from within the family. Maud is slowly cut off geographically— first from the churchyard, then from the grounds; then, once at Bartram-Haugh, she is denied access to the part of the estate where Silas cuts and skins trees. Gradually forbidden to visit Lady Monica or leave the estate, Maud—after the cruelly ridiculous fake journey to Dover—winds up in a jailroom at Bartram-Haugh, then in a corner of the room while the murder takes place. The final incarceration—her grave—awaits her. This claustrophobic sequence in which Maud is continually enclosed into smaller spaces reflects the ultimate terror of intimate murder: that it is inescapable and that all routes lead to the same destination—homicide on the family hearth.

In these romances, extreme and exotic events seem to distance us from the narrative, but the domestication of terror remains both engaging and unsettling. Although Ouida's novel is not as carefully devised as LeFanu's, and her use of conventions is closer to those of melodrama than of fiction, the authors share an interest in homicide, the social and sexual implications of crime, and the idea of the intimate murder. One critic writes of LeFanu what might be said of many works of the mid-Victorian period: in his novels,

> the forces of evil which confront us are implicit and inherent in ordinary people who are quite like ourselves—not Asiatic fanatics a la FuManchu or evil Teutonic scientists and madmen who threaten the existence of the universe. . . . evil does not spring from some murky shadowland, but exists right here among us. (Begnal, 35)

The grittily realistic mid-Victorian worlds of Charles Reade's *Hard Cash* and Dickens's *Bleak House* would seem at first to be continents away from romances like *Strathmore* and *Uncle Silas*. Reade and Dickens purposefully dramatize the inhumane effects of social and bureaucratic injustices. In *Hard Cash* (1863) and other social novels like *It Is Never Too Late To Mend: A Matter of Fact Romance* (1856), *Foul Play* (1868), and *Put Yourself in His Place* (1870), Reade "cast himself in the pleasing romantic role of knight-errant who went striding across a kingdom to find those legal or social wrongs that he believed only the writer of fiction could redress."[12] *Hard Cash* emerged from five years of research on "the corrupt conduct of private asylums in England" (E. Smith, 117). Dickens's dedication to reforming inhumane and unworkable social systems was no less than Reade's. In *Bleak House* (1853), *Hard Times* (1854), *Little Dorrit* (1856), *Great Expectations* (1861), and *Our Mutual Friend* (1865), Dickens lambasts indifferent institutions such as the Court of Chancery and the Circumlocution Office. *Bleak House* might almost be a social and political history of the twenty years preceding its publication:

> The novel accurately reflects the social reality of Dickens's day, in part of the time of publication in 1851–3, in part of the time of Dickens's youth, in the late twenties, when he was a reporter in the Lord Chancellor's court. The scandal of the Court of Chancery, sanitary reform, slum clearance, orphans' schools, the recently formed detective branch of the metropolitan Police Force, Puseyite philanthropists, the Niger expedition, female emancipation, self-perpetuating procrastinations of Parliament and Government—each is represented in some character or scene.[13]

Like Reade, Dickens crusaded for social and political reform in his fiction and his life. Both *Hard Cash* and *Bleak House* share more obvious affinities with the so-called "Newspaper Novel" than with the romance. (Reade, in fact, defensively explained that many of his story ideas came from *The Times*, not his unhealthy imagination [W. Hughes, 76].) As one pamphleteer observes, "the novelist's occupation is gone—his imagination is outdone by reality."[14]

Despite the avowed social purposes of the authors, these novels overflow with adventure, coincidence, and passion; in short, many of the standard conventions and motifs of melodrama and romantic fiction. For all their genuine and significant dissimilarities, *Bleak House* and *Hard Cash* share several themes involving the treatment of murder with *Strathmore* and *Uncle Silas,* as well as with the melodramas and street ballads of the 1850s and 1860s. Crimes are solved with the professional aid of detectives who are protean in appearance and manner. Events and characters become more mysterious through increased narrative secrecy. Most importantly, the fear of public and private crimes that recurs so strikingly in periodical literature and melodrama of the period dominates the presentation of murder in each novel. Sexuality and violence are causally connected in the female criminals and victims; moreover, women become threatening symbols of the physical and moral danger that hovers around the parlor. Additionally, in *Hard Cash* and *Bleak House,* private and public crimes are thematically linked.

Events are so complicated and hectic in these two works that not even professional detectives can unravel them without divine or authorial assistance. The hero of *Hard Cash,* Alfred Hardie, is tricked into incarceration in a madhouse when he discovers that his banker-father has stolen £14,000 from the father of Alfred's intended bride, Julia Dodd. Once trapped in a madhouse, Alfred's life becomes a physical and psychological torment. Surrounded by sane and insane people treated with barbarous cruelty at the hands of their keepers, Alfred is unable to contact anyone or convince doctors of his sanity. When Frank, a weak-minded inmate who adores Alfred, sets fire to the asylum, Alfred escapes with David Dodd, his future father-in-law, who went mad after his money was stolen. In the course of the roller-coaster sequence of events, Alfred's sister is killed by a madman, Alfred is pursued by a lascivious prison matron, and Mrs. Dodd hires a detective to track down her addled husband after he eludes Alfred. Dodd regains his sanity and money, Hardie loses his, and Alfred and Julia are finally married.

*Bleak House* is evidence that "Dickens has almost as good a title as Edgar Allan Poe to be called the father of the detective story."[15] All of the characters, as J. Hillis Miller has pointed out, are obsessed with either protecting or unraveling secrets and clues. The unwieldy, impenetrable case of Jarndyce vs. Jarndyce snuffs out those characters who allow themselves to depend on its eventual resolution. Ada Clare and Richard Carstone, two young wards of the benevolent Mr. Jarndyce, become great friends of his protégée, Esther Summerson. Jarndyce warns them against hoping for financial gain from the endless court case, but Richard does not heed his advice. Meanwhile, Tulkinghorn, an enigmatic, power-loving lawyer to Sir Leicester Dedlock of Chesney Wold, discovers through careful investigation that Lady Dedlock had an affair with a Captain Hawdon before her marriage and had a child out of wedlock. Hortense, Lady Dedlock's French maid, is incensed at her mistress's affection for a young village girl who has been taken into Chesney Wold and vengefully helps the lawyer amass evidence of her past sin. Lady Dedlock and Esther discover that they are mother and daughter.

The chase for information, secrets, and clues to their own identities or those of others takes the characters from the richest country manor of the vain aristocrat Sir Leicester to the most pestilent and neglected slums of Tom's-All-Alone, where Jo, a pathetic street child, dies of disease after providing the kindly doctor whom Esther eventually marries with a key to the interwoven relationships. In the course of the pursuit, Ada and Richard marry, but he dies soon after, his health ruined over his obsession with the Jarndyce case. Lady Dedlock flees Chesney Wold to avoid the shame and shock that Tulkinghorn's revelation of her past sin would bring to her husband. Someone kills Tulkinghorn on the night of her departure, and Inspector Bucket catches up to Lady Dedlock only after she dies miserably in the pauper's graveyard where Hawdon is buried. The detective confronts Hortense with an accusation of murder, and she confesses. Jarndyce vs. Jarndyce resolves, but the costs of the suit absorb the estate. Jarndyce, Esther, her husband, Ada, and her son all live in Bleak House at the story's conclusion.

Both *Bleak House* and *Hard Cash* feature professional detectives. Green, the hired detective in Reade's novel, has both personal desires and business goals in the Dodd-Hardie case; as with Hawkshaw, the situation resolves neatly. Green falls in love with the elder Hardie's servant Peggy. His suspicions of her complicity with her master increase his affection:

> She had led him on, and the pocket-book had been planted for him. If so, why Peggy was a genius, and in his own line; and he would marry her, and so kill two birds with one stone: make a Detective of her (there was a sad lack of female Detectives); and, once his wife, she would split on her master and he should defeat that old soldier at last, and get a handsome slice of the 14,000£.[16]

As Hawkshaw seeks revenge and justice, so Green simultaneously pursues love and financial success. Peggy's duplicity is appealing to Green because it is ingenious. When she is persuaded to step out with him, "he made hot love to her, and pressed her hard to name the day" (304). At her prearranged cough, a policeman jumps out and "collars" Green, who is undaunted: "I'll marry you all the more for this," he cries and escapes, but not before he "caught the astonished Peggy round the neck, kissed her lips violently, and fled like the wind" (304). His admiration for Peggy stems from his commitment to and enthusiasm for his profession: a clever, street-wise woman is far more valuable to him than a virtuous and dull one.

Also, like Hawkshaw, Green is a master of disguise. After his breezy, interrupted courtship, he travels to London "in the character of a young swell, with a self-fitting eyeglass and a long moustache" (304). When telling the Dodds of his investigation, Green sports red hair, a large beard, and the remains of a black eye (304). Using the idiomatic speech of both detective and criminal, Green explains how he caught Hardie with money that had been marked—Dodd's money:

> Here's an unsuspicious gent took by surprise, in moonlight meditation fancy free, and all his little private family matters found in his innocent bosom quite promiscuous; but his beans marked: that don't dovetail nohow. (302)

His use of professional jargon, like Hawkshaw's, indicates that he is a successful detective. Green's easy mastery of the criminal dialect allows him to infiltrate a secret, underground world. He takes energetic pride in his job. When Mrs. Dodd thanks him for locating her husband, she says, "Sir, you inspire me with great confidence." He replies, "And you me with zeal, ma'am . . . . Why I'd go through fire and water for a lady like you, that pays well, and doesn't grudge a fellow a bit of praise" (386).

Although Green displays determination, coincidence solves more problems in the novel than he does. Dodd loses and finds his money half-a-dozen times in a series of storms and robberies at sea before depositing it in Hardie's bank, which teeters on the edge of ruination. Alfred escapes the asylum because his friend sets fire to it, not because authorities discover the injustice of his incarceration. Dodd regains his reason and his cash, but through no brilliant detection or plot of Green's. With a melodramatic finality that renders human detectives irrelevant, Alfred and Julia marry, Edith Archbold—Alfred's lustful suitor—marries Frank, and the young Hardies and older Dodds each have a new baby. Hardie is discovered by his son begging on the street. He lives out the rest of his brief, wretched life in madness, although Alfred forgives him and takes him into his household. The multiple plots resolve with the roccoco "rightness" of Restoration comedy; only a minor character, Green, is incapable of solving mysteries and crimes.

Inspector Bucket of *Bleak House* has been called by Julian Symons "probably the most vividly presented fictional detective before Sherlock Holmes" (78). Although more acute than Green or Hawkshaw, Bucket is as unromantic-looking as his name suggests, a "stoutly built, steady-looking, sharp-eyed man in black, of about the middle-age."[17] His dominant characteristic is persistence. Where Green and Hawkshaw constantly disguise their appearances, Bucket is protean in manner—able to discern the values of those he interviews almost instantly—and brilliant at mirroring their concerns or self-images. When questioning a haughty servant at Chesney Wold, he alternates his questions with insinuating compliments on the man's looks: "Was you ever modelled now?"

(777). Bucket comforts the giddy and self-absorbed Volumnia Dedlock after Tulkinghorn's death: "'You must feel it as a deprivation to you, miss,' replies Mr. Bucket, soothingly, 'no doubt. He was calculated to *be* a deprivation, I'm sure he was'" (774). He controls his interviews with the pugnacious Smallweed, asking that unlovely witness:

> "You don't happen to know why they killed the pig, do you?" with a steadfast look, but without loss of temper.
> "No!"
> "Why, they killed him," says Mr. Bucket, "on account of his having so much cheek. Don't *you* get into the same position because it isn't worthy of you. You ain't in the habit of conversing with a deaf person, are you?" (786)

Even children are not beyond Bucket's reach; he charms the Bagnets and their offspring: "Give us a kiss, my pets. . . . My name's Bucket. Ain't that a funny name?" (728) By the time he and Esther go on their long, desperate journey in search of Lady Dedlock, Esther also falls under his spell. He repeats, "would I put you wrong, do you think? Inspector Bucket. Now you know me, don't you?" She writes, "What could I say but yes" (841). Yet no one knows Bucket, because he reflects the speech and concerns of other characters to further his own discovery of truth.

Strangely, Bucket bears a resemblance to another investigative discoverer of truths in *Bleak House*, the relentless Tulkinghorn. Bucket "is so deep," worries one character, and Tulkinghorn is described as an unopenable oyster (767). He carefully haunts Lady Dedlock in his canny and determined search for her secret. Her incautious interest in the handwriting on some law papers—writing she has recognized as Hawdon's—triggers his dogged efforts to find out what she might have to conceal. Once he learns of her liaison with Hawdon, he dryly informs her of his decision to do nothing at once, but to inform Sir Leicester eventually. Only if she remains at Chesney Wold without altering her life in the least will he hold back for a while the release of her secret. When she sends Rosa, her beloved maid-companion, back to her village on a pretext, Tulkinghorn gives Lady Dedlock warning that she has broken their bargain by altering her circumstances—sending Rosa away to protect her from the shame that will accompany the unmasking—and promises to tell Sir Leicester. His death prevents him from doing so. Where Bucket is persistent in his desire for truth because of his job, and in the implied belief that the truth will free the virtuous and punish the guilty, Tulkinghorn stalks information so that he can use it for his own purposes. The narrator suggests that the lawyer may harbor a long-concealed envy of the aristocratic families he has served or a great desire for power—he may also hope to make the remote, indifferent Lady Dedlock react, to break her composure. Both Tulkinghorn and Bucket reflect the general narrative tendency to involve the reader as detective, to "encourage the reader to consider the names, gestures and appearances of the characters as indications of some hidden truth about them" (J. H. Miller, 14). As Krook attempts to decipher the mystery of written language and Richard Carstone hopes to crack the code of the Court of Chancery, so readers must try to make sense of the enigmatic and carefully revealed clues of character and identity in *Bleak House*.

Reade's narrative methods in *Hard Cash* do not create mystery or sustained suspense. As in *Strathmore,* in which readers wonder when and how events will occur, readers cling steadfastly to the knowledge that Alfred will emerge from the asylum to have his sanity vindicated, Hardie will receive his come-uppance, and the novel will conclude with the long-awaited reunion of Julia's parents. Reade repeatedly surprises the reader with small instances of suspense or excitement. In the long digression from the central plot, Dodd's money is lost and recovered several times. A storm tears away the bottle in which he keeps the money, the bottle surfaces in the water later, having wisely been attached to a "thundering old bladder" of a pouch so that it floats (135). Even after the storm, Dodd reaches Boulogne only to fend off robbers once more; after being rescued in the nick of time, he finally makes it home with his money intact, only to enter Hardie's bank "with a joyful rush" (156). As Reade writes when Dodd loses the money at sea: "In the very moment of that great victory—It was gone" (128).

Sudden reversals are an important characteristic of *Hard Cash*. Several times Alfred thinks he will soon be released from the asylum, only to be informed at the final moment that he is trapped there. Dodd "drowns" when saving someone, after he has escaped from Alfred's care, but revives just before being buried at sea; had a fly not landed on him and drawn blood, he would have been drowned at his burial (458). The overall effect of these constant palpitations is to increase the distance between the realistic portrayal of characters and issues and the way in which they are actually dramatized. Coincidence and accident play so significant a role in the plot that the reader is presented with a world in which human possibility is secondary to the mysterious workings of greater powers. Acute detectives like Green may be on the job, but no matter how determined and ingenious, one character can not control or comprehend the circumstances of the novel.

*Bleak House* also relies heavily on coincidence and narrative symmetry, but its narrative technique is very different from that of *Hard Cash*.[18] Instead of surprising the reader with breathlessly hectic events and dramatic revelations—such as the moment when the trustworthy family doctor reports on Dodd's condition after his apoplexy: "He is a maniac" (200)—*Bleak House* moves toward its ultimate resolution through the gradual emergence of connections, of relationships. In Esther's prophetic, symbolic fever-dream, she sees a "flaming necklace, or ring, or starry circle of some kind, of which *I* was one of the beads" (544). This necklace is a metaphor for the novel's narrative technique: what seem to be unconnected, isolated characters and events are gradually revealed as part of a whole. Thus, Lady Dedlock is Esther's mother, the disease and neglect of Tom's-All-Alone extend to Chesney Wold in the person of Esther's young maid, who brings Jo's illness in the house, and almost all the minor characters provide evidence that leads Bucket to the truth. Coincidences occur, but far more subtly than in *Hard Cash;* the rare dramatic announcements, such as Esther telling her maid that she is blind, do not seem to be of a piece with the rest of the book. "Dickens uses from the first tricks which resemble remarkably those of the modern detective-story writer," writes Symons. "He presents characters whose relation to each other is apparently inexplicably strange," but whose actual connections are revealed by the novel's conclusion (43). Readers, like the central characters, are gently led away from the truth even while Dickens gives enough evidence that we might reach it. As in *Great Expectations,* when Pip believes his fortune to be from Miss Havisham rather than Magwitch, Dickens carefully organizes the events of the lawyer's final night so that it seems as though Lady Dedlock committed the crime, and we can sympathize with the wretchedness that compelled her to it. Yet Hortense's passionate pride, her erratic nature, and her violence toward Tulkinghorn are not concealed. Like *Our Mutual Friend, Bleak House* is "built round a puzzle" (Symons, 79), and the interconnected pieces describe the various, yet morally linked, worlds of the novel. Dickens's masterful use of gradual revelation is thus thematically significant and engages the reader more actively than Reade's constant surprises.

The differences between the narrative techniques and the professional detectives in *Bleak House* and *Hard Cash* suggest that their effects are greatly different. Bucket's capability and ingenuity, his determined competence at tracking down all the disparate elements of the case, would seem to create a confidence that people can solve and control the chaotic tendencies in the world around them. But this confidence does not exist. Like Reade, Dickens gives us large grounds for mistrust that overpower our sense of Bucket's mental agility and his eventual resolution of the mystery. Even Bucket is unable to understand the circumstances of Tulkinghorn's death without nearly divine intervention, as important clues and characters appear before him with regularity. And one individual can not unravel the difficulties of bureaucracies—the case of Jarndyce vs. Jarndyce—or the mysterious desires and jealousies of other people. Tulkinghorn hovers over much of the action of *Bleak House* like an ominous spirit, and the arrogance or indifference of minor characters do not reassure. The squalor of Tom's-All-Alone remains after Esther and Ada retreat to their blissful hermitage. Poverty, urban misery and crime, and heartless bureaucracies are not altered by the resolution of one mystery, no matter how many people that resolution affects. Bucket notwithstanding, *Bleak House* is ultimately a disturbing presentation of systems beyond human control.

Like the ballads and melodramas of the period, *Bleak House* and *Hard Cash* reflect a pervasive fear of private and public crimes. Both novels have several crimes—either murder or murder-related—that are committed secretly by family members or deceptive women. As in novels by Trollope and Thackeray where "fraudulent relations" are "the daily practice of respectable society" (Barickman, 28), so pillars of rectitude reveal themselves to be corrupt and untrustworthy. The poisonous doctors of periodical literature are transformed into dangerous banker and lawyer. A central irony of *Hard Cash* is that after Dodd's perilous and extended adventures at sea, where his money is threatened by pirates and storms, he deposits the £14,000 in Hardie's bank, thinking that his worries are over. They have, of course, only begun. Hardie's greed and dishonesty bring about Alfred's incarceration, Dodd's madness, and the murder of Alfred's sister, Jane, by a client of the bank who goes mad at the news of Hardie's perfidy. Indeed, the lunacy—or temporary madness—of several characters in the novel is directly attributable to Hardie's criminality. Hardie himself disintegrates mentally at the book's conclusion. The educated, professional classes come under suspicious scrutiny; being a doctor or a banker does not guarantee respectability. Indeed, these characters seem more dangerous than their working-class counterparts, because they have more power and expertise to harm a person—in ways that can not be anticipated—without their knowledge. Even dogmatic, short-sighted Jane Hardie entertains a faint suspicion of her beloved father when he learns that Alfred knows of his theft. As she sees her father rushing out to arrange his son's imprisonment, she is aghast at his expression: "Heaven forgive me, it seemed the look of one who meditated a *crime*" (231).

Tulkinghorn also commits a crime from a position of trust. He can blackmail Lady Dedlock only because of his proximity to aristocratic families, his legal resources, and his acute powers of observation, honed by years of protecting the secrets of his clients. As the Dodds—and other customers of the bank and even Alfred—are helpless to defend themselves from Hardie because he is respectable, so Tulkinghorn maneuvers Lady Dedlock into a miserable paralysis. His position enables him to discover her secret and also allows him to make the cruelest, most effective use of his knowledge. Unlike Hardie, Tulkinghorn can not be bought. Lady Dedlock assumes that her secret will be expensive to maintain when Guppy announces that he has located her letters to Hawdon. The lawyer, however, wants something dearer. As Lady Dedlock tells Esther, his "calling is the acquisition of secrets, and the holding possession of such power as they give him" (567). Like Drs. Palmer and Smethurst, Hardie and Tulkinghorn are truly threatening figures because of the knowledge and power their positions give them and because of their eagerness to abuse their trust.

Professional men conceal avarice and the love of power from their acquaintances, but women in *Bleak House* and *Hard Cash* are immoral creatures whose passions drive them to defy social and legal authority. Hortense, the murderer, is based on Maria Manning, and although she is not grotesque or a drunkard, she shares characteristics with Mme. de la Rougierre of *Uncle Silas*. She is French, itself a kind of shorthand for immoral, overly passionate, and mercurial. She would be handsome "but for a certain feline mouth, and general uncomfortable tightness of face, rendering the jaws too eager. . . . she seems to go about like a very neat She-Wolf imperfectly tamed" (209). Dickens's imagery recalls that of numerous authors who wrote about women poisoners for *Blackwood's* and *Fraser's;* these deceptive daughters and wives are "tigresses" who can turn vicious when you feel most secure. Hortense's jealousy of Lady Dedlock's new protégée maddens her. When her mistress sends for Rosa instead of for her, she behaves bizarrely: "without the least discomposure of countenance, [she] slipped off her shoes, left them on the ground, and walked deliberately in the same direction, through the wettest of the wet grass" (312). She is "powerful high and passionate," the groundskeeper tells the astonished spectators; his wife adds that Hortense would just as soon walk through blood as through the wet grass when she was angry. Tulkinghorn uses her, dressed in her mistress's clothing, to help him discover Lady Dedlock's affair. Furious at Lady Dedlock's neglect and the lawyer's cavalier treatment, Hortense demands that he find her another position as he promised. When he contemptuously orders her to leave, threatening to have her "strapped on a board" by the police if she visits again, she warns him to reconsider his words. Not only does she kill Tulkinghorn, she also hopes that her former mistress is hunted down for the crime.

Lady Dedlock is kin to the impassioned, dangerous women in ballads and melodramas, but she is most interesting as a betrayer of her class. She does not kill Tulkinghorn; what she does is—in the context of her rank and marriage— much worse. She conceals her affair and child, allows her beauty to provide an entry into the aristocracy she will deceive, and continues to be haughty and cool after she marries. Dickens is concerned to show her as "a victim of a cruelly oppressive sexual system" (Barickman, 9), yet he also takes pains to show that she is devious and authoritative, as well as loyal to Sir Leicester and loving to Rosa.[19] The discovery of Lady Dedlock's past drives her voluble husband to silence. In *Bleak House,* as in *Hard Cash,* silence is reserved for the indescribably horrible crimes. Some of the tortures practiced on inmates by the female harpies who run the asylum are so terrible that they can not be discussed by Reade's narrator.

But Reade has none of Dickens's inhibitions about presenting the lurid side of women's fallen nature, and he does so in great detail. Edith Archbold, the matron of the asylum to which Alfred is committed, is a supremely energetic woman whose lust is only matched by her determination to seduce Alfred.

Her description suggests that part of her problem is her androgyny: "The mind of Edith Archbold corresponded with her powerful frame, and bushy brows. Inside this woman all was vigour; strong passions, strong good sense to check or hide them; strong will to carry them out" (283). Reade liked "to play with the idea of women who could be the sexual aggressors rather than the tepidly passive recipients of *amour*" (E. Smith, 156). At first she tries to deny her feelings for Alfred by acting coolly toward her handsome young charge. This ploy does not last long, and soon enough the innocent hero dreams of kissing Julia and awakens at the feel of "two velvet lips" on his and "a rustle of flying petticoats" (289). After this stolen pleasure, Archbold throws shame out the window: she "had sucked fresh poison from those honest lips, and filled her veins with molten fire. She tossed and turned the livelong night in a high fever of passion" (289). Writing on the Victorian sensation novel, Thomas Boyle discusses the way woman's sexuality is often "symbolized by her metamorphosis into a part animal creature,"[20] and Archbold's undisguised lust renders her half-kitten, half-tigress. She eventually declares herself: "Let me be your housekeeper, your servant, your slave . . . oh Alfred my heart burns for you, bleeds for you, yearns for you, sickens for you, dies for you" (355). Although desperate for freedom, Alfred declines escape at this price. Archbold's love turns to rage at his rejection: "You couldn't love me like a man; you shall love me like a dog. . . . you shall be my property, my brain-sick, love-sick slave" (356). Her cruelty comes closer to driving Alfred mad—she tells him that Julia is seeing a clergyman, which is true in part—than her passion comes to tempting him from his devotion to his fiancée.

Archbold is the primary representative of female evil and lust in the asylum, but not the only one. Nurse Hannah, another matron, dotes on him: "Together and apart the two women fondle Alfred, kiss him, tickle his feet, and in general subject him to sensuous trials more appropriate to a harem than an asylum."[21] Hannah plans to help him escape and at his departure cries, "Oh, Alfred, for mercy's sake whisper me one kind word at parting; give me one kind look to remember" (292). The other female keepers display more cruelty to inmates than their male counterparts do. Reade describes in detail the process of "tanking," where inmates are nearly drowned in filthy, freezing water, then made to stand outside shivering and sometimes forced to drink the water. The male keepers are unkind and not above bashing Alfred in the head once in a while, but the female keepers alone devise this elaborately cruel punishment. Alfred entreats Archbold to force the keepers to stop tanking inmates; baffled by his eagerness to help a group of women, Archbold, to earn his good favor, punishes the keepers by inviting inmates to tank *them*. Thus, she "bared her own statuesque arms, and, ably aided, soon plunged the offenders, screaming, crying, and whining, like spaniel bitches whipped, under the dirty water" (346). Alfred is delighted with this demonstration and shouts, "There . . . let that teach you men will not own hyaenas in petticoats for women" (346).

Prim Jane Hardie seems to be Edith Archbold's complete opposite, yet she has strong passions, though she deludes herself about their nature. In her diaries, she diligently records her disapproval of Alfred's courtship when her father does not permit their marriage. She also joyfully confides her pleasure at religious discussions with a married clergyman, whose wife is not spiritually on his level: "Poor man, his wife leads him a cat and dog life, I hear, with her jealousy. We had a *sweet* talk" (233). She sees her enthusiasm strictly in religious terms, but the reader is more acute. Thus, even Jane is shown to be sexually passionate; once Reade places her in this light, he "immediately set about denying its [the diary's] implications . . . had to vindicate her by sending her to a bloody, virginal, and saint-like death" (Burns, 224). Even Archbold has a happier ending than Jane; she marries dim-witted Frank, whose intelligence improves through contact with her, and she reforms. Perhaps her genuine misery and confusion over her passion for Alfred exonerates her in part, while Jane's self-delusion and religious wrong-headedness condemn her. Most of the women in *Hard Cash* suggest that in an asylum, where everything is inverted, women reveal their passions and cruelties, but that those outside the madhouse conceal the same potential.

In *Bleak House* and *Hard Cash*, private crimes committed by professional men and passionate women are thematically connected to public crimes. Hardie's avaricious hidden theft drives several people mad and consigns Alfred to an asylum, where similarly self-serving—and sometimes bestial—crimes occur daily. Maxley, the client who goes insane at the loss of his money, visits his wrath on harmless Jane, striking her down unexpectedly, with violence reminiscent of the "Railway Car" murder. The fatal attack is as appallingly unlooked-for as the garroting attacks discussed in mid-Victorian newspapers and periodicals.

The central public crime of *Hard Cash* is, however, that of irresponsible doctors, absentee inspectors, and sadistic keepers of contemporary asylums. Reade abhors the ease with which an inconvenient relative can be fobbed off as insane and incarcerated indefinitely. "Think of it for your own sakes; Alfred's turn to-day, it may be yours to-morrow" (267), he warns the reader. "Once in a mad-house, the sanest man is mad . . . once hobbled and strapped, he is a dangerous maniac" (267). Maddeningly circular logic keeps Alfred in the madhouse. When he is being transferred to another institution, Alfred appeals in turn to a gentleman, a snob, and a kind-looking woman on the train. The gentleman "turned cold directly" after seeing his certificates of madness. The "snob" ignored him: "being called mad was pretty much the same thing as being mad" to him. Only the woman believes his story, until the smug keepers remove his hat to reveal "his shaven crown": "La! so he is . . . dear heart, what a pity! And such a pretty young gentleman" (293–94).

Doctors and inspectors in authority are unreliable, when not actually corrupt. For Dr. Wycherly and the asylum, the only way a patient can be cured is if he first admits to being mad: "A confession of previous delusion is the surest test of a cure" (W. Hughes, 92). When Maxley asks to be committed to a madhouse, Wycherley observes, *"Now, there is a sensible man"* (209). Throughout the novel, the doctors "prove far crazier than their patients" (W. Hughes, 92). Some madhouse authorities may be reasonable and good, but "inspectors who visit a temple of darkness . . . four times a year, know mighty little of what goes on there" the rest of the time (347). Winifred Hughes points out that Reade's Lunacy Commission "suggests at least something of the method, as well as the broader implications, of Dickens's Circumlocution Office" (93). Curing patients can never be accomplished because of the irresponsibility of the doctors and the vicious proclivities of the keepers. Tanking is only one of the horrible punishments devised for the inmates; the others are beyond description, as are the psychological torments the patients suffer: "We can paint the body writhing vainly against its unjust bonds; but who can paint the loathing, agonised, soul in a mental situation so ghastly? . . . Pray think of it for yourselves, men and women, if you have not sworn never to think over a novel" (266). The asylum in *Hard Cash* is a nightmare in which only the patients are, precariously, sane.

Public indifference and social neglect are the larger crimes of *Bleak House*. Jo's death in the dirty, infected, and miserable section of Tom's-All-Alone represents only one example of the multiple murders committed through neglect in the name of progress. "The universe . . . makes rather an indifferent parent," observes Jarndyce (122). When Jo dies, his isolation only artificially bridged by religion as he attempts the Lord's Prayer, the reader, no longer the detective, becomes the murderer. Society is on trial, and Dickens addresses the court: "Dead, your Majesty. Dead my lords and gentlemen. Dead, Right Reverends and Wrong Reverends of every order. . . . And dying thus around us every day" (705). The universe is equally indifferent to the ironically termed "Wards of the Court," Richard and Ada; Jarndyce vs. Jarndyce devours generations of young wards. Instead of protecting Richard, the case obsesses him and leads to his death. Complains one disgruntled character: "I am told, on all hands, it's the system. I mustn't look to individuals. It's the system" (268).

Tulkinghorn's murder sharply contrasts with Jo's death. The night is silent, other-worldly. Places and objects shout soundless warnings to Tulkinghorn: "Every noise is merged, this moonlight night, into a distant ringing hum, as if the city were a vast glass, vibrating" (719). His death seems almost holy; in the strange stillness of the night, it might be a ritual murder. Jo's death is horrible because it is undeserved and impossible to prevent. Tulkinghorn's death is grimly apt. His cruel, vengeful wish for power is connected to the system in which he and Sir Leicester have power and use it to frustrate and to strangle.

Both Dickens and Reade attack social crimes borne of self-interest and indifference. Neither can suggest where the solutions lie; Tulkinghorn and Hardie never undergo a change of character, and virtuous individuals can only influence those around them. The happy ending in *Hard Cash*—where even the Dodds are blessed with a baby—does not counteract the disturbing effect of the novel because significant questions remain unanswered: How can the characters address larger issues instead of only individual cases? Alfred, David Dodd, and Frank are rescued, but the others—both sane and insane—apparently must endure brief lifetimes of tanking. Similarly, the happy characters in *Bleak House* must withdraw from the world to find contentment. Esther has Ada, her husband, her guardian, and her child; life outside Bleak House no longer exists for her. Sir Leicester lives on at Chesney Wold, now deserted, hollow. The fall of foolish and life-denying aristocrats is not, for Dickens, a tragic subject, yet Sir Leicester's devotion to his wife despite her affair arouses pity and some respect. As in melodrama, the virtuous are rewarded, the wicked punished. But not all the suffering is relieved or redressed, and both novels conclude with lingering questions about the subjects for reform, rather than an appreciation of the romantic symmetry with which each principal character and situation is resolved.

As in the ballads and melodrama of the period, these crimes are solved while their implications remain ominous and fearful. Professional detectives can temporarily assuage the anxieties of their clients, but they can really only discover pieces of the truth, and not always in time to do any good. Private crimes committed by trusted family members or employees might happen to anyone. Because the criminal's purposes and passions remain secret, the victim can not be protected. Similarly, public crimes—random or motiveless—can harm the innocent arbitrarily and without warning. The treatment of murder in these social documentaries, as in the contemporaneous romances, reflects an increasing belief that crimes, like those who commit them and the circumstances in which they take place, are moving closer to home. Physical and emotional safety may not longer be possible.

Like Elizabeth Braddon and Mrs. Henry Wood, Wilkie Collins was an enormously popular novelist writing in a characteristically mid-Victorian genre, the sensation novel. *The Woman in White* (1860) was one of the best-selling works of the period, and *The Moonstone* (1868), his second overwhelmingly successful sensation novel, is often cited as the earliest and one of the most ingenious detective stories. As readers of all classes enjoyed Dickens and Ouida, so Collins "succeeded in appealing to a highly diversified public composed of 'porters and boys' as well as intellectuals and public figures such as Matthew Arnold, Edward Fitzgerald, Lord Macaulay and Mrs. Gladstone" (Page, 15). *The Moonstone,* with its intricate structure, multiple narrators, and convenient coincidences, suggests the enclosed and isolated setting of twentieth-century mysteries where red herrings move languidly across the foreground while the murder is symmetrically solved. "Although the action of the novel takes place within a restricted sphere," as Winifred Hughes points out, "there are numerous hints of dimensions beyond it" (155). The tale of the Indian jewel creating havoc in a happy English home shares with mid-Victorian romances and documentaries a concern with the detective as a professional and would-be savior and a complicated presentation of women who are dangerous because of their secret knowledge (and thus, power). The best families in the safest homes can not be protected against social imposters and secret crime. The murder that concludes *The Moonstone* is caused by two simultaneous invasions. The malevolent Indian gem creates chaos and suspicion among the Verinders and their dependents. It also smokes out a respectable, responsible cousin who is a criminal imposter.

In his two most popular sensation novels, Collins explores the criminality and passion beneath respectable surfaces. "Were the proprieties abstractions personified," writes one critic, "they could be imagined pursuing Collins's characters like a Victorian version of the Furies."[22] In *The Woman in White,* Sir Percival Glyde courts Laura Fairlie with the utmost propriety, tact, and delicacy. However, Laura's letters to her sister, Marian, while on their honeymoon grow more guarded and enigmatic. Sir Percival has married for money; he is "almost convincing as a model of courtesy and charm" during their courtship, but by the time Count Fosco—the second villain—enters the story, Glyde's brutality and impulsive violence have emerged (Symons, 13–14). Like Uncle Silas, Sir Percival is the head of a proper British household; when he abandons his disguise, he is fearfully violent and vengeful. Yet because of his irrationality, he proves a less competent and powerful villain than his guide and accomplice, Count Fosco. As in *The Moonstone,* "knowledge rather than strength remains always the basis for power."[23] Witty and eccentric Fosco is Glyde's puppeteer. While Sir Percival commits acts of violence himself, or commissions others to do so, Fosco works "through the mind rather than the body . . . power is derived from Fosco's knowledge of men and of the reasons that they trust him" (Marshall, 63). He is effective because, like Tulkinghorn and Richard Hardie, he gains people's trust. He is, of course, the moonstone of *The Woman in White,* the nefarious, foreign center of the action. Nevertheless, he is more than the Gothic villain some critics consider him. Both Count Fosco and Sir Percival represent different versions of the mid-Victorian notion that villainy hides undetectable among the innocent.

*The Moonstone* combines the fear of crime hidden within respectable citizens with the mid-Victorian fear of passionate, independent women. Women earn suspicion because of their capacity to hide. Secretiveness and passion are the overwhelmingly negative qualities shared by the most central and ambiguous female characters, Rachel Verinder and Rosanna Spearman. Even Clack, a comic hypocrite, provides a grotesque counterpoint that illustrates the same issue. Ridiculous women are capable of the same lusts and ambitions that guide avaricious sirens—or engaging heroines. Rachel charms as the energetic and lovely heroine whose few faults are cited repeatedly by Betteredge, the faithful family servant; Clack, a poor relation; Bruff, the family lawyer; and Rachel's mother, Lady Verinder: she is secretive and self-willed. As Betteredge puts it,

> she had ideas of her own, and was stiff-necked enough to set the fashions themselves at defiance, if the fashions didn't suit her views. . . . She judged for herself . . . never asked your advice; never told you beforehand what she was going to do; never came with secrets and confidences to anybody, from her mother downwards.[24]

Bruff has the same reservations about Rachel; when something shocking occurs, her first instinct is to "shut herself up in her own mind, and to think it over by herself. This absolute self-dependence is a great virtue in a man. In a woman it has the serious drawback of morally separating her from the mass of her sex, and so exposing her to misconstruction by the general opinion" (319). She is "odd and wild, and unlike other girls of her age" (262).

Rachel's passion alarms people as much as her reserve. She is appalled by her love for Franklin Blake even after she has seen him "steal" her jewel, the moonstone; she keeps silent to protect him, but breaks off all relations between them without explanation to anyone. Although she has tried to pull out her feeling for Franklin by the roots, she confesses her lack of success to Godfrey Ablewhite, her religious cousin: "How can I make a *man* understand that a feeling which horrifies me myself, can be a feeling that fascinates me at the same time? It's the breath of my life, Godfrey, and it's the poison that kills me— both in one" (279). Rachel's passion, like her disturbing secretiveness, are integral to the novel's mystery. Were she like other girls her age, Franklin and Lady Verinder would have discovered the source of her rage and antipathy toward her former suitor immediately. But each narrator makes a point of observing that this incident is just one more example of her questionable reserve. Her cautious reticence is also a guard against passion. She protects Franklin, but she does not risk destruction by becoming an open ally in what she thinks to be a crime.

Rosanna Spearman, Rachel's rival and working-class double, is also fatally secretive and solitary. Lady Verinder and Betteredge know that Rosanna is a reformed thief but kindly keep it from everyone else. The other housemaids, nevertheless, do not like her. Betteredge gives the reader the most information about Rosanna and her peers:

> What the servants chiefly resented, I think, was her silent tongue and her solitary ways. She read or worked in leisure hours when the rest gossiped. . . . She never quarrelled, she never

took offence; she only kept a certain distance, obstinately and civilly, between the rest of them and herself. (55)

Her reserve is suspect, and Franklin Blake unconsciously arouses her passions, which are also dangerous to herself and others. After first seeing him on the beach, she goes back to the house where "she had turned . . . all the colours of the rainbow. She had been merry without reason, and sad without reason" (79). Wretchedly aware that she is only a servant, and a plain one, Rosanna resents Rachel, and takes to substituting her own flower for her mistress's in Franklin's vase. She "constantly put herself in Mr. Franklin's way—very slyly and quietly, but she did it. . . . The poor thing's appetite, never much, fell away dreadfully; her eyes in the morning showed plain signs of waking and crying at night" (92). She learns that he "stole" the moonstone and tries to protect him while letting him know that he owes her his safety. He accidentally rebuffs her several times, thinking to ward off her confession of theft. What neither of them—or Rachel—knows is that he took the diamond while in an opium-induced sleepwalk (the local doctor had secretly administered the drug for Franklin's own good) and that Ablewhite stole the jewel after seeing Franklin drop it. Broken-hearted, Rosanna drowns herself, concealing evidence that would have incriminated Franklin with an explanatory note to which he and Betteredge are directed after her death. Her suicide letter confesses love, not crime: "I undressed, and put the nightgown on me. You had worn it—and I had another little moment of pleasure in wearing it after you" (374). Rosanna's passion and silences, like Rachel's, bring suspicion of crime; both women are thought by Detective Cuff to have stolen the gem.

Clack is a comic distortion of the other passionate women in the novel. Cloaking all her prejudices and greed beneath excessive religiosity, she seeks attention, love, and money. Godfrey Ablewhite is a truly godlike Christian hero for her because of his good looks, smooth ways, and ostentatious virtues displayed for various philanthropic groups. In the course of her spying and interference, Clack is appalled by his proposal to Rachel—little knowing that his declaration springs from financial necessity, not love—and easily taken in by his facile explanations for his indifference to the philanthropy groups. Like Jane Hardie in *Hard Cash*, but without her ultimate dignity and selflessness, Clack thinks that her emotional and sexual responses to Ablewhite are signs of righteous spirituality: "He pressed my hands alternately to his lips. Overwhelmed by the exquisite triumph of having got him back among us, I let him do what he liked with my hands. I closed my eyes. I felt my head, in an ecstasy of spiritual self-forgetfulness, sinking on his shoulder" (298–99).

Clack's amorous delusions, and the passions and reserve of Rachel and Rosanna, are a far cry from power-crazed Marion in *Strathmore* or lascivious Archbold in *Hard Cash*. In *The Moonstone*, however, Collins exploits a similar apprehension of the mid-Victorian reading public toward independent and self-willed women. Rachel and Rosanna know they are guilty of protecting Franklin—and perhaps of loving him so passionately. Franklin, however, commits a crime unconsciously, suggesting that our secret urges and desires can betray us. His "crime," though, is much more excusable than those of the two women, although perhaps as frightening in its implication that deep down we are creatures of appetite. Rachel's decision to keep knowledge about the theft to herself exacerbates her strong sexuality. Rosanna's passion and reserve cause her death. Female independence, passion, and ability to conceal are, in *The Moonstone,* suspicious and dangerous.

Dickens called *The Moonstone* "a very curious story—wild, and yet domestic" (Page, 169). Certainly, one of the novel's strengths is in the powerfully unsettling effect of two invasions: a foreign jewel with a curse and a very British confidence man who robs a member of his own family. As the first murder in *Uncle Silas* and Lady Dedlock's affair in *Bleak House* illustrate, old crimes come to light or engender new crimes. After a distant relation steals the moonstone from India, three Indian men come searching for it. They hover on the edges of the central action, eventually regaining the gem by killing Ablewhite. The Indians distract both the reader and the Verinders in the beginning of the novel. The foreign jewel, with its enigmatic significance to the Hindu religion, creates chaos in the Verinder household.

Although Ablewhite steals rather than kills, his crime is as deeply alarming. His hypocrisy, like Sir Percival's, is obvious, and his relatives discern the truth about him long after the reader does. After being attacked, he describes his ordeal with false modesty and courage: "I have only been strangled; I have only been thrown flat on my back, on a very thin carpet, covering a particularly hard floor. Just think how much worse it might have been! . . . I shrink from all this fuss and publicity" (246). He pours his fictitious love into Rachel's ear in hopes of marrying her money and the estate. He displays himself as the most virtuous of community leaders. After Ablewhite's death, Cuff discovers several revelations about his "other" self:

> The side kept hidden from the general notice, exhibited this same gentleman in the totally different character of a man of pleasure, with a villa in the suburbs which was not taken in his own name, and with a lady in the villa, which was not taken in his own name, either. (506)

Rachel and Franklin reconcile following the bizarre recreation of the crime in which Franklin takes the jewel again, and the murder itself becomes almost an epilogue. Ablewhite is killed in a symbolically appropriate way for one who has committed crimes of hypocrisy and hidden theft: "He was killed . . . by being smothered with a pillow from his bed," writes Cuff (503). Ironically, Ablewhite is "hidden" to death. Similarly, no one recognizes him once the pillow is removed because of his disguise. He is killed as the secret criminal, not as a pillar of rectitude.

Cuff arrives at the Verinder household as an expert who will uncover the hidden truths that surround the theft of the moonstone. He proves to be a worthy police detective in the tradition of Inspector Bucket. The "popular hostility to the police and representatives of authority, preserved even by the middle classes" occasioned an authorial compromise; the benevolent detective is often, in mid-Victorian fiction, a private detective like Green in *Hard Cash* or "a police officer from outside the immediate region" (Marshall, 79). Once "a figure of opprobrium and marginal social position in the sensation novel," the detective "gradually becomes the hero as well as the guardian of conventional values" (W. Hughes, 164). Victorian critics sniffed at "the police-court flavour these characters infuse into modern tales" (Page, 176). Yet " 'the great' Sergeant Cuff would almost reconcile one to the type" (Page, 176).

Like Buckett, Cuff is sharp, psychologically attuned to those around him and truly professional without being ruthless. While he disdains disguises, he is never quite what he seems:

> His eyes, of a steely light grey, had a very disconcerting trick, when they encountered your eyes, of looking as if they expected something more from you than you were aware of yourself. . . . He might have been a parson, or an undertaker—or anything else you like, except what he really was. (133)

Gabriel Betteredge, the fiercely loyal Verinder servant, is appalled by Cuff's appearance—"a less comforting officer to look at, for a family in distress, I defy you to discover" (133)—but the reader recognizes the advantage of understatement. When Cuff returns from his retirement to continue the case, he "wore a broad-brimmed white hat, a light shooting jacket, white trousers, and drab gaiters. . . . His whole aim and object seemed to be, to look as if he had lived in the country all his life" (490).

Cuff's professional techniques provide a sharp contrast to those of his plodding and heavy-handed local predecessor. He seems to read minds; more than once he astonished Betteredge with kindness when the servant feels mostly anger toward him: "I feel particularly tender at the present moment, Mr. Betteredge, towards you. And you, with the same excellent motive, feel particularly tender towards Rosanna Spearman, don't you? Do you happen to know whether she has had a new outfit of linen lately?" (158) He cleverly acknowledges Betteredge's worried loyalty to Rosanna while gathering new evidence. His seemingly offhand, unexpected questions are always crucially related to the case. He does not use the colorful jargon of Green and Bucket, but one suspects he could if necessary; he is a thoroughgoing professional. When Betteredge attacks him at the suggestion that Rachel committed the crime, Cuff is tolerant: "If it's any comfort to you, collar me again. You don't in the least know how to do it; but I'll overlook your awkwardness in consideration of your feelings" (173). With determination, he refuses to accept Lady Verinder's payment until he has done what he promised. This impresses even Betteredge: "In those words Sergeant Cuff reminded us that, even in the Detective Police, a man may have a reputation to lose" (202).

In an amusing sequence where Betteredge watches the other servants emerge from private interviews with Cuff, Collins adeptly demonstrates the detective's techniques. Each servant comes out with a different impression of Cuff: "Sergeant Cuff is a perfect gentleman" (153); "If Sergeant Cuff doesn't believe a respectable woman, he might keep his opinion to himself, at any rate" (153); "Sergeant Cuff has a heart; *he* doesn't cut jokes, Mr. Betteredge, with a poor hard-working girl" (153). Betteredge's daughter, Penelope, shows the most imagination: "Sergeant Cuff is much to be pitied. He must have been crossed in love, father, when he was a young man" (153).

Cuff's technique in this instance is a neat microcosm of the author's narrative method and, ultimately, another example of the difficulty of locating and understanding the truth. As Cuff provides various characters with what they expect, causing each to develop a different impression of his personality and opinion, so Collins's multiple narrators function as "witnesses in court" (Wheeler, 93). Each one can only discover and reveal a limited truth. Often they misconstrue the little they do know, so that "the reader is presented with problems of reading or interpretation" as well as plot (Wheeler, 93). Ultimately, as in *Bleak House* and *Hard Cash,* the reader comes to learn that there are truths "beyond the reach of the detective, the appropriate emissary of modern rationality and legal sanctions" (W. Hughes, 165). Cuff is smart but not omniscient. At first drawn to the wrong solution to the robbery and eventual murder, he later arrives at the right one through knowledge brought to him by amateurs stricken with *"detective fever"* and by coincidence (160). The elaborate and pleasing way in which the tale is told and the fact that the crime is eventually solved do not erase the implication that no one person can discover the "truth" about this crime—and indeed, about anything.

The complexity and even incomprehensibility of truth is related to the invasion of the respectable. The world of the novel suddenly does not make the same sense to its inhabitants that it once did, and Cuff must be called in. He is an expert who will diagnose the truth when things are no longer what they seemed to be. Once it is understood that the criminal is among us, our world is shattered. Cuff is—like Green and Bucket—fallible; unlike the story in *Hard Cash,* however, here circumstances must be made right by somebody. We can not hope that they will become right by themselves. *The Moonstone* suggests that although Ablewhite is exposed, his analogously hypocritical or criminal real-life counterparts might remain concealed. The thematic implications of Collins's ingenious narrative method are that events will not unravel themselves and that human beings can not be counted on to solve mysteries without authorial intervention.

"Who ever heard the like of it—in the nineteenth century, mind; in an age of progress, and in a country which rejoices in the blessings of British constitution?" (67) Franklin's amazed and plaintive question informs the whole novel. He comes to disagree with his relative's opinion that "this was the nineteenth century, and any man in his senses had only to apply to the police" (69). The police, as the Verinders learn, can do only so much. Although the story, solved as it is by complicated scientific experiment and the multiple efforts of the characters, seems at first to be self-enclosed and thus reassuring, its implications are nothing of the sort. The series of events that bring about knowledge and the mystery's conclusion, told by an engagingly entertaining series of narrators, result from the techniques and effects of artistry, not life. The power of the individual, even when working with others, is extremely limited. Thus, one of our pleasures in *The Moonstone* is that its formal symmetry and ingenious plotting "work out" the way real life never does: "Solving crimes and conundrums is one way of making order out of one's world. . . . The final consolation of *The Moonstone,* for the reader as well as the self-conscious narrators, most of all for Collins himself, is the triumph of form" (W. Hughes, 165). When knowledge and human control become impossible, form provides comfort and satisfaction. *The Moonstone,* like many Collins novels, "subverts the old maxim that seeing is believing and shows that truth is more complex and reality less easily discernable than one thought."[25] Characters, limited by their human capabilities, see very little and do not usually understand what they can see. Only a single crime, then, may be solved. In *The Moonstone,* as in much midcentury fiction, melodrama, and nonfiction, larger questions about respectable imposters loom over the proceedings and remain unanswered at the work's conclusion.

# Part III

# "The Night-Side of Nature"

# THE WHITECHAPEL TRAGEDY.
## POLICE NEWS EDITION
OF
## THE LIFE AND TRIAL OF
# HENRY & THOMAS WAINWRIGHT,
### WITH VERDICT, &c.

ONE PENNY.
G. PURKESS, Office, 286, Straud, London, W.C.

Pamphlet Cover, 1874
A typical late-century killer, Henry Wainwright, was "a charming companion—a man of most genial nature."
*(Courtesy of the Michael Sadleir Collection, Lilly Library)*

# Introduction to Part III

"The highest type of man may revert to the animal if he leaves the straight path of destiny," warns Sherlock Holmes in "The Creeping Man."[1] Both men and women return to the bestial in late-century crime literature. The paths they creep along lead to conscienceless villainy. People devolve into animals as their moral and spiritual lives decay. The characteristic genres of the period—journalism, melodrama, and fiction—reveal a belief in the criminality of human nature. This pervasive criminality unravels the workings of justice. Murders are solved accidentally or belatedly. Citizens form faceless conspiracies that stymie detectives. In other works, policemen or detectives are themselves criminal. Killers in late-century writing are no longer psychotic outsiders or social imposters. Instead, they belong to the community they assault and have respectable motives for committing crimes.

Individuals hired to protect people are capably criminal or criminally inept. In *Michael Dred, Detective: The Unravelling of a Mystery of Twenty Years* (1899) by Robert and Marie Leighton, the detective is, in fact, the killer. Dred murders a romantic rival through jealous rage. He is perfectly willing to frame almost every other character in the novel for his crime. His professional skills make him a very slippery criminal to track. Grodman, the wry investigator of *The Big Bow Mystery* (1892) by Israel Zangwill, is a retired police detective who kills a philanthropist, then pretends to hunt the murderer. His nerve and wit enable him to kill a man in front of a witness without getting caught. Only his last-minute confession identifies him as the killer. Policemen in Arthur Conan Doyle's stories bumble in the wake of Sherlock Holmes, struggling to steal credit from him and each other in an unlovely display of vanity and hypocrisy. Holmes himself has a criminal side, often turning vigilante, as Marcello Truzzi points out, when he finds it "necessary to go outside the law to assure justice."[2] He lies habitually, faking "illness, accidents, information, and even his own death"; he also lets "known felons go free" more than a dozen times (Truzzi, 74). "I am the last and highest court of appeal," Holmes declares, exempting himself from the laws that bind others (Clausen, 112). Whether for justice, love, money, or sport, late-century police and detectives often become criminals.

The motives behind crimes committed by those who solve them have ominous implications. Holmes and other detectives break laws because they have been handcuffed by bureaucracy. The legal system sometimes provides loopholes through which killers can leap. Only those with the courage and moral certainty of a Sherlock Holmes can break the law in the name of justice. Works with detectives who steal, burgle, or kill raise several disturbing questions. First of all, why do laws permit some criminals to escape? How can wrongdoers be protected by the rules they ignore? Secondly, who can track criminal detectives? The skills they cultivate to solve murders instruct them when they choose to kill. Lastly, Holmes may trespass and free felons to serve the innocent and punish the guilty, but what of detectives whose purposes are less noble? When laws are selectively bent or broken by those engaged to uphold them, the criminal justice system teeters on anarchy.

Indeed, other late-century detectives share Holmes's occasional willingness to commit crimes but lack his strong sense of morality. Michael Dred kills a romantic rival, showing that those hired to solve crimes are sometimes driven by the same passions that govern ordinary people. Grodman kills Arthur Constant because he wants to commit the perfect murder. Constant has nothing to do with his own death—Grodman likes him, in fact—but he is sacrificed to the investigator's sense of crime as art. Grodman wants to design a homicide with panache and to outwit his successor at Scotland Yard.

This rash of criminal detectives indicates more than a lack of faith in the system, although public confidence suffered when, in the late 1870s, Scotland Yard "endured a scandal that resulted in its reorganization" (Clausen, 111). In late-century literature, nursemaids, sailors, and doctors are as fallen as policemen and detectives. Respectable people of all ranks and stations commit murder, often because of motives that are not in themselves criminal. Mathias, the villain of *The Bells* (1871) by Leopold Lewis, has killed a wealthy merchant for his money long before the action of the play begins. He has not, in the interim, suffered years of anguish. Instead, he has accomplished everything he had hoped. Mathias used the money to save his inn, consolidate his reputation, and become a dignified member of the community. He plans as carefully as any businessman. Unlike Lady Audley, he is a genuinely respectable and generous person. Similarly, Wilfred Denver of *The Silver King* (1883), written largely by Henry Arthur Jones, is falsely accused of murder, but he might as well have killed the victim. Denver drinks heavily and gambles away his family's security. In desperation and rage, he threatens to kill Ware, his wife's former suitor, and later believes he has done so. Only a peculiar quirk of timing prevents him from becoming a murderer. Although he has not killed anyone, he is nevertheless a criminal hero whose vices are as genuine as his virtues.

In *Dr. Jekyll and Mr. Hyde* (1886), readers might find the clearest vision of the respectable murderer. Robert Louis Stevenson houses both the middle-class killer and the criminal hero in his central character. Dr. Jekyll's scientific experiments result in his occasional transformation to wicked, bestial Hyde. As Hyde, Jekyll behaves shamefully. Eventually, the doctor can not control his experiment and becomes Hyde without choosing. Significantly, Jekyll and Hyde are *not* two separate personalities: the murderous creature springs from the doctor's animal nature. Jekyll comes to realize that his smug sense of moral superiority triggers the appearance of Hyde. Like many characters in late-century popular genres, he is his own monster.

Journalism, melodrama, and fiction present a range of murders that show criminality taking shape in middle-class homes or minds. In their treatment of homicide, melodramas such as *The Silver King* and *The Bells* show killers with respectable motives. Crime journalism and fiction suggest that society may be morally corrupt to its roots. In these works, people "revert to the animal" with disheartening regularity, and all roads lead to crime.

# 7

# Nonfiction, 1870–1900

In 1873, a writer for *Macmillan's Magazine* observes: "Crime follows in the wake of civilization—the demon that dogs its footsteps and revels in its shadow."[1] After arguing for moral education in prison rather than punitive, mind-deadening physical tasks, the author concludes: "There will always be a night-side of nature, where the spawn of evil will fructify unseen, sometimes spreading into the light of day, scattering its poison, diffusing its noxious power around it" (DeMauley, 154). By the last quarter of the nineteenth century, many writers on crime and murder are convinced of the "night-side of nature" and the difficulty in controlling it. Writers for middle-class journals such as *The Spectator, Fortnightly Review, Macmillan's Magazine,* and *All the Year Round* tend to discuss crime as if civilization itself was the target of a deep-rooted conspiracy: "Talents of a high order are exerted for the subversion, not the support of society" (DeMauley, 154). The midcentury fear of being attacked from within apparent security still exists, but instead of focusing on wily doctors and women poisoners, late-century authors take a more dour and resigned view of crime. It is not just that women and professional men are capable of great deceit. All of society has somehow changed for the worse: "A well-grounded impression has fixed itself upon the public mind, that our social condition is unhealthy . . . with all our philanthropy, crime is increasing" (De-Mauley, 145). "The Epidemic of Murder," as one article is titled, has spread, and decent, thoughtful people—those who read and write sociological articles for middle-class magazines, in short—are forced to the conclusion that society is unequipped to deal with "modern" violence, amorality, and criminality.

The professionalism of police and criminals is still a topic of great concern in late Victorian journalism. Respect for the British police, however, has given way to a straightforward and uneasy belief that English police are not as efficient as English thieves and murderers. London detectives are not canny enough to abate the epidemic of murder, and crime has grown beyond the capabilities of ordinary British police, hampered as they are by bureaucracy. Indeed, so desperate is the situation that several writers suggest learning from French detectives.

Articles that compare British police unfavorably to their French colleagues usually take the form of an interview or series of adventures with a French detective. Suspicious writers come to fear that London policemen are obvious and easy to spot, cartoon figures unequal in every way to their determined criminal counterparts. In "A French Detective Story," an "elderly, very gentlemanly-looking" detective expresses astonishment at the methods of English detectives: "Your secret police . . . are no more secret than your police in uniform. Everybody knows them, and they even dress so exactly alike that they might as well wear the blue tunic with the number on the collar."[2] Although winningly polite, the detective adds: "If my appearance and my vocation were known, even to my landlord and my concierge, I would be of no more use to the secret police of Paris than a pair of boots without soles would be to an infantry soldier" ("A French Detective Story," 370). Later, the same detective bets the writer a good dinner that he can fool him: "I will speak on three separate occasions to monsieur, that he will not on either occasion recognise who I am until I disclose myself, and that each time I will speak to him for at least five minutes" ("A French Detective Story," 370). In an impressive display of ingenuity and expertise, the detective fools the author three times, and the "history of the finding of the bonds" that brought the Englishman to Paris unravels in "three or four days" after his arrival ("A French Detective Story," 373).

A similar article in *Macmillan's Magazine* by M. Laing Meason expresses doubts about the efficiency of the British police.[3] When a French friend's home is burgled, the author has an opportunity to observe the pragmatic and canny French detectives. The police detective explains his methods: "We don't send constables . . . to make a fuss and put every one on their guard; we like to do things quietly, the result is better" ("The French Detective Police," 297). The detective in France is "hidden from public view," solving crimes in secrecy rather than in the circuslike atmosphere surrounding a sensational case in England ("The French Detective Police," 299). While tactfully admiring the British police who keep public order, the detective has "a very low opinion" of the detectives in England: "No sooner is a robbery committed . . . than the utmost publicity is given to the whole affair, and the thieves are as well aware of what steps are being taken to unravel the matter as the police themselves" ("The French Detective Police," 299).

Meason argues for the necessity of secrecy—and, by implication, the adoption of criminal methods and disguises—to solve crimes. Lawbreakers are so efficient that their nemeses must adopt their methods to contest them. At Charing Cross station, he asks a youth whether two "well-built, well-set-up, active-looking men" nearby are soldiers:

> "No, sir, them beant soldiers; they's detectives, they is." "How do you know?" said I. "Oh, sir," was the answer, "*we* knows all them plain-clothes officers. They try to look like other folks; but it's no good. We can tell them as well as if they wore helmets and blue coats." ("The French Detective Police," 301)

In "The London Police," Meason anticipates that any move for a more efficient police force would be stymied by well-meaning but hopelessly innocent citizens:

> There is in England such a strong, and in this case such an unreasoning feeling against anything like secrecy, or not doing everything in the light of day, that if the French detective system were introduced into this country we should no doubt have scores of petitions against it, and gushing letters . . . written to prove that it was in every way un-English and demoralising.[4]

Only by becoming better at criminal methods than the criminals—more ingenious at disguise, more sneaky and secretive—will British police succeed in quelling outbreaks of robbery and murder.

Articles on crime, murder, and the police are characterized by concern about police laziness as well as want of wit. Police make easy arrests rather than hard ones. The detective in "The French Detective Police" relates an incident in which three or four quiet, well-behaved men were apprehended by several policemen: "Much astonished, the Frenchman made up his mind that they were guilty of some political offence. He followed them to Bow Street, and there found out that they had been guilty of betting" ("The French Detective Police," 300). Later, he sees more men gambling at "Victoria, the great betting club," without being disturbed by police ("The French Detective Police," 300). The obvious implication is that one law works for the wealthy and upper-middle class, while another operates for ordinary people; however, the author is most concerned to show that the inability to keep law-breaking of different kinds in proportion is damaging to British detectives:

> If our *employees* of Scotland Yard took half as much pains to find the outs and ins of the classes who live by thieving, as they do to convict publicans in whose houses a glass of ale has been drunk after hours, the general public of London would benefit greatly by their knowledge. ("The French Detective Police," 300)

Police foolishly waste time on petty law breakers when offensive and dangerous criminals pose a larger threat to "the community at large" ("The London Police," 195). Frighteningly, "vice and crime of every kind is to be met with at any time" in London, and criminals get the upper hand because they are smarter and more efficient than those employed to stop them ("The London Police," 195).[5]

These articles express the growing belief that detectives must use illegal or criminal methods to fight crime. In earlier nonfiction and street ballads, ordinary citizens who happen upon evidence of the crime itself solve murders. In other cases, criminals reveal themselves through guilt and remorse or a bestial stupidity that renders them unable to wash the accusatory blood from their clothing. By the end of the century, some writers believe that "without some secret system by which the perpetrators of such crimes can be discovered, law and order, nay, the safety of life itself, will become unknown in the land" ("The London Police," 200). Murderers and thieves seem to become more professional, unhampered by virtuous attitudes about what is cricket and what is not. Their maneuvers require desperate measures. Police are almost clownlike—easy to identify—as they follow idiotic rules about drinking after hours while letting real criminals escape. Detectives can no longer afford to indulge in these leisurely antics. Hawkshaw's disguises may have amazed when *The Ticket-of-Leave Man* first appeared, but by the end of the century, his opponents would have "twigged him" at once, and he would have been obliged to do more than eavesdrop to solve crimes.

Articles that discuss murder, as well as those about the police force, reflect a fear of "the night-side of nature" gaining complete ascendancy over goodness in contemporary society. "The epidemic of murder" and other crimes can be battled defensively but not definitively. Authors of articles for middle-class journals can only note the situation and offer suggestions as to how the epidemic might be quarantined. Like the critics who believed that Newgate novels caused crime by romanticizing criminals, so late Victorian writers of nonfiction accuse newspapers of fomenting further offenses against the community. In "The Epidemic of Murder," the writer observes: "We believe that the morbid excitement which the story of the murders has produced has done far more to stimulate the active criminal impulse, than the failure to detect the criminal has done to diminish the dread of consequences."[6] After providing several examples, the author suggests that a fear of punishment is "a feeble antiseptic at best," less effective than "the virulence of the poison spread by a constant study of the horrible details of sensational crime" ("The Epidemic of Murder," 45). Crime reporting exacerbates crime, which is then reported to repeat the deadly cycle: "The publicity which is necessarily given to every great crime, and still more to every great series of crimes, in itself fosters the moral ferment that produces such crimes" ("The Epidemic of Murder," 45). The implication is that the disposition to crime is widespread. Some writers see even the reporting of crime as a dangerous part of criminality's contagious effects.

Violence, some believe, must be met and answered by legal violence. In "The Hangman's Office," the author argues that hanging must be retained as the means of capital punishment because it is disgraceful: "Men ought not to lose the sense that there is something rough and brutal about capital punishment, that it is essentially a last appeal to force in its most direct and savage form."[7] Increased brutality in punishment may help to abate the tide of crime and murder. In earlier nonfiction and street literature, execution always provides an appropriate climax to the terrible lives of criminals. By the century's end, with capital punishment under attack from some quarters and sympathy for criminals running high, defenders of the gallows argue explicitly for rough and brutal measures to curtail rough and brutal crimes.

Where some articles blame newspapers and the human interest in sensational details for the epidemic of crime, another on "The Poisons of the Day; a New Social Evil" is appalled by the ease with which people can purchase lethal medications. In an experiment to prove his point, Henry Hubbard sends an eleven-year-old girl into a variety of stores that sold "Patent Medicines."[8] "Without hesitation or inquiry of any kind," merchants provided the child with every dangerous substance she asked for: "Had we extended our journey onwards with the same object, this little child could have procured sufficient poisons to have converted any parish in London into 'a city of the dead'" (Hubbard, 243). Significantly, Hubbard is as despairing of genuinely improving criminal behavior as those who discuss sensational newspaper articles are of reducing crime. Altering the laws on the purchase of poison might "lessen the number of luckless and uninitiated victims" (Hubbard, 244). But "moral and social influences, or legislative enactments, can avail but little to restrain the deeds of desperate men and women. The hand of the reckless poisoner cannot thereby be stayed" (Hubbard, 244). While suggesting reforms that would make it more difficult to buy poison, Hubbard is nevertheless convinced that *"murders* will ever and anon occur and be brought to light while human nature remains what it is, in spite of the severest legislation" (Hubbard, 241). Crimes may be uncovered but not prevented.

There are still echoes in these articles of mid-Victorian paranoia about murders committed from within apparent security. In "The Bernays Tragedy," the author indirectly expresses the suspicion of women that characterized earlier writing: "Of all motives influencing educated men to commit murder, jealousy is probably the most frequent, as we should all perceive" if the motives of duels were recorded.[9] The most fascinating, fearful murders are those that attack decent people who do not expect it, in safe places, as we suppose our homes to be. In "Murder as a Fine Art in Scotland," the unsolved attempted murder of a hard-working elderly housekeeper is particularly distressing because "half the horror of the crime . . . was that it broke in upon the long summer night of one of the quietest villages in rural Scotland."[10] The author of "The Motives of Murder" agrees: "We all unconsciously shudder more violently when the offchance of misfortune overtakes the apparently secure."[11] Yet although the threat of murder in a presumably safe environment is chilling, what is truly gripping is the sense that criminality is rooted in human nature. It can not be exorcised or executed. When ordinary people and police do not even understand crimes, they certainly can not prevent or solve them.

In "The Motives of Murder," the author uses several examples to demonstrate that "in a great number of the recorded cases the murderer had no adequate motive at all, and was moved either by small greed, or petty fear . . . or revenge for apparently trifling injury" ("The Motives of Murder," 1544). "No murder, if it is a true murder at all," the author argues ominously, "can have an adequate motive" ("The Motives of Murder," 1544). What is also appalling is that killers do not understand the enormity of their crimes; only afterward do they realize the horror of their offenses. In arguing for capital punishment, the author concludes that trying to find motives for murderers "is almost to waste time, for anything is a motive, just as it used to be to the duellist by profession. He had in his long impunity lost the perception of what killing meant" ("The Motives of Murder," 1544).

That growth of amoral insensitivity to human life is the subject of "The Fenayrou Trial," an exploration of the attitudes displayed by a husband-and-wife team of murderers: "The woman . . . bargains with her husband for forgiveness for her unfaithfulness to him, on condition that she betrays one of her former lovers to a horrible death."[12] They include his mother and brother in the dangerous plans, and three of them have a hearty supper before the murder itself. The "stolidity" and indifference to morality with which the criminals conspire and commit the murder disturbs the author more than anything else. Crimes of passion, like those of the enraged, frustrated suitors or rejected lovers of early street ballads, are more sympathetic because they are more understandable. Indifferent, amoral murders seem worse than the calculating crimes of Drs. Palmer and Pritchard or of Madeline Kent. Those, at least, had clear if reprehensible purposes: greed or the disentangling of a liaison that would have impeded a convenient marriage. In the Fenayrou case, the wife had other lovers, but the husband made no attempt to kill them, and while planning the murder, none of the criminals allowed any interference in the humdrum course of daily events and obligations: "The world was not out of joint for them, either before the bloody act or after it" ("The Fenayrou Trial," 1078). Remorse is completely alien to these killers. Even his own execution strikes the husband indifferently; on being condemned, he remarks, "What does it matter?—one man the less" ("The Fenayrou Trial," 1078).

The Fenayrous' indifference previews the chaotic criminality of the future: "Is not that the form which the . . . wickedness of the present and future tends more and more to assume?" The author attributes this "hardening of the heart" to "the slenderer hold which religious faith has of the modern world." Apathy and spiritual decay bring on

> a new phase in the history of moral evil, the phase in which evil has much fewer terrors, much fewer guilty starts, much fewer auguries of the intolerable misery of self-knowledge, than it used to have,—the age in which evil is stolid, and careful, and prudent, and obtuse, and far better disposed to live the small life of petty animal enjoyments, than it has ever been during the past. ("The Fenayrou Trial," 1078)

Calculation and secrecy marked mid-Victorian murder, but a stolid return to pre- or amoral primitivism characterizes the crimes discussed in late-century issues of *The Spectator* and *Macmillan's Magazine*. In "The Moral Muddle about

Murder," the author blames the public's reluctance to condemn criminals to death on a "decrease in fortitude," not a "decrease in ferocity."[13] People display too much sympathy for living criminals and not enough for deceased victims. Using for an example a grotesque case of cannibalism at sea, the writer observes that people have too acute a compassion for the "sufferings of the men in the boat" while failing to realize "that the unhappy boy who perished bore all these sufferings like his comrades, and a violent death besides" ("The Moral Muddle about Murder," 1694). Journalists must "help the people out of their moral muddle" or else witness society "relapse into the old savagery" ("The Moral Muddle about Murder," 1695). Rather than indicating an increased respect for human life, the public outcry against capital punishment convinces the writer of a new indifference to life and crime: "If it is a trifle to kill a man because you have only him to eat, what is it to kill him because his wealth would make whole families happy?—the very creed of the poisoners" ("The Moral Muddle about Murder," 1695). Logic has eroded with an older, more just morality.

Whether they blame journalism, bureaucracy, or human nature itself for the phenomenon, articles on crime and murder in late nineteenth-century periodicals are unified in their depiction of a degenerative and contagious criminality, one that is less controllable because of its increasing distance from recognizable human passions and motives. Infected by sensational reporting, the public will either exonerate or become criminals. Writers argue for capital punishment, yet recognize its inadequacy as a deterrent. Implied in the support of hanging is the belief that criminality must be answered with more severe, if nominally righteous, criminality. This wholehearted endorsement of execution had existed in the first part of the century, but by the seventies and eighties, writers see the gallows as the last alternative for a crumbling and morally disintegrating society. In the thirties and forties, execution was thought to discourage other wrongdoers with its harsh finality. By the end of the century, writers seem to hope, rather than believe, that murderers and other criminals might be deterred by brutal, public justice. But hanging, they argue, would be a desperately needed moral sign that virtuous people have the courage and energy of their criminal counterparts.

# 8

# Melodrama, 1870–1900

By the end of the nineteenth century, popular theatre had begun an "escape from the escapism of melodrama."[1] Playwrights grew ambitious for critical as well as popular success; the conventional midcentury melodrama filled theatres but aroused journalistic contempt. Tom Taylor, who became editor of *Punch* in 1874, spoke for many viewers in his dismissal of the theatre to which he had contributed *The Ticket-of-Leave Man:*

> There are many, of all classes, who have ceased to frequent the theatre, because they have ceased to find what they want there—comedy which will amuse without disgusting by excess or offending by indecency; tragedy which will move and elevate without repelling by imperfectness and bad taste in impersonation; drama which will stir and enthrall without condescending to vulgar claptrap, crawling realism, or the mere physical excitement, now christened Sensation.[2]

Critics called for a new theatre, one that would shed the excess and bombast of the old. George Augustus Sala complains in 1883 that

> the public are growing as weary of murderers and forgers, fraudulent cashiers, insolvent stockbrokers, hired bravoes . . . stage detectives, stage children, stage convicts, and stage Israelites as they are of stage houses on fire, explosions . . . .[3]

Tom Robertson had worked to raise the level of mid-Victorian drama in realistic comedies like *Society* (1865) and *Caste* (1867). He also influenced the theatre by virtually inventing, as W. S. Gilbert believed, the art of stage management.[4] Robertson supervised productions down to the smallest detail— doorknob, saucer, and moonlight—and with the Bancrofts at the Prince of Wales Theatre, helped to draw "polite society" back into a once "unfashionable playhouse" (Rowell, *Victorian Theatre,* 83). George Rowell describes "the return of respectability" to the late-nineteenth-century stage in *The Victorian Theatre 1792–1914*. As audiences in some theatres became more "respectable," they began to seek images of themselves and their concerns on stage.

The desire for exciting drama that mirrored middle-class sensibilities resulted in two distinctive strains of criminal melodrama. The first has been called the "guilty secret" or "women with a past" play, in which social misdeeds have the effect of actual crimes. Works in this subgenre examine the dilemma of the fallen woman. *The Second Mrs. Tanqueray* (1893) by Arthur Wing Pinero, *Mrs. Dane's Defence* (1900) by Henry Arthur Jones, and *Lady Windermere's Fan* (1892) by Oscar Wilde attempt a greater understanding of women with compromising histories. In some of these plays, the fallen characters are permitted to disappear into social exile instead of suffering the more traditional fate of death by murder, remorse, or sin. This type of criminal melodrama reflects both the Victorian obsession with chastity[5] and the return of the middle and upper classes to the theatre. Except for Paula Tanqueray's poignant self-murder, however, these plays tend to feature symbolic rather than actual killings.

The other strain of criminal melodrama of the period includes actual murders that somehow comment on issues of class, respectability, and honor. In the two immensely popular late-century plays I will discuss, murderers are not outside society, like killers in early Victorian literature. Nor have they insinuated themselves into the middle or upper classes. Instead, they are esteemed, longstanding members of the respectable community they assault. *The Bells* (1871) by Leopold Lewis and *The Silver King* (1882) by Henry A. Jones and Henry Herman are "two of the best-known melodramas of crime" (Booth, *English Melodrama,* 160) that raise significant questions about respectability and the criminality of human nature.

The opening night of *The Bells* at The Royal Lyceum Theatre on November 25, 1871 has been considered "a turning-point in the fortunes of the Victorian theatre."[6] Henry Irving's performance as Mathias, the Burgomaster tortured by memories of the murder he committed years before, established him as a brilliant actor. George Rowell observes that, like David Garrick's Richard III and Edmund Kean's Shylock, Irving's interpretation of Mathias made him "not merely famous but foremost in his profession" (*Irving,* 1). Rowell also notes that Irving's triumph in the role saved "Colonel" Hezekiah Bateman, manager of the Lyceum, from bankruptcy (*Irving,* 13). Nevertheless, as James O'Neill "became" the Counte of Monte Cristo for years after his first performance in the role, so Irving both benefitted and suffered from his unforgettable association with Mathias:

> The measure of his success was that more than thirty years after his first triumph in the part he could still pack theatres by his performance as Mathias in *The Bells.* The measure of his failure was that he had no choice but to do so. (Rowell, *Irving,* 171)

Most critics agree that *The Bells* became famous first and last because of its riveting central performance:

> Two eminent scene designers had been hired to lavish money on decoration, some dazzling

new machinery was employed for special effects, and the music director of the Theatre Cluny had been especially brought over from Paris for the occasion, but essentially it was Sir Henry Irving as Sir Henry Irving in *The Bells* that firmly established both Irving and the Lyceum. (Ashley, 315)

Certainly Mathias, itself a double role of murderer and esteemed father of the bride, is an actor's part, rich and complex.

But *The Bells* has a power independent of Irving's genius. Leonard Ashley rather grudgingly grants the play some credit while urging readers to read it with sympathetic imagination:

> *The Bells* may seem old-fashioned now, but it was stunning then. It may read badly, but (whether at the Lyceum or a command performance at Sandringham) it played well; its characters may seem as synthetic as those in George Du Maurier's *Trilby* (1894), but Mathias, once experienced, is as unforgettable as Svengali. (316–17)

Based on the French melodrama *Le Juif Polonais* by Emile Erckmann and Alexandre Chatrian, *The Bells* employs "the technical resources of the theatre with discretion and real force" (Rowell, *Irving,* 98) in the two sensation scenes. It also uses sensation to explore the two worlds of Mathias—"an outer world that is ever smiling, and an inner world which is a purgatory" (Ashley, quoting Wilson, 316)—in a chilling examination of a murderer who is, in a way, never found out by the community he betrays.

Lewis's play begins on a snowy night at a village inn in Alsace, where the Burgomaster's daughter, Annette, prepares for the arrival of her fiancé, Christian. The snow reminds villagers of "the Polish Jew's winter,"[7] when the snow was also very heavy and a Jewish seed merchant was brutally murdered. Although suspicion fell on two brothers, Mathias helped to clear their names and the crime remained unsolved. More village reminiscing touches on the Burgomaster: "Mathias is fortunate in finding so good a son-in-law, but everything has succeeded with Mathias for the last fifteen years" (325). The Burgomaster enters and tells his family and friends about an astonishing mesmerist he saw perform; the man could make people fall asleep and confess what weighs on their consciences. The mention of "the Polish Jew's winter" a few moments later brings about a remarkable but secret change in Mathias: he stops eating and hears the sound of sleigh bells that no one else hears. After the others leave, he is haunted by a vision of the merchant.

When he recovers the next day, Mathias is eager to see Annette and Christian wed. He still hears bells and discusses the case of the Polish Jew with Christian, who became interested enough in the story to reread accounts of the murder. The young man thinks he knows who might have killed the merchant—someone with a limekiln, which might have destroyed the body—and Mathias jokes: "Take care, Christian—take care. Why, I, myself had a limekiln burning at the time the crime was committed" (334). They laugh at the improbability of the thought, but later Mathias is driven nearly to distraction by the sound of bells at the wedding and afterward. That night, he dreams he is on trial for the Jew's murder. Although he denies the crime, the bells torment him, and the mesmerist he saw at the fair draws out the truth. As the dream-judge pronounces the sentence—death by hanging—death bells become wedding bells, the scene returns to the inn, and Mathias fails to answer knocking at the door. Christian breaks in to discover the Burgomaster "haggard, and ghastly pale":

> (*in a voice of strangulation*) The rope! the rope! Take the rope from my neck! (*He falls suddenly, and is caught in the arms of HANS and WALTER, who carry him to the chair in centre of stage. The Bell heard off. . . . His hand clutch[es] at his throat as if to remove something that strangles him. . . . his head falls on his breast.* (346)

"Dead!" cries his wife. The bells stop, and the curtain falls on a tableau.

That tableau—striking, sad, impossibly familiar—is one of the many melodramatic conventions *The Bells* shares with earlier plays. Murderers are often haunted by their crimes: Mathias's dream and hallucination recall the supernatural agonies of William Corder before he is hanged in *The Murder in the Red Barn*. The Burgomaster's guilty madness echoes that of Sweeney Todd on the witness stand. Characters in Lewis's play are also familiar. Annette is the standard two-dimensional heroine, while Christian could be any of the strong, virtuous, and rather dim heroes of earlier works. Mathias has the arrogance of a Lady Audley. Justice serves him out with relentless authority: murderers, as in much Victorian literature, do not escape their crimes and even pursue themselves to their punishment. Yet for all its similarity to most melodramas, *The Bells* is distinctive. Murder does *not* out. For the other characters, the story is simply one of a wedding and the sad death of the bride's father. The private nature of the retribution, the ineptitude of the detectives, and the relative success of the respectable killer raise questions especially relevant to late Victorian crime literature.

Like *The Bells, The Silver King* (1883) has some of the attributes of typical melodrama but transforms them to influence the theatre of the period. Jones's story of an innocent man who believes he has committed a murder was hailed as a work of startling brilliance and glory in part because of what preceded it. That same year, *Pluck,* a play by Augustus Harris and Henry Pettit, included

> a double train-crash, the interruption of a wedding breakfast (with the arrest of the bridegroom), the placing of the corpse of a murdered banker inside a Chatwood safe, the chance appearance of most of the surviving characters outside the Criterion Restaurant during a snowstorm at dead of night and the reunion in the same place and at the same time of a father and his long-lost child.[8]

Little wonder that Sala greeted *The Silver King,* a strong play that is far from a work of genius, as though it were divine: "There is a rift in the clouds, a break of blue in the dramatic heavens, and it seems as if we were . . . fairly at the end of the unlovely" (Jackson, 5). No less a critic than Matthew Arnold thought Jones's play a work of art:

> The diction and sentiments are natural, they have sobriety and propriety, they are literature. It is an excellent and hopeful sign to find playwrights capable of writing in this style, actors capable of rendering it, a public capable of enjoying it.[9]

In contrast to *The Bells, The Silver King* has been considered excellent independent of its cast, "an actor-proof play."[10] With it, Jones won "the support of intelligent critics" (Cordell, 39).

The triumph of hero Wilfred Denver over his enemies met with strong popular as well as critical approval. *The Silver King* "was selected by the King for the Actors' Benefit performance in 1914" (Cordell, 38), thirty-two years after its debut. Jones had hoped to receive a knighthood for his work at the time, although as Richard Cordell points out, that honor was not bestowed on those who satirized political hypocrisy and title-buying, as Jones did in *Mary Goes First* (235). As late as 1925, Jones claimed that his play "had been performed every week night somewhere, since its initial production" (Cordell, 37). The Wilson Barrett company played *The Silver King* as a serious drama, along with *East Lynne* and *Maria Martin,* both during and after World War II (Booth, *English Melodrama,* 177). Its success is particularly impressive in view of Shaw's complaint in 1895: "Nowadays an actor cannot open a letter or toss off somebody else's glass of poison without having to face a brutal outburst of jeering" (Booth, *English Melodrama,* 178).

Hailed as the long-awaited marriage of art and theatre, *The Silver King,* like *The Bells,* used many stock melodramatic characters and devices. The play opens with that famous figure of temperance drama, the good-hearted hero who has drunk himself nearly into the gutter. Wilfred Denver loses his last cent betting on the horses, then goes into deeper debt by gambling in an attempt to win enough money to save his house and family. Taunted about his bad luck and drunkenness by Geoffrey Ware, a man who had unsuccessfully courted Denver's wife, Nelly, before they were married, Denver vows vengeance. A criminal gang led by elegant Captain Skinner starts to rob Ware's house in his absence. Interrupted by Denver, the thieves chloroform him. Ware returns before they can leave. Skinner tries to talk his way out of the house but resorts regretfully to killing Ware when Ware will not believe the Captain's story. When Denver awakens, he speaks to Ware's porter and then discovers himself alone with the corpse of the man he threatened to kill. As in *The Ticket-of-Leave Man* and *Jonathan Bradford,* an innocent man is believed to have committed a terrible crime.

In *The Silver King,* Denver too believes he is a killer and returns to confess his crime to his wife. She protects him and urges him to escape. He catches a train and plans to leave it at an early stop, hoping to lead the police into thinking he is still on board. When the train crashes after Denver leaves it, he realizes that everyone—the police and his family—will think him dead and that he will have to remain silent for his own protection. He escapes to America, assumes a new name, John Franklin, and gets rich by discovering silver in Nevada. The "Silver King" returns to England to watch his family from a distance more than three years later; he fears telling them his identity because he is still a wanted man. They are dreadfully poor and ill, but with the constancy of melodrama, they speak kindly of Denver. He reveals himself to Jaikes, the faithful servant who works for Nelly long beyond her ability to pay his wages. Through Jaikes, Denver gives his wife and children money.

Denver tracks the gang who killed Ware, disguising himself to discover the truth, and learns of Skinner's guilt. Skinner tries to blackmail him into silence, but one of the gang turns state's evidence. Baxter, the police detective, is thus able to arrest the murderer. "I've no desire for revenge—my only wish is to clear my name,"[11] declares Denver at the play's end. The family kneels together in thankful prayer.

Both *The Silver King* and *The Bells,* with their arrogant villains and haunted hero-villains, draw on the stereotypes of earlier melodramas, but their emphasis on the ineptitude of detectives and on "respectable" criminals is significantly new. Walter tells his listeners about the fruitless efforts of Quartermaster Kelz, who was investigating the Polish Jew's murder: "How he travelled about! What witnesses he badgered! What clues he discovered! What information and reports were written! and how the coat and cap were analysed, and examined by magistrates and doctors!—but it all came to nothing" (324). Audiences would likely have remembered similar searches described in *The Times*—in the Waterloo Bridge case, for example—with identical and frustrating results. Kelz is capable of great activity but not of cerebration, and he arrests two brothers who owned an old bear:

> The report was that they had caused the Jew to be eaten by the dogs and the bear, and that they only refrained from swallowing the cloak and cap, because they had had enough. They were arrested, and it would have gone hard with the poor devils, but Mathias interested himself in their case, and they were discharged, after being in prison fifteen months. (324–25)

How Mathias helped them earn a relatively light sentence is not clear, but his interest in the case would seem to be another example of why he is so well-respected in the community: he is fair and just.

Official and unofficial detectives in *The Bells* can not approach the crime's solution because they are blinded by Mathias's rank and seeming virtue. Like the foolish, bumbling police detectives he resembles in late Victorian journalism, Kelz remains wholly ineffective. Mathias led him away from the truth—that he is the murderer—while bringing him toward the truth that the brothers were innocent. A generation later, Christian takes up the case to no avail. Although he realizes that the body must have been burned in a limekiln, his respect for Mathias renders his insight useless. He discusses the murderer's intelligence with the murderer and, like earlier villains, Mathias is pleased with the recognition:

CHRISTIAN: The man who committed that murder must have been a clever fellow.
MATHIAS: Yes, he was not a fool.
CHRISTIAN: A fool! He would have made one of the cleverest gendarmes in the department.
MATHIAS (*with a smile*): Do you really think so? (333–34)

Later, Mathias's high opinion of his future son-in-law soars higher when Christian explains the difficulty of escaping such a thorough search as Kelz's: "I quite agree with you, Christian; and what you say shows your good sense. . . . I should think it requires a great amount of courage to resist the first success in crime" (334). Christian may be smarter than Kelz—he draws the right conclusion about the limekiln—but there is no evidence that he would have realized that the Burgomaster—Mathias, the man who "deserves all the success he has achieved" (325)—could have committed the murder. Authority and depositions help neither Christian nor Kelz: the bells alone accuse Mathias, and they are his own creation.

Curiously, in the Burgomaster's final dream, it is the mesmerist who becomes detective, priest, and avenger. He hypnotizes the resistant Mathias, who sleeps within his sleep, and commands him to reenact the crime while narrating his thoughts:

MESMERIST: Have you already decided to attack him?
MATHIAS (*after a short silence*): That man is strong. He has broad shoulders. I am thinking that he would defend himself well, should any one attack him. (*He makes a movement.*)
MESMERIST: What ails you?
MATHIAS (*in a low voice*): He looks at me. He has grey eyes. (*As if speaking to himself.*) I must strike the blow!
MESMERIST: You are decided?
MATHIAS: Yes—yes; I will strike the blow! I will risk it! (343)

As Franklin Blake accuses himself under opium in *The Moonstone*, so Mathias shows dreamed witnesses how he killed the Jew. But while Franklin thinks himself innocent, Mathias knows that he is guilty, and his own psyche, disintegrating with fear of discovery, betrays him to his enemies. Like a magician, the mesmerist pulls the crime from Mathias in a few moments of mental legerdemain, fixing the criminal with his strong voice and unrelenting commands. The official detectives can not uncover criminals as esteemed and intelligent as Mathias: the job is left to Mathias and to the mesmerist he creates to undo himself in his dream.

In *The Silver King,* Baxter, the police detective, fares only a little better than Kelz. Hawkshaw can mislead criminals by sitting quietly in a public house, watching them. Baxter has no such luck. Skinner recognizes him immediately. When Baxter tries to unnerve him, Skinner manages to conceal his fear:

> BAXTER:   They've caught the man who committed the jewel robbery at Lady Fairford's. (*giving him paper and indicating paragraph*) It may interest you, it seems he was quite a swell, as well dressed as you are!
> SKINNER:   Was he? The cheek of these fellows!
> BAXTER:   You're right—they are cheeky¹ (*Looks straight at SKINNER for some moments. SKINNER's face remains perfectly impassive. BAXTER speaks aside.*) A cucumber isn't in it with him. (43)

Shortly afterward, Skinner leads the detective from the crime about to take place: "Follow me up! I'll lead you a pretty dance tonight" (44). Sure enough, Baxter trails him and misses important conversation.

Baxter's powers of deduction exist only in moderation. Just three-and-a-half years later, he meets John Franklin, the "Silver King," while tracking down Franklin's criminal secretary. The stage directions tell us that Denver's hair has turned almost all white and that he looks older, sadder. But three-and-a-half years is not a long time. Baxter knows he looks familiar but is unable to place him. Later, Denver uncovers the truth of the murder, while Baxter only knows "there's some big swag about here tonight" (97). It is the falsely accused man, not Baxter, who has watched the killer "day and night for the last five months" (100). Baxter muddies the waters and can not solve crimes, raising, as do Kelz and the actual police detectives scorned in late-century journalism, serious questions about the ability of the police force to protect its citizenry.

Murderers in these plays are much smarter than those paid to pursue them, and their lives as respectable community members are not faked. Mathias and Skinner really *are* respected members of their communities. The villagers consider the Burgomaster to have been "born under a lucky star," and he has the authority and dignity of a country squire (325). He treats Christian with generosity, hoping, of course, that in case of trouble later, his son-in-law will protect him:

> CHRISTIAN:   You know, Burgomaster, I do not bring much.
> MATHIAS:   You bring courage and good conduct—I will take care of the rest; and now let us talk of other matters. (333)

The wedding of Annette and Christian brings the whole village on stage to celebrate, and Mathias is the focus of the occasion as Burgomaster, father of the bride, and, unknown to all except the audience, anguished murderer. Mathias behaves well. He acts with good sense and kindness. He killed the Jew to insure the success of the inn and his crime brought him hoped-for security. Unlike Lady Audley, who marries above herself and conceals her bigamy, Mathias is unsuspected of duplicity. He is not, in fact, duplicitous: after committing one crime, he returned to living the life of the just. Though haunted by the bells, he lived untroubled for many years after the murder because of his wit and position.

Mathias's arrogance seems justified. He is the only one who can catch up with himself, since the villagers are respectful and slow-witted. After worrying about his reaction to the bells, he thinks: "what a lesson! Would anyone believe that the mere talk about the Jew could bring on such a fit? Fortunately the people about here are such idiots that they suspect nothing" (331). Mathias is also proud of his self-control—he kills once, then renounces crime—and of his foresight in selecting Christian to marry Annette. Once the young man is part of the family, Mathias will have brought a loyal official into his home as a final security. Where Sweeney Todd feigns membership in the middle classes, Mathias genuinely belongs there. His motive for murder and his behavior in the years since the crime award him his position as rightfully as his talent does.

Captain Skinner possesses the taste, temperament, and values of the aristocracy, and, like Mathias, is clearly superior to those who pursue him. Closer to Raffles than to Corder, the Spider is elegant, even fastidious. He appears to be "very well dressed; light summer overcoat and faultless evening wear" (43). Called to the robbery at Ware's, Skinner waits while a henchman removes his coat for him to uncover another set of "faultless" dress clothes (50). "What the plague did you want me for tonight?" he complains. "I was just starting for Lady Blanche Wynter's dinner party" (50). A "West End villain" for the newly respectable theatre audiences (Booth, *English Melodrama,* 163), Skinner alone knows how to behave correctly and tries hopelessly to teach the other criminals how to be gentlemen. When he suggests that Cripps has been impolite to Mrs. Skinner, Cripps is disgusted:

> CRIPPS:  I hates politeness. I hates folks as are civil and stuck up.
> SKINNER:  My dear fellow, consider the dignity of our profession. There's no reason why we shouldn't be gentlemen.
> CRIPPS:  Gentlemen! There's nothing of the gentleman about me.
> SKINNER:  Hush, don't tell us so, or we shall begin to believe it by and by. (64)

Also fluent and unflappable, Skinner tries to slip out of Ware's house before resorting to violence: "We are friends of your clerk—we met him at the Derby, and he insisted on our coming here to spend the evening with him, and so naturally, as a matter of course—(*coolly putting tools in box*)—excuse me, I have an appointment" (51). His tastes, talents, and manners seem to have earned him his "luxuriously furnished apartment" in Bromley, a location "in much favour with City merchants" for its "quiet air of conscious respectability" (Jones 63, 63n.).

Skinner displays a curious upper-crust fastidiousness about what is and is not done. His squeamishness about the murder of Ware seems to spring as much from a sense of etiquette as it does from remorse: more so. "I've gone a step too far this time," he worries as he leaves the murder weapon near Denver. "Why wouldn't he let me pass?" (51) Oddly compulsive, he wipes his hands after shaking with Coombe, a gang member: "'It's damned dirty—what of that? It's honest! The shake of an honest hand does me good.' (*Takes out his handkerchief and wipes his hand behind his back.*)" (90) Coombe's hand is about as honest as Iago's, but Skinner divides the work: he provides the brains and the public relations, others supply violence. His uneasiness about the murder springs from a kind of disgust with the lower task. When threatening Coombe, he and Cripps play a hot-and-cool duet:

> CRIPPS:   . . . Handle me gentle, use me well, fair and square, I've got the temper of a sucking lamb, haven't I, Spider?
> SKINNER:   You have, Mr. Cripps, and also its playfulness and innocence.
> CRIPPS:   But rub me the wrong way—come any dodge, try to do me out of my fair share of the swag, and then—! (*Brings fist down on the table with tremendous force.*)
> SKINNER:   Then you have the ferocity of the British lion in mortal combat with the apocryphal unicorn. Now, Coombe, once more, where are Lady Blanche's diamonds? (93)

He prefers not to play rough, and this odd preference explains his cruelty to Nelly even when he is unaware of her identity as Denver's "widow." She and her children have been living on his land in a small, rundown cottage, but they can not pay their rent. His wife pleads for the family:

> OLIVE:   Herbert, you don't really mean to turn that poor woman and her children out of that wretched cottage?
> SKINNER:   Yes, I do!
> OLIVE:   Why?
> SKINNER:   They are starving, one of the children is dying. I object to people starving and dying on my property. (63)

When Nelly herself makes her case, Skinner refuses to let her stay for what seem like aesthetic reasons:

> SKINNER:   Now please don't make a scene. I've made up my mind to pull down that cottage. It isn't fit for a dog to live in.
> NELLY:   Then let me live in it, and my children, only for a few days—only till my child is better—or dead.

SKINNER:  Yes, that's just it! Your child may die—and I don't wish him to die on my property, a hundred yards from my door. I dislike death, it's a nuisance, and I don't wish to
be reminded of it. (67)

His "peculiar abstract distaste for the poor" reflects his later assertion that poverty, not theft, is the real crime in England (Jackson, 7; Jones, 63).

The motives of murderers in these two plays are sensible and pragmatic.
Mathias needs money to continue life in the middle class: "If I have not three
thousand francs by the 31st," he broods while hypnotized, "the inn will be
taken from me" (342). He hesitates at the thought of murder, but his necessity,
the Jew's anonymity, and the heavily laden money belt persuade him to act.
There is nothing of Todd's psychosis or Corder's demonic energy here.
Mathias has simply identified the answer to his problem—and he is right. Once
he murders and steals, his life *is* better, and he remains undiscovered by guilt
for years, until the heavy Christmas eve snows and the village conversation
bring back the night of his crime. Skinner is similarly pragmatic. Far from
"mysteriously evil . . . he simply needs to save his own skin" (Jackson, 7). Although he regrets having to kill Ware—he is a thief and prefers to specialize—
he must do so in order to survive. When Denver finally confronts the real murderer with his crime, Skinner hopes to make a practical bargain: "We are both
in a devil of a mess. Why not make a mutual concession, silence for silence—
you keep quiet on my affairs, I will keep quiet on yours—you allow me to pursue my business, I allow you to pursue yours" (101). Like Brecht's version of
the West End villain, Macheath, Skinner sees himself primarily as a
businessman who makes decisions based on common sense rather than on rage
or an irrelevant distinction between right and wrong.

The breast-beating, hand-wringing remorse of murderers in earlier popular
literature has been reduced to Mathias's advice to himself—"You must be
cleverer than that, Mathias; you mustn't run your neck into a halter. . . . You
will die an old man yet, Mathias" (331)—and his desire to escape the bells and
the Jew's eyes. Skinner's remorse is really worried distaste, and Denver, believing himself to be the killer, co-opts the traditional haunted dreams:

Do you know what a murderer's sleep is? It's the waking time of conscience! It's the whip-
ping-post she ties him to while she lashes and stings his poor helpless guilty soul! Sleep! it's
a bed of spikes and harrows! It's a precipice over which he falls sheer upon the jags and forks
of memory! It's a torchlight procession of devils, raking out every infernal sewer and cranny
of his brain! (84)

Here is the traditional remorse of the murderer, except the real killer does not
experience these torments. Skinner is only afraid of getting caught. In these
late-century plays, criminals may get what they deserve, but not with the conviction that characterized earlier works.

The respectable women in *The Silver King* are accomplices to the men they marry. Where midcentury female criminals pretended to be decent women, Nelly Denver and Olive Skinner really *are* nice women who help to cover up crimes. Mrs. Skinner begs her husband to do the right thing in the ringing tones of any melodramatic heroine: "Herbert, can't you make some reparation, can you not do something to wipe the stain off that man's memory?" (64) Yet although she frightens Skinner briefly with a whispered reference to the murder, he is himself again in a moment, and she can not follow up her advantage:

> OLIVE:    You're not quite deaf to the voice of conscience, it seems.
> SKINNER:    I wish to goodness I could be deaf to your voice occasionally. (64)

At first, Mrs. Skinner delights when her husband's retribution appears to be at hand. Her loyalty and love, however, overpower her sense of justice. She races to help Skinner escape. "Will you do as I tell you?" he asks. "You know I will—if it's to save you," she replies (95). She has her own moral qualms— her own fastidiousness—about what Skinner does for a living, but she continues to live with him in their luxurious home and, one assumes, to dress for dinner.

Nelly Denver resembles many virtuous melodramatic heroines of earlier plays, but she also acts as her husband's accomplice for good and proper reasons. "Isn't a wife's place by her husband's side?" she asks when Denver winces at seeing her in the skittle alley (45). She will not abandon him, even when she believes he has killed Ware. His confession elicits only a request for more details—"How did it happen?" (53)—and a "great cry of pity" (54). The symbolic "blood on his hands" does not cause horror. Instead, Nelly urges him to hide. While he speaks darkly of "trying to get away from him and from myself," Nelly plans:

> You mustn't stay here! This will be the first place they will search. You must go to one of the big railway stations and take a ticket for a long distance—do you see—make it appear you are trying to leave the country, and then you must leave the train at the first station, and so throw them off the scent. (54)

Even Denver seems astonished by her fast thinking. When he asks, "Why don't you curse me?" she responds: "Because you never had so much need of my love and of my prayers as you have now. We're wasting time. What money have you?" (54). Nelly becomes both accomplice and instructor. She and Olive conceal crimes for reasons as proper as Mathias's wish to prosper as an innkeeper: they are good, loyal wives.

Women in *The Silver King* are criminal even in the low comedy of the village. When Jaikes, the Denvers' servant, tells people that he has inherited money to keep Wilfred's return a secret, an old flame tries to wheedle her way into his affections. Tabby, a woman who once "set her cap" at Jaikes, has been thrice-married and thrice-widowed. When she proposes to him, he is aghast: "Married! Me marry you! Why, you old Mormon, (*TABBY starts back horrified*) you old female Henry the Eighth! You old wolf in sheep's clothing! You—you, you old Bluebeard in petticoats! Me marry you! Never! Never!" (83) The connection between sexuality and violence that was so significant in early and midcentury works returns in *The Silver King* as a joke, but all the women in the play have the potential to be criminals.

Jones's play, more inventive and sophisticated in design than Lewis's, features a range of subplots in which respectability is an issue. The criminality of the ordinary middle class is quite wonderful. Selwyn, John Franklin's private secretary, forges his name on a check; Denver, as Franklin, kindly covers for him in Baxter's presence and later sets him on the right path (78). The "nice" children do not play with Denver's daughter Cissy because their "fathers and mothers are respectable" (71). The one scrap of comfort a girl offers her— "don't you tell anybody—I love you if the others don't" (72)—must be given in secret. And the tradesmen and parish clerk at an inn where Denver hides relish murders as particular delicacies:

> BROWNSON:    . . . It's my belief that women never look at a newspaper for anything except these spicy little bits.
>
> BINKS:   Well, a divorce is all very well in its way, but I say give me a jolly good murder, one as ain't found out for a month or two, and puzzles judge and jury and everybody. That's what I like.
>
> BROWNSON:   Ah! and where you ain't quite certain it's the right man till after he's hung, eh? (*regretfully*) Ah! we don't get such murders nowadays. (58)

The comedy stems from their detachment and offhand discussion of Denver's crime—uninteresting because he obviously did it—but the implications about the criminality of nice people are clear in the serious scenes as well as the light ones.

People in the play do terrible things in the name of respectability; Corkett's desire to be a gentleman is both amusing and symbolic. He lights a cigar with currency to show that "money ain't no object to me" (42). He steals his employer's money to bet on horses so that he might sooner behave as aristocrats do. His loud imitation of Skinner's spare elegance shows the difference between spurious and real class. After blackmailing the Spider about Ware's murder, Corkett saunters in wearing an "outrageous tweed suit, eyeglass, crutch-stick, white hat, light kid gloves" (92). Skinner seems as appalled by his outfit as he does by his blackmail, and the news that Corkett has charged his clothes to Skinner at his own tailor causes him to lose his temper. Eventually, Corkett turns state's evidence but not before participating in several crimes. When Coombe arrives at the cottage to evict Nelly, he does the wrong thing in the right way:

COOMBE: Now, my dear good lady, there's a pleasant way of doing things and an unpleasant, and I always try the pleasant way first.
NELLY: Oh, don't make any words about it. You have come to turn me out, is it not so?
COOMBE: Oh, dear no. I've only come to ask you in the kindest possible manner to pay
your rent. Three pounds five shillings. (77)

He knows she is penniless, but Skinner has trained him to use respectable manners when committing legal or moral crimes. The gang breaks up in a dither
of theft—Corkett steals the money the Spider stole from Coombe, which was
stolen from Lady Blanche—and the play concludes with the lines between the
criminal and the respectable barely visible.

In many ways, Denver is, like Mathias, a criminal hero. He has not committed murder, but he sometimes behaves with abominable self-absorption.
When learning that the train he escaped crashed, burning all the passengers to
cinders, he falls to his knees to thank God for answering his prayers. His most
animated, tortured speeches involve his own guilt and suffering, not Nelly's.
Although he has tried to send her money without success—she and the children
change addresses several times—it is hard not to wonder whether he could
have devised some more effective way of helping them. While his family drags
on, ill and barely alive, he lives in wealth as the "Silver King," an important
and esteemed exile. He behaves generously toward Selwyn and Skinner, but
Jones, like the author of *Eugene Aram,* must work hard to make his hero's actions explicable and admirable.

Denver, Skinner, and Mathias suggest many disturbing questions about the
nature of respectability and of criminality. Unlike the criminals of earlier plays,
Mathias, in many ways, does escape culpability. No one ever knows he is a
murderer, and he lives safely with his homicide for many happy years. While
he does not wind up living to the old age he plans, he still gets away with murder for a long time. His overscaled guilt only torments him when circumstances
conspire against him. Skinner does not impersonate the aristocrats he robs: he
is of them already. His pride in his servants perversely mirrors that of any
wealthy householder:

My coachman has just done eighteen months; my cook's a jewel—she's the one that stole
Lord Farthinghoe's silver—I always like to encourage enterprise. My housemaid was born
in Durham jail, and my footman I took out of charity when his father went to do his fourteen
years. In fact, I haven't a soul about the place that I can't trust. (65)

In extremity, Skinner decides to "cut the gang" after their next theft, "disappear, retire to some quiet country place, go to church regularly, turn church-
warden and set an example to the parish" (67). There is no reason to suppose
that he would be less worthy a churchgoer than those who forgo murder.

Skinner is a philosopher as well as a businessman. He argues that crime
is part of the natural cycle:

My dear Olive, all living creatures prey upon one another. The duck gobbles up the worm, the man gobbles up the duck and then the worm gobbles up the man again. It's the great law of nature. My profession is just as good as any other, till I'm found out. (63)

Influenced more by Charles Darwin than by Jack Sheppard, Skinner suggests that his crime is both natural and necessary for the community as a whole. Denver's gambling and drinking may also be part of this cycle. Jaikes explains that his master is "a bit wild" because "he's got too much nature in him, that's where it is" (40). Like his father, he is always "larking, hunting, drinking, fighting, steeple-chasing—any mortal spree under the sun" (40). Both the criminal hero and the respectable villain behave as their natures dictate.

In both *The Bells* and *The Silver King*, then, nature is criminal, and crime is natural. Respectability does more than simply conceal murder and theft. The motives for being respectable and prosperous are the same as those for committing crimes. Mathias and Skinner purchase respectability with their murders and thefts. It becomes difficult to distinguish between motives for crime and motives for evicting the poor or being generous to a son-in-law who can be helpful. Similarly, Olive Skinner and Nelly Denver behave with admirable loyalty to their husbands, but this very loyalty makes them accomplices and then criminals. In these works, normal motives—even Skinner's desire to appear as a proper gentleman—bring people to crime. Stage murderers, then, no longer kill only through madness or passion. They kill with the same motives that make members of the audience consider themselves good citizens.[12]

# 9

# Fiction, 1870–1900

"There is nothing in this world that has not happened," detective Martin Hewitt remarks, "or is not happening in London." A world-weary Sherlock Holmes echoes Hewitt's observation: "There is nothing new under the sun. It has all been done before."[1] Late-century crime fiction reflects this grim perception of crime as unchanging, ever-present, relentlessly repetitive. In many novels and stories that feature murder, crime is highly organized and implacable. The calculating, coldblooded murders of mid-Victorian popular genres are replaced by a larger, more completely amoral threat to decent society. Although ruthless doctors like Palmer and Pritchard committed premeditated rather than impassioned murders, their motives were simply financial. Lady Audley's improvisational violence springs from her terror of exposure and the ensuing loss of her social standing. Late-century murderers in popular fiction kill for more removed and distressing reasons. Individuals or gangs murder for religious or intellectual—occasionally even aesthetic—motives. The accounts of conspiracies, gangs, and cults in popular writing stress the stark proficiency, inhumanity, and moral depravity of late-century murder.

Detectives and their criminal counterparts show strong and ominous resemblances to each other; virtuous and murderous impulses are often lodged within one person. In order to combat highly organized professional criminals, police and detectives adopt criminal methods. But sometimes the crime solvers become criminals themselves for other reasons than the desire to see rough justice done. For revenge, for love, or for sport, detectives discard their professional responsibilities with alacrity, occasionally even using their special knowledge to escape punishment. Their liability to moral failings and human passions eliminates the final protection against thieves and murderers. Their deductive powers and their attention to the minutiae of crime only further undermine any hope for safety and justice. Holmes's special knowledge—of exotic cigarette ash, for example—might have helped him to become a master criminal, as he sometimes muses; the more adeptly police and detectives solve crimes, the better equipped they are to commit them.

Like police and detectives in late-century popular fiction, ordinary characters are also capable of extraordinary criminality. No one is incorruptible and no trusted member of the community or family is above the most hateful deeds or motives. In earlier fiction, sly murderers like Hortense, the maidservant in *Bleak House,* or Madeline Smith, who killed her former lover to protect her future marriage, shock because they are unexpected and incongruous; their crimes erupt from within protected middle- or upper-class settings. By the end of the century, friends, lovers, servants, and relatives are exactly those who commit murders: it is no longer incongruous for anyone to kill. Late Victorian popular fiction reflects a disintegration of faith in human nature and despair at the prospect of curbing crime. "There's the scarlet thread of murder running through the colorless skein of life," Holmes intones, and the very blandness of the "skein" becomes a constant threat of violent crime (Doyle I, 36).

A *Study in Scarlet,* "The Sign of Four," "The Five Orange Pips," and "The Final Problem" are Sir Arthur Conan Doyle's most significant contributions to the late-century literature of conspiracy. In A *Study in Scarlet,* a man is killed violently, the word "RACHE" painted in blood on the wall above his body. "There was something so methodical and so incomprehensible about the deeds of this unknown assassin," Watson shudders, "that it imparted a fresh ghastliness to his crimes" (47). Holmes discovers that RACHE refers to a secret criminal society that is not involved in this murder, a blind to conceal the identity of the murdered man and the motive for the crime. Later, the man is identified as Drebber, and his secretary, Joseph Strangerson, is also killed. After the surprise arrest of Jefferson Hope, the American who committed the crimes, the story unfolds in flashback: Hope killed both men because they caused the death of his fiancée, Lucy Ferrier, years ago in Utah. Drebber and Strangerson were Mormons, and Lucy's father had been murdered by them because he refused to permit his daughter to marry into the Mormon faith and become one of a group of wives.

Doyle depicts the Mormons as cold, frightening, and all-powerful religious fanatics. They kill those who believe differently or who present obstacles. The Ferriers come to live among them after being saved by Mormons in the desert. Converting to Mormonism is a condition of their rescue: "Better far that your bones should bleach in this wilderness than that you should prove to be that little speck of decay which in time corrupts the whole fruit," the spokesman for the Mormons says ominously (57). Ferrier becomes a useful and respected member of the Mormon community, although he would not "set up a female establishment after the manner of his companions" (59). Lucy falls in love with Jefferson Hope after he saves her when a bull gores her horse. But John Ferrier is told that Lucy has interested the sons of two important Mormons, Drebber and Strangerson, and that she must choose between them in thirty days or else: "It were better for you . . . that you and she were now lying blanched skeletons upon the Sierra Blanco, than that you should put your weak wills against the orders of the Holy Four" (59).

Unfortunately for the Ferriers, this warning is not hollow. The devotion to the Mormon creed is obsessive and inhumane; individual preferences must be erased for the common "good," lack of conformity punishable by death. A retributive force within the Mormon camp, called the "Danite Band," polices the behavior and speech of the faithful: "Even the most saintly dared only to whisper their religious opinions with bated breath, lest something which fell from their lips might be misconstrued, and bring down a swift retribution upon them" (62). No one knew the members of this avenging group: "The very friend to whom you communicated your misgivings . . . might be one of those who would come forth at night with fire and sword to exact a terrible reparation" (63). The band was conceived as a way to punish recalcitrants who wanted to leave or distort the Mormon faith; yet soon "it took a wider range" and a shortage of women was followed by "fresh women" who "bore upon their faces the traces of an unextinguishable horror" (62, 63).

Horribly efficient, the "Danite Band" strikes mysteriously. After insulting the two young Mormon suitors who come to wrangle over marrying Lucy, John Ferrier starts receiving bizarre warnings. The first is a note pinned to his bed covers while he sleeps: "Twenty-nine days are given you for amendment, and then—" (67). Every day a new warning appears in a different place, counting down the days, and Ferrier can not stop them or find out how they are posted: "Sometimes the fatal numbers appeared on the walls, sometimes upon the floors, occasionally they were on small placards stuck upon the garden gate or the railings. . . . A horror which was almost superstitious came upon him at the sight of them" (67). Ferrier sends a desperate message to Hope, who arrives two days before the month is out. Although Hope sneaks the Ferriers out of Mormon territory, he returns from fetching food to discover Ferrier dead and buried beneath a newly dug grave identified by a handmade sign. Lucy has been kidnapped. Hope's pioneering ingenuity is no match for the Mormons' relentless organization. He cannot prevent Ferrier's murder or Lucy's marriage to Drebber; by the time he locates her, she has "pined away and died" (74), and he spends the next twenty years pursuing Drebber and Stangerson to revenge the deaths of the Ferriers. Finally, nearly dead himself from an aortic aneurism, Hope achieves his life's aim.

"The Sign of Four," "The Five Orange Pips," and "The Final Problem" also focus on organized gangs and criminal alliances. In "The Sign of Four," Major Sholto dies of shock when seeing a threatening face in the window, and his son is killed later; the murderer leaves a note reading "The sign of the four" by Bartholomew Sholto's body. Greed and revenge animate these fatal events. Four men sign a treasure map indicating vast riches that are inaccessible because Jonathan Small, their leader, was in prison; two officers who learn of the treasure rob the men, and Bartholomew Sholto, one conspirator's son, is killed by Small's savage associate. As in *A Study in Scarlet,* alliances quickly become criminal with fatal consequences for innocent people. "The Five Orange Pips" presents the fatal "outrages" of the Ku Klux Klan, who murder opponents after sending them a warning "in some fantastic but generally recognized shape—a sprig of oak-leaves in some parts, melon seeds or orange pips in others."[2] Like the "Danite Band," the KKK is omnipotent and fearfully effective: "So perfect was the organization of the society, and so systematic its methods, that there is hardly a case upon record where any man succeeded in braving it with impunity, or in which any of its outrages were traced home to the perpetrators" (Doyle I, 226). Although Holmes discovers the identities of two KKK murderers, he does not uncover the entire group to which they belong.

In "The Final Problem," organized crime is given a face: that of "the Napoleon of crime," Professor Moriarty.[3] Brilliant, evil Moriarty invents the most various and sophisticated crimes in London; as with the "Danite Band" or the KKK, criminals under his direction may be captured without impeding the murderous activities of the whole organization. Holmes is frustrated by Moriarty's invisibility, which seems to accentuate his triumph over the great detective: "The man pervades London, and no one has heard of him. That's what puts him on a pinnacle in the records of crime," Holmes explains to Watson (Doyle I, 470). His evil intellect directs a vast criminal network: "He is the organizer of half that is evil and of nearly all that is undetected in this great city. . . . He sits motionless, like a spider in the centre of its web, but that web has a thousand radiations, and he knows well every quiver of each of them" (471). His anonymity is a taunting reminder of his brilliance, and only Holmes, a genius of the same order, even knows Moriarty exists.

*The Valley of Fear* (1915), written near the end of Doyle's career as a crime writer, returns to the theme of conspiracy with chilling energy. Dangerous, impulsive McMurdo joins Lodge 341 in Vermissa (a "most desolate corner of the United States of America")[4] by undergoing a savage ceremony. McGinty, the "Bodymaster" of the Lodge, "sat at the head with a flat black velvet cap upon his shock of tangled black hair, and a coloured purple stole round his neck; so that he seemed to be a priest presiding over some diabolical ritual" (115). It was "difficult to believe" that the ordinary members of the Lodge "were in very truth a dangerous gang of murderers, whose minds had suffered such complete moral perversion that they took a horrible pride in their proficiency at the business" (115). Whatever ideological, political motives inspired their early crimes have degenerated into a few desultory remarks about differences among the classes. The Lodge members have sunk into the most ruthless, inhumane crimes, and their murders develop their own aesthetic:

> To their contorted natures it had become a spirited and chivalrous thing to volunteer for service against some man who had never injured them, and whom in many cases they had never seen in their lives. The crime committed, they quarreled as to who had actually struck the fatal blow, and amused one another and the company by describing the cries and contortions of the murdered man. (116)

After being branded, McMurdo becomes a full-fledged member of the Lodge. Dissension in the ranks is quelled before it begins; one brother whose conscience has not atrophied frets: "Whatever we say, even what we think, seems to go back to that man McGinty" (130). After reducing Vermissa's population further, the Lodge is finally halted by McMurdo, a wily detective in disguise. But years later, he is murdered, and Holmes recognizes the hand of Moriarty, whom the American gang consulted and to whom it contracted the murder of McMurdo. Even Holmes can not save this courageous, virtuous man. The story ends on a dark note as Holmes broods about Moriarty's success: " 'I don't say that he can't be beat. But you must give me time—you must give me time!' We all sat in silence for some minutes while those fateful eyes strained to pierce the veil" (174–75). It is no wonder Holmes needs time; he is called upon, as Christopher Clausen observes, to defend "an entire social order . . . deeply threatened by forces that only he is capable of overcoming."[5] Secret societies mean more than the sum of their individual victims. Crime is relentless and hydra-headed, as in earlier Doyle stories.

In order to combat crime that is so organized and ruthless, police and detectives adopt criminal methods. At times they circumvent, bend, or merely avoid the law when traditional systems of justice can not reach the criminals. "I shall be my own police," Holmes announces in "The Five Orange Pips," and with biblical appropriateness, he sends the killers their own warning; although the pips never reach the murderers, they go down on a ship in mysteriously severe gales (228). Holmes shares many qualities with Raffles, the debonair creation of Doyle's brother-in-law, E. W. Hornung. Although both are outsiders who are smarter than the rest of society, Raffles is a criminal, Holmes a detective. "Between them the two brothers-in-law evolved a conception of crime as a perfectly planned military operation," one critic notes.[6] After seeing Holmes force open the catch of a locked window, Inspector Gregson remarks: "It is a mercy that you are on the side of the force, and not against it, Mr. Holmes!"[7]

The worry about inept police that characterizes late-century nonfiction becomes, in popular fiction, the uneasy suspicion that police detectives are corrupted by desires for publicity and bureaucratic advantage rather than for justice. In the Holmes stories and Israel Zangwill's *The Big Bow Mystery* (1892), the authors depict police as competitive thieves of credit. Capturing dangerous criminals and understanding what causes their behavior is secondary to receiving public acclaim for brilliant detective work, work that is often done by others. Not only are Inspectors Gregson and Lestrade less than smart, they also are distressingly plagued with petty rivalries; as Holmes observes: "They have their knives into one another. . . . They are as jealous as a pair of professional beauties" (Doyle I, 27). The police constantly steal credit from Holmes, and the sycophantic tone of the newspaper articles that often conclude one of Sherlock Holmes's brilliant demonstrations of deductive reasoning act as ironic epilogues:

> It is an open secret that the credit of this smart capture belongs entirely to the well-known Scotland Yard officials, Messrs. Lestrade and Gregson. The man was apprehended, it appears, in the rooms of a certain Mr. Sherlock Holmes, who has himself, as an amateur, shown some talent in the detective line and who, with such instructors, may hope in time to attain to some degree of their skill. It is expected that a testimonial of some sort will be presented to the two officers as a fitting recognition of their services. (Doyle I, 86)

Officers receive applause even for the wrong guess; after Inspector Athelney Jones arrests innocent Thaddeus Sholto, a newspaper article sings his praises: "The prompt and energetic action of the officers of the law shows the great advantages of the presence on such occasions of a single vigorous and masterful mind" (Doyle I, 229). The inspectors' dishonesty is minor and amusing; the implication that their top priority is rising in the ranks of Scotland Yard rather than helping to halt criminal activities is not.

The vanity and bureaucratic ambition that cause Scotland Yard inspectors to steal credit from Holmes and from each other seems to infect every character in *Michael Dred, Detective: The Unravelling of a Mystery of Twenty Years* (1899). Using a now well-worn convention, authors Marie and Robert Leighton present a victim whom every character in the novel has good reason to kill. Choleric and mean-spirited Lord Luxmore is murdered, and police arrest his daughter Lena's suitor, the virtuous but poor Paul Wingrove, for the crime. Wingrove had argued openly with Luxmore about his refusal to permit Lena to marry him. However, a duplicitous butler, a vengeful housekeeper who is jealous over Lord Luxmore's upcoming marriage, an erratic and secretive daughter, Beatrix (Lena's younger sister), and a ne'er-do-well aristocratic cousin, Reginald, all have sturdy reasons for wanting Luxmore dead. The possibilities for criminal alliances among them are almost infinite. Dred, the mysterious and moody detective Wingrove consults, uncovers evidence that points in turn to each member of the household and every character. The coroner, in his investigative capacity, addresses the possibility of conspiracy, although he is not aware of the multiplicity of motives that would inspire such plots:

> There appears to have been a remarkable unanimity among the various members of the household in desiring that on this particular evening the rooms should be left in darkness—a unanimity which would suggest, were such a thing not practically impossible, that every member of the family was accessory to the crime, either before or after the fact.[8]

As it turns out, Luxmore has been killed twice, and each of his murderers had no knowledge of the other. Mrs. Vayne, the malicious housekeeper, gave him arsenic to prevent his marriage. When Dred, in love with Luxmore's fiancée, entered the room shortly after, he found the victim in what seemed to be a fit and poisoned him on the spot using a syringe. Although no conspiracies actually existed, the Luxmore residence was alive with motives to murder Lord Luxmore, and only Lena, a stock melodramatic heroine who is less convincing a character than her selfish family and associates, grieves at his death. The grotesque "double" murder might well have been a quadruple crime, and the seething atmosphere of hatred, fear, and greed nurtured a kind of contagious criminality.

In *Michael Dred*, both hero and detective share the criminality of the other characters. Charming, self-sacrificing Paul Wingrove eagerly eavesdrops on Dred's courtship of Luxmore's former fiancée without shame: "I desired to gain information, and I had—and have still—too much at stake to care how I gained it. There is no way of meeting cunning except with equal cunning" (294). Dred's courtship is desperate, sickly: "If you were the worst and cruellest woman living—if you were guilty of the blackest of crimes—I should not love you less" (289). Later, Dred sends Paul a confession, explaining how he killed Luxmore—he removed the dying man's shirt and injected poison into his body—while pretending to help him. With ruthless efficiency, Dred spends the next weeks trying to endanger everyone who might be suspected of the murder he committed: "I occupied myself in accumulating evidence indiscriminately against any and every other person who could possibly be implicated in the affair. I felt no malice against any one of those whom I endeavoured to convict" (320). Because it is not vengeful, Dred's pursuit of the other characters is perhaps even more distressing.

The most successful detectives in late-century crime fiction are those who recognize the inexorable way in which evil runs through "the colourless skein of life." "There is a strong family resemblance about misdeeds, and if you have all the details of a thousand at your finger ends," Holmes tells Watson, "it is odd if you can't unravel the thousand and first" (Doyle I, 24). Holmes's observation and his general ennui imply that a boring brutality infests Victorian London. Crime and criminals are the norm, not the deviation. Mrs. G., the dogged detective in Andrew Forrester's *The Unknown Weapon*, shares Holmes's suspicion of human nature: "We have to believe every man a rogue till, after turning all sorts of evidence inside out, we can only discover that he is an honest man. And even then I am much afraid we are not quite sure of him—."[9] Grodman, the wry investigator of *The Big Bow Mystery*, concurs: "All men—and women—have something to conceal, and you have only to pretend to know what it is."[10]

Detectives could not possess too cynical a vision of human nature. Readers of late Victorian fiction repeatedly witness the homicidal natures of "decent" as well as underworld characters. In "The Poisoner," investigator Paul Beck is saddened but unsurprised to learn that Susan, "a quiet, shy little body" beloved for her placidity and good nature, is a two-time murderer.[11] After she and her accomplice, Dr. Coleman, are discovered, she commits suicide, and her romantic death jars with what the reader now knows to be her terrible ruthlessness:

> Behind the bright chintz curtains, on the white counterpane, Susan Coolin lay dead—soft, pure, and beautiful as a white lily. The wealth of light golden hair lay scattered loose on her pillow like a saint's halo—a tender smile was on her dead lips. She seemed a statue of sleeping innocence, carved by a master-hand. (209)

"It's wonderful," observes Beck, "that a fiend should look so like an angel" (210). Especially grotesque is her lack of viciousness; we never really see what lies beneath her gentle exterior except when she flees, terrified, as Beck invites her to eat a piece of poisoned cake she intended for someone else. Unlike Lady Audley's sotto voce triumph, or the energetic lust of Edith Archbold, we have no way to understand Susan's evil; one character concludes that Dr. Coleman "tempted her to this," and her devotion to him may be one explanation, but it is insufficient (210). Similarly, in "Murder by Proxy," jovial, affectionate Eric commits a murder and does his best to indict his cousin for the crime, while pretending to save him. Only under Beck's canny questioning does Eric break down, changing to a nearly bestial killer in a matter of moments; a voice escaped him, "a voice unlike his own—loud, harsh, hardly articulate; such a voice might have been heard in the torture chamber in the old days when the strain on the rack grew unbearable."[12] Like Sweeney Todd, Eric falls in a timely fit after confessing. But where even his less-than-bright apprentice suspects Todd of crime, Eric remains untarnished by his beleaguered cousin's accusations. Only Beck figures out the truth, and his complete lack of faith in human nature makes him an acute detective.

Israel Zangwill's *The Big Bow Mystery,* a distinctive story that was greatly popular in its time, illustrates many late-century themes in popular crime fiction, especially the corruption of the police by desires for publicity, the criminality of the detective, and the murderer's impersonal motive. In this novel, suspicion of and contempt for the police are palpable. When observing that there were no suspects in the shocking murder of middle-class philanthropist Arthur Constant, the narrator dryly remarks: "The police could not even manufacture a clue" (219). George Grodman, a famous former inspector of Scotland Yard, is summoned to Constant's room by his neighbor Mrs. Drabdump when Constant, her tenant, does not awaken. Grodman lives to humiliate his successor, posh and progressive Edward Wimp. Unconcerned with Wimp's effectiveness as a detective, although Wimp indeed is notorious for "putting two and two together to make five," Grodman fears that his own accomplishments will fade because of his successor's good fortune or deceit: "He [Wimp] almost threatened to eclipse the radiant tradition of Grodman by some wonderfully ingenious bits of workmanship" (243). Grodman writes a letter to the *Pell Mell Press,* taunting Wimp for his inability to quickly solve the case: "The Department has had several notorious failures of late. It is not what it used to be. Crime is becoming impertinent" (230). A letter signed "Scotland Yard" retorts that Grodman's "judgment is failing him in his old age," and the rivalry continues even at Christmas dinner; Wimp has invited Grodman so that he might pump him for information (232). Grodman attends for the same reason.

The drama of agitator Tom Mortlake's arrest by Wimp at a working-class gathering, where Gladstone is to dedicate a portrait of Constant, is followed by the excitement of Mortlake's conviction, over working-class and liberal protests. But to Grodman, it is all merely background to his professional duel with Wimp. At the moment Mortlake is convicted, Grodman feels no pity or outrage, although he knows Mortlake is innocent: "Wimp had won; Grodman felt like a whipped cur" (285). Grodman is ready to have Denzil Cantercot, the ghostwriter of Grodman's best-selling memoirs, arrested to punish him for bringing information about the murder to Wimp. (Even Grodman's book, *Criminals I Have Caught,* is false, written entirely by Cantercot, who receives no credit for it.) Although their competitiveness and dishonesty is humorous, Wimp is morally corrupt—he will arrest anyone to get credit for solving the crime—and Grodman turns out to be corrupt *and* criminal.

Like other detectives in late Victorian fiction, Grodman breaks the law. The night before Mortlake's execution, after Grodman had organized several unsuccessful actions for his release, the former detective visits the Home Secretary. During a lengthy, abstract lecture on the vagaries of evidence and human psychology, he informs the Home Secretary that since Mrs. Drabdump *expected* to see Constant dead when she and Grodman burst into his room, that is what she saw, although Constant was really only "sleeping the sleep of the just" under the influence of a sleeping powder Grodman had given him the night before for his toothache (294). When Grodman cries out as if he saw something horrible, "a mist as of blood swam before Mrs. Drabdump's eyes. She cowered back . . . she shut off the dreaded sight with her hands. In that instant I made my cut" (299). Thus, Grodman commits murder in front of a witness and confesses only to thwart Wimp's victory. Saving the innocent Mortlake is secondary:

> That Wimp should achieve a reputation he did not deserve, and overshadow all his predecessors by dint of a colossal mistake, this seemed to be intolerable. . . . As the overweening Wimp could not be allowed to go down to posterity as the solver of this terrible mystery, I decided that the condemned man might just as well profit by his exposure. (301)

Grodman kills Constant for the pleasure of devising a crime that can not be solved. Where Lord Luxmore deserves his death, Constant is preternaturally good, and Grodman's decision to kill him is simply perverse: "I do not know when I have ever taken to a man more. . . . It is a pity humanity should have been robbed of so valuable a life. But it had to be" (297). He shares with Cantercot an appreciation of the aesthetic: "And yet criminals would go on sinning, and giving themselves away, in the same old grooves—no originality, no dash, no individual insight, no fresh conception!" He longed to show criminals "their lack of artistic feeling and restraint" (296, 297). Grodman is eventually robbed even of his confession when the Home Secretary reveals that last-minute evidence clearing Mortlake had arrived just before Grodman did, and the former detective shoots himself. Yet Grodman comes dangerously close to achieving his goal, and only an ironic twist of plot prevents him from getting away untouched.

Robert Louis Stevenson's *Dr. Jekyll and Mr. Hyde* (1886) may be the most vivid late-century work exposing the criminality of human nature. Although Nabokov warns the reader against interpreting Stevenson's work as an allegory about warring decency and wickedness in ordinary people, Stevenson himself invited such an interpretation.[13] "The gnome is interesting, I think," he wrote to his American friend, W. H. Low, "and he came out of a deep mine, where he guards the fountain of tears. . . . The gnome's name is JEKYLL AND HYDE: I believe you will find he is likewise quite willing to answer to the name of Low or Stevenson."[14] The novel abounds with monstrous imagery—Jekyll's "other" is variously described as "some damned Juggernaut" and "something troglodytic"[15]—but Jekyll's similarity to ordinary people, not his freakishness as Hyde, emerges as more deeply distressing (28, 44). Hyde, the murderer and brutal half-man, exists within Jekyll embryonically before the good doctor ever conceives of the experiment that helps to conjure him up in fact. Reserved, rational Utterson, Dr. Jekyll's lawyer, suspects an evil he cannot name, and goes to Dr. Lanyon to inquire about their philanthropic, strangely preoccupied, mutual friend. Lanyon has had a falling-out with his fellow medical man because of Jekyll's theories: "It is more than ten years since Henry Jekyll became too fanciful for me. He began to go wrong, wrong in mind" (39). We learn, when reading Jekyll's confession, that his dangerous proclivities existed even before Lanyon's disapproval of his impractical experiments.

The doubleness of his nature was an accomplished fact by the time Jekyll reached "years of reflection":

> And indeed the worst of my faults was a certain impatient gaiety of disposition such as has made the happiness of many, but such as I found it hard to reconcile with my imperious desire to carry my head high, and wear a more than commonly grave countenance before the public. . . . I concealed my pleasures. . . . I stood already committed to a profound duplicity of life. (123)

As he begins to consider his own duality, Jekyll comes to believe that "man is not truly one, but truly two" (124). He is, he realizes, "radically both" sides of the duality, and Hyde springs directly from the evil side of the doctor's nature (125). Hyde does not victimize the doctor because of his respectability, but because of his amoral desires. Stevenson's reference to Jekyll's secret pleasures "hints at the stereotype of the 'respectable' gentleman's . . . pecadilloes in the upper regions of the Victorian underworld."[16] Jekyll's experiments release "the beast within" (Wheeler, 177).

Jekyll is not morally different from other citizens, but his medical knowledge enables him to become entirely his bestial self. He knows he must choose between his two natures:

> Strange as my circumstances were, the terms of this debate are as old and commonplace as man; and it fell out with me, as it falls with so vast a majority of my fellows, that I chose the better part, and was wanting in the strength to keep to it. (137)

Tellingly, it is as Jekyll, not as Hyde, that he eventually "was once more tempted to trifle with my conscience; and it was as an ordinary secret sinner that I at last fell before the assaults of temptation" (141). After Hyde has brutally murdered Sir Danvers Carew and Jekyll resolves never to indulge his other self again, he reflects one day: "I was like my neighbours; and then I smiled, comparing myself with other men, comparing my active goodwill with the lazy cruelty of their neglect" (141). At that "vainglorious" thought, he turns into Hyde. His unconscious is his murderer, and he is afraid to sleep: "If I sleep, or even dozed for a moment in my chair, it is always as Hyde that I awakened" (145). By ordinary standards, Jekyll is, as a philanthropist and friend, a good person; his eruption into Hyde is caused by his slyness and his humanity. Moreover, Hyde's wickedness is stronger than Jekyll's virtue. This essential possibility for evil we keep repressed, but sooner or later it will burst out.

Detectives and philanthropists are as dangerous as those they seek to capture or reform. Behind this late-century belief in the essential criminality of human nature is a loss of faith in divine justice. As Hyde, Jekyll scrawls terrible blasphemies in a pious work, and Utterson is partly right when he concludes at first that his friend is driven by some past sins: "In the law of God there is no statute of limitations" (46). But if characters in late-century fiction believe in God, they only believe in a punishing deity; events are generally considered to be ruled by an amoral, careless fate. "Chance!" observes Mrs. G. "In the history of crime and its detection chance plays the chief character" (54). Tormented Jefferson Hope tries to discover whether human events are determined randomly or purposefully when he confronts Drebber. Instead of shooting or strangling him, he gives him the choice of two pills, one poisoned: "Choose and eat. There is death in one and life in the other. I shall take what you leave. Let us see if there is justice upon the earth, or if we are ruled by chance" (81). Drebber's death suggests that justice exists, but, as Umberto Eco notes, "in fictional possible worlds things go better."[17] And even in the possible world of Jefferson Hope, belief in a beneficient, guiding presence is compromised by the shadow of the "Danite Band," Lucy's awful marriage and death, and Hope's blighted life. Justice is not divine; instead, it is a lucky toss of the dice.

# Epilogue

In early street ballads, murders required little investigation because evil could not be hidden. Murderers died on the gallows after contrite, remorseful prayers, and those who did not suffered the more for their recalcitrance. In early melodramas like *Maria Martin; or, The Murder in the Red Barn*, visions informs against the killers, who die in ceremonial tableaux. Fiction of the 1830s and 1840s depicts a corrupt society, but the individual murderers are captured and punished with poetic and often divine justice. By the end of the century, however, faith in justice being done has been eroded so far that the very people who are employed to stop crime become violent and brutal. The difference between good people and criminals shrinks until it is minimal or arbitrary. In *The African Millionaire*, a comical series of stories in which insolent, ingenious Colonel Clay bilks capitalist millionaire Sir Charles Vandrift repeatedly, the reader recognizes the justice in one of Clay's taunts. As he abandons Vandrift and his secretary on an island at the end of "The Episode of the Drawn Game," Clay cries: "Sir Charles Vandrift, we are a pair of rogues. The law protects *you*. It persecutes *me*. That's all the difference."[1] Respectable, successful citizens are as criminal as underworld elements.

When Sherlock Holmes concludes that "crime is commonplace," readers of popular Victorian literature might conclude even more. Throughout the century, responsibility for murder moves closer and closer to the ordinary citizen or reader. In early street literature, melodrama, and fiction, readers could identify with the concerns of diligent passers-by who discover mangled bodies or with the endangered heroines and bereaved relatives. The urgent desire for social status in *Catherine* and the criminal neglect of oversized, indifferent governmental systems in *Oliver Twist*, like the inhumane distance between classes in *Mary Barton*, stand accused of complicity in the murders they cause. With the intimate and public crimes of popular writing in the mid-Victorian years, anxiety about being attacked from within the community and the family circle increases. Responsibility for crime moves toward the hearth and, more distressingly, into the mirror. The hero of *The Ticket-of-Leave Man* steadfastly resists the pressure to become a criminal, but he could hardly have been condemned for doing otherwise: the society that abandons its former convicts without a trace of concern for the possibility of their rehabilitation might well be blamed for any robberies or murders he might have committed. Dickens's angry narrator wheels from the tragic death of Jo in pestilent Tom's-All-Alone to face the reader with accusatory emphasis. Those who ignore Reade's warnings in *Hard Cash* are as culpable for the cruel mistreatment of people in institutions, the author suggests, as the keepers and doctors who actually mistreat them. Lady Audley, Edith Archbold, Marion Vavasour, and Madame de la Rougierre display ambitious, cruel, and lustful qualities, demonstrating that women conceal the potential for dangerous passions, that sexuality and sexual drives experienced by all people can result in horrific, shocking violence. Detectives may be employed to stop or uncover crime, but they must struggle against the determined wickedness around them. Moreover, they can only discover pieces of the truth, and sometimes a Green, Hawkshaw, Cuff, or even Bucket can not learn enough in time to help.

By the end of the century, murder in popular literature becomes an emblem of moral decay. Because criminality is wide-ranging and intrinsic to human nature, evil can not be exorcised with the resonant execution of a single murderer. A resigned belief in "the night-side of nature" informs crime fictions of the eighties and nineties. Evil is as commonplace and unstoppable as the faceless criminals in Moriarty's gang. Most disturbingly, moral authority has gone awry. After the gradual erosion of sexual, institutional, and religious authority that characterized much Victorian crime writing, authors and their readers could not fall back on the hope of divine justice or heavenly rewards. As Holmes broods in "The Adventure of the Veiled Lodger": "The ways of Fate are indeed hard to understand. If there is not some compensation hereafter, then the world is a cruel jest."[2] In fictional worlds where every character is capable of murder, the grim joke reflects a cultural fear of degenerating morality and, as such, points the way to the nihilism of twentieth-century crime literature.

# Notes

**Prologue**

1. Garrett Stewart, *Death Sentences: Styles of Dying in British Fiction* (Cambridge, Mass.: Harvard Univ. Press, 1984), p. 8.

2. Ian Ousby, *The Bloodhounds of Heaven: The Detective in English Fiction from Godwin to Doyle* (Cambridge, Mass.: Harvard Univ. Press, 1976), p. viii.

3. Richard Altick, *Victorian Studies in Scarlet* (New York: W. W. Norton and Company, 1970), p. 9.

4. Christopher Clausen, "Sherlock Holmes, Order, and the Late-Victorian Mind," *Georgia Review* 38:1 (Spring 1984), 106.

5. Kirby Farrell, "Heroism, Culture, and Dread in *The Sign of the Four*," *Studies in the Novel*, 16:1 (Spring 1984), 32.

**Introduction to Part I**

1. Henry Mayhew, *London Labour and the London Poor*, 4 vols. (1861–62; rpt. New York: Dover, 1968), I, 222.

2. Richard Barker, *The Fatal Caress: And Other Accounts of English Murders From 1551 to 1888* (New York: Duell, Sloan & Pearce, 1947), p. 155.

3. Vivian DeSola Pinto and Allan Edwin Rodway, eds., *The Common Muse: An Anthology of Popular British Ballad Poetry, XVth–XXth Century* (London: Chatto & Windus, 1957), p. 189.

4. Charles Hindley, *Curiosities of Street Literature* (1871; rpt. New York: Augustus M. Kelley, 1970), p. 189.

5. Mayhew, *London Labour and the London Poor*, I, 284. The Mannings especially fascinated the public.

6. George Rowell, *The Victorian Theatre 1792–1914: A Survey*, 2nd ed. (Cambridge: Cambridge Univ. Press, 1978), p. 45.

**Chapter 1**

1. Michael Hughes, foreword in Hindley, *Curiosities of Street Literature*, p. 10. Previous generations read about rural, legendary, and traditional subjects.

2. Martha Vicinus, *The Industrial Muse: A Study of Nineteenth Century British Working Class Literature* (New York: Harper & Row, 1974), p. 9.

3. Hindley, *Curiosities of Street Literature,* table of contents; Martha Vicinus, *Broadsides of the Industrial North* (Newcastle upon Tyne: Frank Graham, 1975), p. 15.

4. Vicinus, *The Industrial Muse,* p. 8; Victor E. Neuburg, *Popular Literature: A History and Guide* (Harmondsworth: Penguin, 1977), p. 142.

5. John Holloway, "Cherry Girls and Crafty Maidens," *The Listener,* 83 (1970), 684.

6. Louis James, *English Popular Literature 1819–1851* (New York: Columbia Univ. Press, 1976), p. 260.

7. In his discussion of journalistic murder reports in midcentury America, James Fulcher explores reader identification as one of the "aesthetic" reasons for becoming involved in the newspaper account; see Fulcher, "Murder Reports: Formulaic Narrative and Cultural Context," *Journal of Popular Culture,* 18:4 (Spring 1985): 31–42.

8. Stephen Knight, *Form and Ideology in Crime Fiction* (Bloomington: Indiana Univ. Press, 1980), p. 16.

9. Garrett Stewart, *Death Sentences: Styles of Dying in British Fiction* (Cambridge, Mass.: Harvard Univ. Press, 1984), p. 12.

10. John Ashton, *Modern Street Ballads* (London: Chatto & Windus, 1888), pp. 389, 393.

11. James Walvin, *Leisure and Society, 1830–1950* (London: Longman, 1978), p. 27.

12. Peter Bailey, *Leisure and Class in Victorian England: Rational Recreation and the Contest for Control, 1830–1885* (London: Routledge & Kegan Paul, 1978), p. 24.

13. Peter Webb, "Victorian Erotica," in Alan Bold, ed., *The Sexual Dimension in Literature* (London: Vision, 1982), pp. 93–94.

14. Maurice Charney, *Sexual Fiction* (London: Methuen, 1981), p. 91.

15. Elaine and English Showalter, "Victorian Women and Menstruation," *Victorian Studies,* 14 (1970), 85.

16. Nina Auerbach, *Woman and the Demon: The Life of a Victorian Myth* (Cambridge, Mass.: Harvard Univ. Press, 1982).

**Chapter 2**

1. Edward Fitzball, *The Fortunes of Nigel; or, King James I and His Times* (London: John Lowndes, 1822), p. 4.

2. George Rowell, Michael Booth, and Robertson Davies are among the critics who show a thorough and imaginative understanding of melodrama's significance.

3. Michael R. Booth, "A Defence of Nineteenth-Century English Drama," *Educational Theatre Journal,* 26 (1974), 7.

4. Robertson Davies, *The Mirror of Nature* (Toronto: Univ. of Toronto Press, 1983), p. 9.

5. Clive Barker, "A Theatre for the People," in Kenneth Richards and Peter Thomson, eds., *Essays on Nineteenth Century British Theatre* (London: Methuen, 1971), p. 3.

6. Earl F. Bargainnier, "Melodrama as Formula," *Journal of Popular Culture,* 9 (1975), 730.

7.  Michael R. Booth, *English Melodrama* (London: Herbert Jenkins, 1965), p. 14.

8.  Gilbert B. Cross, *Next Week—East Lynne: Domestic Drama in Performance 1820–1874* (Lewisburg: Bucknell Univ. Press, 1977), p. 50.

9.  Douglas Jerrold, *Black-Ey'd Susan,* in Leonard R. N. Ashley, ed., *Nineteenth-Century British Drama* (Glenview, Ill.: Scott, Foresman & Company, 1967), p. 125.

10.  Peter Haining, *The Mystery and Horrible Murders of Sweeney Todd The Demon Barber* (London: Frederick Muller, 1979), p. 75.

11.  Michael Kilgarriff, ed., *The Golden Age of Melodrama* (London: Wolfe, 1974), p. 204.

12.  After Corder buried Marten in the red barn, he left town and forged a letter to her mother pretending that Maria was his happy wife. He advertised for a spouse and found one; Douglas Jerrold's *Wives by Advertisement* (1828) is a farce based on that element of the sensational crime. Ten thousand people came to see Corder hanged. The report of the trial, which was bound in his skin, is at the Moyse's Hall Museum, Bury St. Edmunds (Kilgarriff, 210–11).

   Sweeney Todd's exploits, probably fictitious, are connected to several true stories. Critic Peter Haining, who stalks rumors of Todd's existence with the avidity formerly reserved for Kipling's Janeites and the Joyce scholars who annually walk where Bloom "walked," traces the barber to a fourteenth-century French ballad purporting to be true. The Parisian barber also killed people and baked them into pies. The translation from which Haining quotes has the same grim, energetic humor as Pitt's play: "And he said of his customers when defunct, / They are gone—'pork creatures'" (Haining, 95). Whether anyone ever baked customers or not, the issue must have been discussed, especially by those who passed playbills outside the theatre reading "FOUNDED ON FACT!" (Haining, 87)

13.  Anonymous, *Maria Martin; or, The Murder in the Red Barn,* in Kilgarriff, *The Golden Age of Melodrama,* p. 215. All subsequent quotations from the play will be noted by page number within the text.

14.  George Dibdin Pitt, *The String of Pearls,* in Kilgarriff, *The Golden Age of Melodrama,* p. 246. All subsequent quotations from the play will be noted by page number within the text.

15.  Davies delineates the recurring motifs in nineteenth-century popular drama, including: unrecognized merit showing itself superior to external circumstances, great value found in the despised, renunciation, remorse, and the fated man (90–91).

16.  A. Radcliffe's novels are among the Gothic works that feature lascivious and violent villains whose designs on the heroines are multiple.

17.  J. R. Planché, *The Vampire,* in Kilgarriff, *The Golden Age of Melodrama,* p. 73.

18.  Gershon Legman, *Love and Death: A Study in Censorship* (New York: Hacker Art Books, 1963), p. 11.

19.  Sally Mitchell, *The Fallen Angel: Chastity, Class and Women's Reading 1835–1888* (Bowling Green, Ohio: Bowling Green Univ. Popular Press, 1981), p. 23.

20.  *Sweeney Todd,* Stephen Sondheim's operetta, develops these implications. Todd and Mrs. Lovett—now his would-be lover—see themselves as imaginative survivors in a post-Darwinian "dog eat dog" society.

## Chapter 3

1.  Keith Hollingsworth, *The Newgate Novel, 1830–1847: Bulwer, Ainsworth, Dickens, and Thackeray* (Detroit: Wayne State Univ. Press, 1963), p. 69.

2. William M. Thackeray, *Catherine: A Story,* in *The Complete Works of William Thackeray,* 20 vols. (1840; rpt. Boston: Dana Estes, 1882–84), IV, 395. All subsequent quotations from the novel will be noted by page number within the text.

3. Albert I. Borowitz, "Why Thackeray Went to See a Man Hanged," *Victorian Newsletter,* 48 (1975), 16.

4. Borowitz points out that Thackeray wrote the biography of Cartouche, an eighteenth-century French con man, thief, and murderer (16).

5. Nancy Jane Tyson, *Eugene Aram: Literary History and Typology of the Scholar-Criminal* (Hamden, Conn.: Archon Books, 1983), p. 89.

6. Ina Ferris, *William Makepeace Thackeray* (Boston: Twayne, 1983), p. 13.

7. Edward Bulwer-Lytton, *Eugene Aram* (1831; rpt. London: Chapman & Hall, 1853), p. 7. All subsequent quotations from the novel will be noted by page number within the text.

8. Charles Dickens, *Oliver Twist* (1837; rpt. New York: New American Library, 1961), p. 418. All subsequent quotations from the novel will be noted by page number within the text.

9. "Thackeray punctures Bulwer with skill, exposing the vanity, arrogance, and emptiness of his fictional world" (Ferris, 14).

10. Frederick C. Cabot, "The Two Voices in Thackeray's *Catherine,*" *Nineteenth Century Fiction,* 28 (1974), 411.

11. William M. Thackeray, "Catherine," *Fraser's Magazine,* February 1840, p. 209. Most editors delete this section of the novel, considering it inappropriate for inclusion.

12. Elizabeth Gaskell, *Mary Barton* (1848; rpt. Harmondsworth: Penguin, 1970), p. 61. All subsequent quotations from the novel will be noted by page number within the text.

13. Elaine Jordan, "Spectres and Scorpions: Allusion and Confusion in *Mary Barton,*" *Literature and History,* 7:1 (Spring 1981), 55.

14. Coral Lansbury, *Elizabeth Gaskell* (Boston: Twayne, 1984), p. 13.

15. Sibylla J. Flower, "Charles Dickens and Edward Bulwer-Lytton," *Dickensian,* 69 (1973), p. 81.

16. Jane Flanders, "The Fallen Woman in Fiction," in Diane Fowlkes and Charlotte S. McClure, eds., *Feminist Visions: Toward a Transformation of the Liberal Arts Curriculum* (University: Univ. of Alabama Press, 1984), p. 102.

**Introduction to Part II**

1. "Cautionary Hints to Speculators on the Increase of Crimes," *Blackwood's Magazine,* 3 (1818), 176.

2. J. J. Tobias, *Crime and Industrial Society in the Nineteenth Century* (London: B. T. Batsford, 1967), p. 123.

3. "The Moral Philosophy of Garotting, by a Retired Practitioner of the Science," *Fraser's Magazine,* 67 (1863), 261.

4. *The Whitechapel Mystery,* pamphlet, Sadleir Collection of the Lilly Library, p. 3.

5. James Fulcher, "Murder Reports: Formulaic Narrative and Cultural Context," *Journal of Popular Culture,* 18:4 (Spring 1985), 31.

6. Anthea Trodd discusses the case of Constance Kent in "The Policeman and the Lady: Significant Encounters in Victorian Fiction," *Victorian Studies,* 27:4 (Summer 1984): 435–60.

7. John G. Cawelti, *Adventure, Mystery, and Romance* (Chicago: Univ. of Chicago Press, 1976), p. 102.

8. Kellow Chesney, *The Anti-Society: An Account of the Victorian Underworld* (Boston: Gambit, 1970), p. 369.

**Chapter 4**

1. Noel Annan, "Magsmen, Macers, Gonophs, Footpads and Pimps," rev. in *The New York Times Review of Books,* 15 (17 December 1970), p. 39.

2. Margaret Dalziel, *Popular Fiction 100 Years Ago: An Unexplored Tract of Literary History* (London: Cohen & West, 1957), p. 122.

3. Auerbach, *Woman and the Demon: The Life of a Victorian Myth,* p. 63.

4. James Walvin, *A Child's World: A Social History of English Childhood, 1800–1914* (Harmondsworth: Penguin, 1982), p. 148.

5. Bernd Weisbrod, "How to Become a Good Foundling in Early Victorian London," *Social History,* 10:2 (May 1985): 193–209.

6. Dana Brand discusses this anxiety in relation to Poe; "Reconstructing the 'Flâneur': Poe's Invention of the Detective Story," *Genre,* 18:1 (Spring 1985): 36–56.

7. Jane Austen, *Northanger Abbey* (1818; rpt. London: Allan Wingate, 1948), p. 162.

8. "Murder Will Out: Being Singular Instances of the Manner in Which Concealed Crimes Have Been Detected," *Cassell's Illustrated Family Paper,* 160 (22 December 1860), 53.

9. "Murder Will Out: Being Singular Instances . . . ," *Cassell's Illustrated Family Paper,* 165 (26 January 1861), p. 140.

10. "Murder Will Out: Being Singular Instances . . . ," *Cassell's Illustrated Family Paper,* 162 (5 January 1861), p. 92.

11. "Capital Punishments," *Fraser's Magazine,* 69 (1864), 758.

12. "The Demeanour of Murderers," *Household Words,* 13 (14 June 1856), 507.

13. M. Jeanne Peterson, *The Medical Profession in Mid-Victorian London* (Berkeley: Univ. of California Press, 1978), p. 285.

14. "The Ursinus," *Household Words,* 12 (22 September 1855), 176.

15. "The Criminal Law and the Detection of Crime," *Cornhill Magazine,* 2 (1860), 697.

16. "The Modern Science of Thief-Taking," *Household Words,* 1 (1850), 372.

17. "Injured Innocents," *All the Year Round,* 1 (1869), 414.

18. "Switzerland in Summer and Autumn: Part Two," *Blackwood's Magazine,* 98 (1865), 493.

**Chapter 5**

1. James Smith, ed., *Victorian Melodramas: Seven English, French and American Melodramas* (London: Dent, 1976), p. xix.

2. Richard Barickman, Susan MacDonald, and Myra Stark discuss the significance of the sexual crime or fraud in the Victorian novel. They argue persuasively that the emphasis on crime in nineteenth-century fiction "can be as significant a fictional motif for Victorian culture as the corruption of the monarchy was for Elizabethan culture"; *Corrupt Relations: Dickens, Thackeray, Trollope, Collins, and the Victorian Sexual System* (New York: Columbia Univ. Press, 1982), p. 25.

3. Rowell, *The Victorian Theatre, 1792–1914: A Survey,* p. viii.

4. Booth, *English Melodrama,* p. 157.

5. Cross, *Next Week—East Lynne: Domestic Drama in Performance 1820–1874,* p. 113. Devil figures in medieval dramas and villains like Barabas in *The Jew of Malta* always had red hair. Lady Audley's coloring, and that of similar female villains, may stem from this dramatic tradition.

6. George Rowell, Introduction to *Nineteenth-Century Plays* (London: Oxford Univ. Press, 1953), p. viii.

7. C. H. Hazlewood, *Lady Audley's Secret,* in George Rowell, ed., *Nineteenth-Century Plays* (London: Oxford Univ. Press, 1953), p. 236. All subsequent quotations from the play will be noted by page number within the text.

8. Auerbach, *Woman and the Demon: The Life of a Victorian Myth,* p. 139.

9. Tom Taylor, *The Ticket-of-Leave Man,* in Rowell, *Nineteenth-Century Plays,* p. 236. All subsequent quotations from the play will be noted by page number in the text.

10. Laurence Senelick provides a list of famous dramatic tags from the Victorian stage, including "I know you, Jack Dalton" and other lines from criminal melodramas; "'Dead! And Never Called Me Mother!': The Legacy of Oral Tradition from the Nineteenth-Century Stage," *Theatre Studies,* nos. 26/27 (1979/80–1980/81): 7–20.

11. T. W. Robertson, *Caste,* in Ashley, *Nineteenth-Century British Drama,* p. 313.

**Chapter 6**

1. Michael Wheeler, *English Fiction of the Victorian Period 1830–1890* (New York: Longman, 1985), p. 94.

2. Barickman, MacDonald, and Stark, *Corrupt Relations: Dickens, Thackeray, Trollope, Collins, and the Victorian Sexual System,* p. 26.

3. Norman Page, ed., *Wilkie Collins: The Critical Heritage* (London: Routledge & Kegan Paul, 1974), p. 122.

4. Winifred Hughes, *The Maniac in the Cellar: Sensation Novels of the 1860s* (N.J.: Princeton Univ. Press, 1980), p. 32.

5. R. C. Terry, *Victorian Popular Fiction,* 1860–80 (London: Macmillan Press, 1983), p. 56.

6. Sheridan LeFanu, *Uncle Silas* (1864; rpt. New York: Dover Publications, 1966), p. 146. All subsequent quotations from the novel will be noted by page number in the text.

7. Patrick Brantlinger suggests that truth in sensation novels is "hidden, buried, smuggled away behind the appearances"; Maud can not understand her circumstances until she is so well hidden that she becomes, to her would-be killer, invisible. See "What is 'sensational' about the 'Sensation Novel'?", *Nineteenth-Century Fiction,* 37 (1982), 26–27.

8. Michael H. Begnal, *Joseph Sheridan LeFanu* (Lewisburg, Penn.: Bucknell Univ. Press, 1971), p. 36.

9. Eileen Bigland, *Ouida: The Passionate Victorian* (London: Jarrolds, 1950), p. 33.

10. Yvonne Ffrench, *Ouida: A Study in Ostentation* (London: Cobden-Sanderson, 1938), p. 358.

11. Ouida (Louise de la Ramée), *Strathmore* (1865; rpt. London: 1925), p. 358. All subsequent quotations from the novel will be noted by page number in the text.

12. Elton E. Smith, *Charles Reade* (Boston: Twayne Publishers, 1976), p. 104.

13. J. H. Miller, introduction to *Bleak House* (1853; rpt. Harmondsworth: Penguin, 1971), p. 361.

14. "Full Account of the Chelsea of Uxbridge Murders," Sadleir Collection of the Lilly Library.

15. Julian Symons, *Charles Dickens* (London: Arthur Barker Limited, 1951), p. 78.

16. Charles Reade, *Hard Cash: A Matter of Fact Romance* (1863; rpt. London: Chatto & Windus, 1888), pp. 303–4. All subsequent quotations from the novel will be noted by page number in the text.

17. Charles Dickens, *Bleak House* (1853; rpt. Harmondsworth: Penguin, 1971), p. 361. All subsequent quotations will be noted by page number in the text.

18. Deborah Clarke provides an excellent discussion of narrative in *"Bleak House:* Divided against Itself." An early version of this essay was presented at the Midwest Modern Language Association Conference in November 1985, St. Louis, Missouri.

19. John C. Ward, "The Virtues of the Mothers: Powerful Women in *Bleak House,"* *Dickens Studies Newsletter,* 14:2 (June 1983), 40.

20. Thomas F. Boyle, " 'Fishy Extremeties': Subversion of Orthodoxy in the Victorian Sensation Novel," *Literature and History,* 9:1 (Spring 1983), 95.

21. Wayne Burns, *Charles Reade: A Study in Victorian Authorship* (New York: Bookman Associates, 1961), p. 220.

22. Jerome Meckier, "Wilkie Collins's *The Woman in White:* Providence Against the Evils of Propriety," *The Journal of British Studies,* 22:1 (Fall 1982), 113.

23. William H. Marshall, *Wilkie Collins* (New York: Twayne, 1970), p. 63.

24. Wilkie Collins, *The Moonstone* (1868; rpt. Harmondsworth: Penguin, 1973), p. 87. All subsequent quotations from the novel will be noted by page number in the text.

25. Jeanne F. Bedell, "Wilkie Collins," in Earl F. Bargainnier, ed., *Twelve Englishmen of Mystery* (Bowling Green, Ohio: Bowling Green Univ. Popular Press, 1984), p. 29.

## Introduction to Part III

1. Christopher Clausen, "Sherlock Holmes, Order, and the Late-Victorian Mind," *Georgia Review,* 38:1 (Spring 1984), 116. Clausen's discussion of Holmes as a cultural weathervane for his time is extremely thoughtful and persuasive.

2. Marcello Truzzi, "Sherlock Holmes: Applied Social Psychologist," in Umberto Eco and Thomas A. Sebeok, eds., *The Sign of Three: Dupin, Holmes, Peirce* (Bloomington: Indiana Univ. Press, 1983), p. 73.

**Chapter 7**

1. DeMauley, "Crime, Criminals, Punishment," *Macmillan's Magazine,* 29 (1873), 145.

2. "A French Detective Story," *All The Year Round,* 19 (1877), 368–69.

3. M. Laing Meason, "The French Detective Police," *Macmillan's Magazine,* 45 (1881), 296–301.

4. M. Laing Meason, "The London Police," *Macmillan's Magazine,* 66 (1882), 199.

5. "A Night with the Thames Police" (*Strand Magazine,* 1 (1891), 124–31) displays an admiring attitude toward police. Yet the history of the Thames police may distinguish them from their detective colleagues and offer an explanation for the differing journalistic treatment. Rather than functioning as cogs in a huge machinery of justice, the Thames police work together like members of a guild or union to protect property. They are a hardy group of individuals, not a faceless police force (125).

6. "The Epidemic of Murder," *The Spectator,* 62 (1889), 44.

7. "The Hangman's Office," *The Spectator,* 57 (1884), 343.

8. Henry W. Hubbard, "The Poisons of the Day; a New Social Evil," *Macmillan's Magazine,* 66 (1882), 243.

9. "The Bernays Tragedy," *The Spectator,* 55 (1882), 1536.

10. "Murder as a Fine Art in Scotland," *The Spectator,* 61 (1888), 994.

11. "The Motives of Murder," *The Spectator,* 57 (1884), 1544.

12. "The Fenayrou Trial," *The Spectator,* 55 (1882), 1078.

13. "The Moral Muddle about Murder," *The Spectator,* 57 (1884), 1694.

**Chapter 8**

1. Ashley, *Nineteenth-Century British Drama,* p. 16.

2. Martin Banham, ed., *Plays by Tom Taylor* (Cambridge: Cambridge Univ. Press, 1985), p. 4.

3. Cited by Booth, *English Melodrama,* p. 172.

4. George Rowell, *The Victorian Theatre 1792–1914: A Survey,* p. 83.

5. Flanders, "The Fallen Woman in Fiction," p. 97.

6. George Rowell, *Theatre in the Age of Irving* (Oxford: Basil Blackwell, 1981), p. 154.

7. Leopold Lewis, *The Bells,* in Ashley, *Nineteenth-Century British Drama,* p. 324. All further quotations from the play will be cited in the text.

8. Russell Jackson, ed., *Plays by Henry Arthur Jones* (Cambridge: Cambridge Univ. Press, 1982), p. 5.

9. Quoted by James Woodfield, *English Theatre in Transition 1881–1914* (London: Croom Helm, 1984), p. 15.

10. Richard A. Cordell, *Henry Arthur Jones and the Modern Drama* (Port Washington, N.Y.: Kennikat Press, 1932; rpt. 1968), p. 174.

11. Henry Arthur Jones, *The Silver King,* in Jackson, *Plays by Henry Arthur Jones,* p. 102. All further quotations from the play will be cited in the text.

12. The incisive and thoughtful comments of Donald Gray on this chapter helped shape my conclusion.

**Chapter 9**

1. Arthur Morrison, "The Case of the Missing Hand," in *Best Martin Hewitt Detective Stories,* ed. E. F. Bleiler (New York: Dover Publications, 1976), p. 77; Arthur Conan Doyle, *A Study in Scarlet,* in *The Complete Sherlock Holmes,* 2 vols. (Garden City, N.Y.: Doubleday and Company, 1905), I, 29. All subsequent quotations will be cited by page number in the text.

2. Arthur Conan Doyle, "The Five Orange Pips," in *The Complete Sherlock Holmes,* 2 vols. (Garden City, N.Y.: Doubleday and Company, 1905), I, 223. All subsequent quotations will be cited by page number in the text.

3. Arthur Conan Doyle, "The Final Problem," in *The Complete Sherlock Holmes,* 2 vols. (Garden City, N.Y.: Doubleday and Company, 1905), I, 471. All subsequent quotations will be cited by page number in the text.

4. Arthur Conan Doyle, *The Valley of Fear* (1915; rpt. New York: Berkley Publishing, 1981), p. 87. All subsequent quotations will be cited by page number in the text.

5. Christopher Clausen, "Sherlock Holmes, Order, and the Late-Victorian Mind," *Georgia Review* 38:1 (Spring 1984): 104–123.

6. Anthony Curtis, preface to E. W. Hornung's *Raffles: The Amateur Cracksman* (1899; rpt. London: Chatto & Windus, 1972), p. 4.

7. Arthur Conan Doyle, "The Green Interpreter," in *The Complete Sherlock Holmes,* 2 vols. (Garden City, N.Y.: Doubleday and Company, 1905), I, 445.

8. Marie Connor Leighton and Robert Leighton, *Michael Dred, Detective: The Unravelling of a Mystery of Twenty Years* (London: Grant Richards, 1899), p. 196. All subsequent quotations will be cited by page number in the text.

9. Andrew Forrester, Jr., *The Unknown Weapon,* in *Three Victorian Detective Novels,* ed. E. F. Bleiler (New York: Dover Publications, 1978), p. 41. All subsequent quotations will be cited by page number in the text.

10. Israel Zangwill, *The Big Bow Mystery,* in *Three Victorian Detective Novels,* ed. E. F. Bleiler (New York: Dover Publications, 1978), p. 240. All subsequent quotations will be cited by page number in the text.

11. M. McDonnell Bodkin, "The Poisoner," in *Paul Beck, The Rule of Thumb Detective* (London: C. Arthur Pearson Ltd., 1898), p. 200. All subsequent quotations will be cited by page number in the text.

12. M. McDonnell Bodkin, "Murder by Proxy," in *Paul Beck, The Rule of Thumb Detective* (London: C. Arthur Pearson, Ltd., 1898), p. 123.

13. Vladimir Nabokov, "Dr. Jekyll and Mr. Hyde," in *Lectures on Literature* (New York: Harcourt, Brace, Jovanovich, 1980), p. 180.

14. John Hampden, introduction to Robert Louis Stevenson's *Dr. Jekyll and Mr. Hyde* (1886; rpt. London: The Folio Society, 1948), pp. 19–20.

15. Ed Block, Jr., provides an interesting interpretation of the animal imagery in *Dr. Jekyll and Mr. Hyde* in "James Sully, Evolutionist Psychology, and Late Victorian Gothic Fiction," *Victorian Studies,* 25 (1982), 443–69.

16. Michael Wheeler, *English Fiction of the Victorian Period 1830–1890* (New York: Longman, 1985), p. 177.

17. Umberto Eco, "Horns, Hooves, Insteps: Some Hypotheses on Three Types of Abduction," in *The Sign of Three: Dupin, Holmes, Peirce,* ed. Umberto Eco and Thomas A. Sebeok (Bloomington: Indiana Univ. Press, 1983), p. 220.

**Epilogue**

1. Grant Allen, "The Episode of the Drawn Game," *An African Millionaire: Episodes in the Life of the Illustrious Colonel Clay* (1897; rpt. New York: Dover Publications, 1980), p. 136.

2. Arthur Conan Doyle, "The Adventury of the Veiled Lodger," in *The Final Adventures of Sherlock Holmes,* ed. Edgar W. Smith, 3 vols. (1927; rpt. New York: Heritage Press, 1957), III, 1752.

# Bibliography

**Primary Sources**

Allen, Grant. "The Episode of the Drawn Game." In *An African Millionaire: Episodes in the Life of the Illustrious Colonel Clay*. 1897; rpt. ed., New York: Dover Publications, 1980.

Anonymous. *Maria Martin; or, The Murder in the Red Barn*. In *The Golden Age of Melodrama*. Ed. Michael Kilgarriff. London: Wolfe, 1974, pp. 214–35.

Ashton, John, ed. *Modern Street Ballads*. London: Chatto & Windus, 1888.

"The Bernays Tragedy." *The Spectator*, 55 (1882), 1536–37.

Bodkin, M. McDonnell. "Greased Lightning." In *Paul Beck, The Rule of Thumb Detective*. London: C. Arthur Pearson Ltd., 1898.

Bulwer-Lytton, Edward. *Eugene Aram*. 1831; rpt. ed., London: Chapman & Hall, 1853.

"Capital Punishments." *Fraser's Magazine*, 69 (1864), 753–72.

Carpenter, Mary. *Our Convicts*. 2 vols. London: Longman, Green, Longman, Roberts & Green, 1864.

"Cautionary Hints to Speculators on the Increase of Crimes." *Blackwood's Magazine*, 3 (1818), 176–78.

Collins, Wilkie. *The Moonstone*. 1868; rpt. ed., Harmondsworth: Penguin, 1973.

"The Criminal Law and the Detection of Crime." *Cornhill Magazine*, 2 (1860), 697–708.

"A Criminal Trial." *Household Words*, 13 (1856), 529–34.

de la Ramée, Louise. *Strathmore*. 1865; rpt. ed., London: Chatto & Windus, 1925.

DeMauley. "Crime, Criminals, Punishment." *Macmillan's Magazine*, 29 (1873), 145–54.

"The Demeanour of Murderers." *Household Words*, 13 (1856), 505–7.

DeSola Pinto, Vivian and Allan Edwin Rodway, eds. *The Common Muse: An Anthology of Popular British Ballad Poetry, XV–XXth Century*. London: Chatto & Windus, 1957.

Dickens, Charles. *Bleak House*. 1853; rpt. ed., Harmondsworth: Penguin, 1971.

―――. *Oliver Twist*. 1837; rpt. ed., New York: New American Library, 1961.

Doyle, Arthur Conan. "The Final Problem," "The Five Orange Pips," "The Greek Interpreter," and *A Study in Scarlet*. In *The Complete Sherlock Holmes*. 2 vols. Garden City, New York: Doubleday and Company, 1905.

―――. *The Valley of Fear*. 1915; rpt. ed., New York: Berkley Publishing, 1981.

"The Epidemic of Murder." *The Spectator*, 62 (1889), 44–45.

"The Fenayrou Trial." *The Spectator*, 55 (1882), 1078.

Forrester, Andrew, Jr. *The Unknown Weapon*. In *Three Victorian Detective Novels*. Ed. E. F. Bleiler. New York: Dover Publications, 1978.

"A French Detective Story." *All The Year Round*, 19 (1868), 368–73.

Gaskell, Elizabeth. *Mary Barton*. 1848; rpt. ed., Harmondsworth: Penguin, 1970.

"The Hangman's Office." *The Spectator*, 57 (1884).

Hindley, Charles, ed. *Curiosities of Street Literature*. 1871; rpt. ed., New York: Augustus M. Kelley, 1970.

Hubbard, Henry W. "The Poisons of the Day; A New Social Evil." *Macmillan's Magazine*, 66 (1892), 238–44.

Jones, Henry Arthur and Henry Herman. *The Silver King*. 1883; rpt. ed., *Plays by Henry Arthur Jones*. Ed. Russell Jackson. Cambridge: Cambridge Univ. Press, 1982.

LeFanu, Sheridan. *Uncle Silas*. 1864; rpt. ed., New York: Dover Publications, 1966.

Leighton, Marie Connor and Robert Leighton. *Michael Dred, Detective: The Unravelling of a Mystery of Twenty Years*. London: Grant Richards, 1899.

Lewis, Leopold. *The Bells*. 1871; rpt. ed., *Nineteenth-Century British Drama*. Ed. Leonard R. N. Ashley. Glenview, Ill.: Scott, Foresman & Company, 1967.

Mayhew, Henry. *London Labour and the London Poor*. 4 vols. 1861–62; rpt. ed., New York: Dover, 1968.

Meason, M. Laing. "The French Detective Police." *Macmillan's Magazine*, 45 (1881), 296–301.

———. "The London Police." *Macmillan's Magazine*, 66 (1892), 192–202.

"The Modern Science of Thief Taking." *Household Words: A Weekly Journal*, 1 (1850), 368–72.

"The Moral Muddle about Murder." *The Spectator*, 57 (1884), 1694–95.

Morrison, Arthur. *Best Martin Hewitt Detective Stories*. Ed. E. F. Bleiler. New York: Dover Publications, 1976.

"The Motives of Murder." *The Spectator*, 57 (1884), 1544–45.

"Murder as a Fine Art in Scotland." *The Spectator*, 61 (1888), 994–95.

"Murder Will Out: Being Singular Instances of the Manner in Which Concealed Crimes Have Been Detected." *Cassell's Illustrated Family Paper*, 7 (1860), 53–54, 92, 125–26, 139–40.

"A Night with the Thames Police." *Strand Magazine*, 1 (1891), 124–31.

Pike, Luke Owen. *History of Crime in England*. 2 vols. London: Smith, Elder, & Co. 1876.

Pitt, George Dibdin. *The String of Pearls*. In *The Golden Age of Melodrama*. Ed. Michael Kilgarriff. London: Wolfe, 1974, pp. 244–62.

"Poison." *Household Words*, 13 (1856), 220–24.

"Poison in Flounces." *Cassell's Illustrated Family Paper*, 4 (1857), 206.

"The Predatory Art." *Household Words*, 15 (1857), 241–46.

Reade, Charles. *Hard Cash: A Matter-of-Fact Romance*. 1863; rpt. London: Chatto & Windus, 1888.

"Switzerland in Summer and Autumn: Part Two." *Blackwood's Magazine*, 98 (1865), 493.

Thackeray, William Makepeace. *Catherine: A Story*. In *The Complete Works of William Thackeray*. 20 vols. 1840; rpt. ed., Boston: Dana Estes, 1882–84.

"The Ursinus." *Household Words*, 12 (1855), 176–80.

*The Whitechapel Mystery*. Pamphlet. Sadleir Collection of the Lilly Library.

Zangwill, Israel. *The Big Bow Mystery*. In *Three Victorian Detective Novels*. Ed. E. F. Bleiler. New York: Dover Publications, 1978.

**Secondary Sources**

Altick, Richard D. *Victorian Studies in Scarlet*. New York: Norton, 1970.

Anderson, Nancy F. "The 'Marriage with a Deceased Wife's Sister Bill' Controversy: Incest Anxiety and the Defense of Family Purity in Victorian England." *The Journal of British Studies*, 21:2 (Spring 1982): 67–86.

Annan, Noel. "Magsmen, Macers, Gonophs, Footpads and Pimps." *New York Review of Books*, 15 (1970): 39–42.

Ashley, Leonard R. N., ed. *Nineteenth-Century British Drama*. Glenview, Ill.: Scott, Foresman and Company, 1967.

Auerbach, Nina. *Woman and the Demon: The Life of a Victorian Myth.* Cambridge, Mass.: Harvard Univ. Press, 1982.

Bailey, Peter. *Leisure and Class in Victorian England: Rational Recreation and the Contest for Control, 1830–1885.* London: Routledge & Kegan Paul, 1978.

Banham, Martin. Introduction to *Plays by Tom Taylor.* pp. 1–18. Cambridge: Cambridge Univ. Press, 1985.

Bargainnier, Earl F. "Melodrama as Formula." *Journal of Popular Culture,* 9 (1975): 726–33.

Barickman, Richard, Susan MacDonald, and Myra Stark. *Corrupt Relations: Dickens, Thackeray, Trollope, Collins, and the Victorian Sexual System.* New York: Columbia Univ. Press, 1982.

Barker, Clive. "A Theatre for the People." In *Essays on Nineteenth Century British Theatre.* Eds. Kenneth Richards and Peter Thomson. London: Methuen, 1971, pp. 3–23.

Barker, Richard. *The Fatal Caress: And Other Accounts of English Murders From 1551 to 1888.* New York: Duell, Sloan & Pearce, 1947.

Bedell, Jeanne F. "Wilkie Collins." In *Twelve Englishmen of Mystery.* Ed. Earl F. Bargainnier. Bowling Green, Ohio: Bowling Green Univ. Popular Press, 1984, pp. 8–32.

Begnal, Michael H. *Joseph Sheridan LeFanu.* Lewisburg, Penn.: Bucknell Univ. Press, 1971.

Bigland, Eileen. *Ouida: The Passionate Victorian.* London: Jarrolds, 1950.

Block, Ed, Jr. "Evolutionist Psychology and Aesthetics: *The Cornhill Magazine, 1875–1880.*" *Journal of the History of Ideas,* 45:3 (July/September 1984): 465–75.

———. "James Sully, Evolutionist Psychology, and Late Victorian Gothic Fiction." *Victorian Studies,* 25 (1982): 443–69.

Bogel, Fredric V. "Fables of Knowing: Melodrama and Related Forms." *Genre,* 11 (1978): 83–108.

Booth, Michael R. "A Defence of Nineteenth-Century English Drama." *Educational Theatre Journal,* 26 (1974): 5–13.

———. *English Melodrama.* London: Herbert Jenkins, 1965.

Borowitz, Albert I. "Why Thackeray Went to See a Man Hanged." *Victorian Newsletter,* 48 (1975): 15–21.

———. *The Woman Who Murdered Black Satin: The Bermondsey Horror.* Columbus: Ohio State Univ. Press, 1981.

Boyle, Thomas F. "'Fishy Extremities': Subversion of Orthodoxy in the Victorian Sensation Novel." *Literature and History,* 9:1 (Spring 1983): 92–96.

Brand, Dana. "Reconstructing the 'Flâneur': Poe's Invention of the Detective Story." *Genre,* 18:1 (Spring 1985): 36–56.

Brantlinger, Patrick. *Bread and Circuses: Theories of Mass Culture as Social Decay.* Ithaca, N.Y.: Cornell Univ. Press, 1983.

———. "What is 'Sensational' about the 'Sensation Novel'? " *Nineteenth-Century Fiction,* 37 (1982): 1–28.

Burns, Wayne. *Charles Reade: A Study in Victorian Authorship.* New York: Bookman Associates, 1961.

Cabot, Frederick C. "The Two Voices in Thackeray's Catherine." *Nineteenth-Century Fiction,* 28 (1974): 404–16.

Cawelti, John G. *Adventure, Mystery, and Romance.* Chicago: Univ. of Chicago Press, 1976.

Charney, Maurice. *Sexual Fiction.* London: Methuen, 1981.

Chesney, Kellow. *The Anti-Society: An Account of the Victorian Under-World.* Boston: Gambit, 1970.

Clarke, Deborah. *"Bleak House:* Divided Against Itself." Unpublished essay; an early version was presented at the Midwest Modern Language Association Conference, St. Louis, Missouri, November 1985.

Clausen, Christopher. "Sherlock Holmes, Order, and the Late-Victorian Mind." *Georgia Review,* 38:1 (Spring 1984): 104–23.

Cohen, Anne B. *Poor Pearl, Poor Girl! The Murdered-Girl Stereotype in Ballad and Newspaper.* Austin: Univ. of Texas Press, 1981.

Collins, Philip. *Dickens and Crime.* Bloomington: Indiana Univ. Press, 1962.

————. "'Sikes and Nancy': Dickens's Last Reading." *Times Literary Supplement,* 11 (1971): 681–82.

Cordell, Richard A. *Henry Arthur Jones and the Modern Drama.* 1932; rpt. ed., Port Washington, N.Y.: Kennikat Press, 1968.

Craig, Patricia, and Mary Cadogan. *The Lady Investigates: Women Detectives and Spies in Fiction.* London: Victor Gollancz Ltd., 1981.

Cross, Gilbert B. *Next Week—East Lynne: Domestic Drama in Performance 1820–1874.* Lewisburg, Penn.: Bucknell Univ. Press, 1977.

Curtis, Anthony. Preface to *Raffles: The Amateur Cracksman,* by E. W. Hornung. 1899; rpt. ed., London: Chatto & Windus, 1972.

Dalziel, Margaret. *Popular Fiction 100 Years Ago: An Unexplored Tract of Literary History.* London: Cohen and West, 1957.

Davies, Robertson. *The Mirror of Nature.* Toronto: Univ. of Toronto Press, 1983.

Degen, John A. "Victorian Drama." *Indiana University Bookman,* 17 (1977): 5–25.

Dunae, Patrick A. "Penny Dreadfuls: Late Nineteenth Century Boys' Literature and Crime." *Victorian Studies,* 22 (1978): 133–50.

Dye, William S., Jr. *A Study of Melodrama in England from 1800 to 1840.* State College, Penn.: Nittany, 1919.

Eco, Umberto. "Horns, Hooves, Insteps: Some Hypotheses on Three Types of Abduction." In *The Sign of Three: Dupin, Holmes, Peirce.* Eds. Umberto Eco and Thomas A. Sebeok. Bloomington: Indiana Univ. Press, 1983, pp. 198–220.

Faber, Richard. *Proper Stations: Class in Victorian Fiction.* London: Faber & Faber, Ltd., 1971.

Farrell, Kirby. "Heroism, Culture, and Dread in *The Sign of the Four.*" *Studies in the Novel,* 16:1 (Spring 1984): 32–51.

Ferris, Ina. *William Makepeace Thackeray.* Boston: Twayne, 1983.

Flanders, Jane. "The Fallen Woman in Fiction." In *Feminist Visions: Toward a Transformation of the Liberal Arts Curriculum.* Eds. Diane L. Fowlkes and Charlotte S. McClure. University: Univ. of Alabama Press, 1984, pp. 97–109.

Flower, Sibylla J. "Charles Dickens and Edward Bulwer-Lytton." *Dickensian,* 69 (1973), 79–89.

Foucault, Michel. *The History of Sexuality: An Introduction.* New York: Pantheon Books, 1978.

Ffrench, Yvonne. *Ouida: A Study in Ostentation.* London: Cobden-Sanderson, 1938.

Fulcher, James. "Murder Reports: Formulaic Narrative and Cultural Context." *Journal of Popular Culture,* 18:4 (Spring 1985): 31–42.

Hacking, Ian. "Nineteenth-Century Cracks in the Concept of Determinism." *Journal of the History of Ideas,* 44:3 (July/September 1983): 455–75.

Haining, Peter. *The Mystery and Horrible Murders of Sweeney Todd The Demon Barber.* London: Frederick Muller, 1979.

————, ed. *The Penny Dreadful: Or, Strange, Horrid and Sensational Tales!* London: Victor Gollancz, 1975.

Hampden, John. Introduction to *Dr. Jekyll and Mr. Hyde,* by Robert Louis Stevenson. 1886; rpt. ed., London: The Folio Society, 1948.

Hartman, Mary S. *Victorian Murderesses: A True History of Thirteen Respectable French and English Women Accused of Unspeakable Crimes.* New York: Schocken Books, 1977.

Hollingsworth, Keith. *The Newgate Novel, 1830–1847: Bulwer, Ainsworth, Dickens, and Thackeray.* Detroit: Wayne State Univ. Press, 1963.

Holloway, John. "Broadside Verse Traditions." *The Listener,* 83 (1970), 710–14.

————. "Cherry Girls and Crafty Maidens." *The Listener,* 83 (1970), 680–85.

Hughes, Michael. Foreword to *Curiosities of Street Literature,* by Charles Hindley. New York: Augustus M. Kelley, 1970.

Hughes, Winifred. *The Maniac in the Cellar: Sensation Novels of the 1860s.* Princeton: Princeton Univ. Press, 1980.

Humphreys, Ann. "G. W. M. Reynolds: Popular Literature and Popular Politics." *Victorian Periodicals Review,* 16:3 & 4 (Fall and Winter 1983): 79–89.

Hutter, Al. "Dreams, Transformation, and Literature: The Implications of Detective Fiction." *Victorian Studies,* 18 (1974), 181–210.

Jackson, Russell. Introduction to *Plays by Henry Arthur Jones.* Cambridge: Cambridge Univ. Press, 1982.

James, Louis. *English Popular Literature 1819–1851.* New York: Columbia Univ. Press, 1976.

———. "The Rational Amusement: 'Minor' Fiction and Victorian Studies." *Victorian Studies,* 14 (1970), 193–99.

Jordan, Elaine. "Spectres and Scorpions: Allusion and Confusion in *Mary Barton.*" *Literature and History,* 7:1 (Spring 1981): 48–61.

Keating, P. J. *The Working Classes in Victorian Fiction.* New York: Barnes & Noble, 1972.

Kennedy, George E., II. "Women Redeemed: Dickens's Fallen Women." *Dickensian* 74 (1978), 42–48.

Kilgarriff, Michael, ed. *The Golden Age of Melodrama.* London: Wolfe, 1974.

Knight, Stephen. *Form and Ideology in Crime Fiction.* Bloomington: Indiana Univ. Press, 1980.

Lansbury, Coral. *Elizabeth Gaskell.* Boston: Twayne, 1984.

Leavis, L. R. "The Late Nineteenth Century Novel and the Change Towards the Sexual—Gissing, Hardy and Lawrence." *English Studies: A Journal of English Language and Literature,* 66:1 (February 1985): 36–47.

Legman, Gershon. *Love and Death: A Study in Censorship.* New York: Hacker Art Books, 1963.

Lerner, Laurence. "Thackeray and Marriage." *Essays in Criticism,* 25 (1975), 279–303.

McCormack, W. J. *Sheridan LeFanu and Victorian Ireland.* Oxford: Clarendon Press, 1980.

McMaster, Juliet. "Diabolic Trinity in *Oliver Twist.*" *Dalhousie Review,* 61:2 (Summer 1981): 263–77.

Marlow, James E. "English Cannibalism: Dickens After 1859." *Studies in English Literature 1500–1900,* 23:4 (Autumn 1983): 647–66.

Marshall, William H. *Wilkie Collins.* New York: Twayne, 1970.

Matossian, Mary Kilbourne. "Death in London, 1750–1909." *The Journal of Interdisciplinary History,* 16:2 (Autumn 1985): 183–97.

Maxwell, Richard C., Jr. "G. M. Reynolds, Dickens, and *The Mysteries of London.*" *Nineteenth-Century Fiction,* 32 (1977), 188–213.

Meckier, Jerome. "Wilkie Collins's *The Woman in White:* Providence Against the Evils of Propriety." *The Journal of British Studies,* 22:1 (Fall 1982): 104–26.

Miller, J. Hillis. *Charles Dickens: The World of His Novels.* Bloomington: Indiana Univ. Press, 1958.

———. Introduction to *Bleak House,* by Charles Dickens. Harmondsworth: Penguin, 1971.

Mitchell, Sally. *The Fallen Angel: Chastity, Class and Women's Reading 1835–1888.* Bowling Green, Ohio: Bowling Green Univ. Popular Press, 1981.

Most, Glenn W. and William W. Stowe, eds. *The Poetics of Murder: Detective Fiction and Literary Theory.* New York: Harcourt Brace Jovanovich, 1983.

Nabokov, Vladimir. "Dr. Jekyll and Mr. Hyde." In *Lectures on Literature.* Ed. Fredson Bowers. New York: Harcourt Brace Jovanovich, 1980.

Neuburg, Victor E. *Popular Literature: A History and Guide.* Harmondsworth: Penguin, 1977.

Ousby, Ian. *Bloodhounds of Heaven: The Detective in English Fiction From Godwin to Doyle.* Cambridge: Harvard Univ. Press, 1976.

Page, Norman, ed. *Wilkie Collins: The Critical Heritage.* London: Routledge & Kegan Paul, 1974.

Peterson, M. Jeanne. *The Medical Profession in Mid-Victorian London.* Berkeley: Univ. of California Press, 1978.

Radway, Janice A. *Reading the Romance: Women, Patriarchy, and Popular Literature.* Chapel Hill: Univ. of North Carolina Press, 1984.

Rogers, Katharine M. "The Pressure of Convention on Thackeray's Women." *Modern Language Review,* 67 (1972): 257–63.

Rowell, George. Introduction to *Nineteenth-Century Plays.* London: Oxford Univ. Press, 1953.

——. *Theatre in the Age of Irving.* Oxford: Basil Blackwell, 1981.

——. *The Victorian Theatre 1792–1914: A Survey.* 2nd ed. Cambridge: Cambridge Univ. Press, 1978.

Schachterle, Lance. "*Oliver Twist* and Its Serial Predecessors." *Dickens Studies Annual,* 3 (1974): 1–13.

Senelick, Laurence. "'Dead! And Never Called Me Mother!': The Legacy of Oral Tradition from the Nineteenth-Century Stage." *Theatre Studies,* nos. 26/27 (1979/80–1980/81): 7–20.

——. "Ladykillers and Lady Killers: Recent Popular Victoriana." *Victorian Studies,* 21 (1978), 493–500.

Sharps, John G. *Mrs. Gaskell's Observation and Invention: A Study of Her Non-Biographic Works.* Sussex: Linden Press, 1970.

Showalter, Elaine. "Desperate Remedies: Sensation Novels of the 1860s." *Victorian Newsletter,* 49 (1976): 1–5.

——, and English Showalter. "Victorian Women and Menstruation." *Victorian Studies,* 14 (1970): 83–89.

Smith, David. "*Mary Barton* and *Hard Times:* Their Social Insights." *Mosaic: A Journal for the Comparative Study of Literature and Ideas,* 5 (1971), 97–112.

Smith, Elton E. *Charles Reade.* Boston: Twayne, 1976.

Stephens, J. R. "*Jack Sheppard* and the Licensers: The Case Against Newgate Plays." *Nineteenth Century Theatre Research,* 1 (1973): 1–14.

Stewart, Garrett. *Death Sentences: Styles of Dying in British Fiction.* Cambridge, Mass.: Harvard Univ. Press, 1984.

Symons, Julian. *Charles Dickens.* London: Arthur Barker Limited, 1951.

Taylor, John Russell. *The Rise and Fall of the Well-Made Play.* London: Methuen, 1967.

Terry, R. C. *Victorian Popular Fiction, 1860–80.* London: Macmillan Press, 1983.

Tobias, J. J. *Crime and Industrial Society in the Nineteenth Century.* London: B. T. Batsford, 1967.

Trodd, Anthea. "The Policeman and the Lady: Significant Encounters in Victorian Fiction." *Victorian Studies,* 27:4 (Summer 1984): 435–60.

Truzzi, Marcello. "Sherlock Holmes: Applied Social Psychologist." In *The Sign of Three: Dupin, Holmes, Peirce.* Eds. Umberto Eco and Thomas A. Sebeok. Bloomington: Indiana Univ. Press, 1983, pp. 55–80.

Tyson, Nancy Jane. *Eugene Aram: Literary History and Typology of the Scholar-Criminal.* Hamden, Conn.: Archon Books, 1983.

Vernon, Sally. "Trouble Up at T'Mill: The Rise and Decline of the Factory Play in the 1830's and 1840's." *Victorian Studies,* 20 (1976), 117–39.

Vicinus, Martha. *Broadsides of the Industrial North.* Newcastle upon Tyne: Frank Graham, 1975.

——. *The Industrial Muse: A Study of Nineteenth Century British Working Class Literature.* New York: Harper & Row, 1974.

——. "The Study of Victorian Popular Culture." *Victorian Studies,* 18 (1975), 473–83.

Walkovitz, Judith R. "Jack the Ripper and the Myth of Male Violence." *Feminist Studies,* 8:3 (Fall 1982): 543–74.

Wall, Geoffrey. "'Different from Writing': *Dracula* in 1897." *Literature and History,* 10:1 (September 1984): 15–23.

Walton, John K. and James Walvin, eds. *Leisure in Britain 1780–1938*. Manchester: Univ. of Manchester Press, 1983.

Walvin, James. *A Child's World: A Social History of English Childhood, 1800–1914*. Harmondsworth: Penguin, 1982.

———. *English Urban Life, 1776–1851*. London and Dover, N.H.: Hutchinson, 1984.

———. *Leisure and Society, 1830–1950*. London: Longman, 1978.

Ward, John C. "The Virtue of the Mothers: Powerful Women in *Bleak House*." *Dickens Studies Newsletter*, 14:2 (June 1983): 37–42.

Watson, Colin. *Snobbery with Violence: Crime Stories and Their Audience*. London: Eyre & Spottiswoode, 1971.

Webb, Peter. "Victorian Erotica." In *The Sexual Dimension in Literature*. Ed. Alan Bold. London: Vision, 1982, pp. 93–94.

Weisbrod, Bernd. "How to become a good foundling in early Victorian London." *Social History*, 10:2 (May 1985): 193–209.

Wheeler, Michael. *English Fiction of the Victorian Period 1830–1890*. New York: Longman, 1985.

Wildman, John H. "Thackeray's Wickedest Woman." In *Essays in Honor of Esmond Linworth Marilla*. Eds. Thomas A. Kirby and William J. Olive. Baton Rouge: Louisiana State Univ. Press, 1970, pp. 53–58.

Williams, Raymond. "Social Environment and Theatrical Entertainment: The Case of English Naturalism." In *English Drama: Forms and Development*. Eds. Marie Axton and Raymond Williams. Cambridge: Cambridge Univ. Press, 1977, pp. 203–23.

Woodfield, James. *English Theatre in Transition 1881–1914*. London: Croom Helm, 1984.

# Index